Race and the Cultural Industries

Race and the Cultural Industries

ANAMIK SAHA

polity

The right of Anamik Saha to be identified as Author of this Work has been asserted in accordance with the UK Copyright, Designs and Patents Act 1988.

First published in 2018 by Polity Press

Polity Press
65 Bridge Street
Cambridge CB2 1UR, UK

Polity Press
101 Station Landing, Suite 300
Medford, MA 02155, USA

ISBN-13: 978-1-5095-0530-2
ISBN-13: 978-1-5095-0531-9 (pb)

A catalogue record for this book is available from the British Library.

Library of Congress Cataloging-in-Publication Data

Names: Saha, Anamik, 1977- author.
Title: Race and the cultural industries / Anamik Saha.
Description: Malden, MA : Polity Press, [2017] | Includes bibliographical
   references and index.
Identifiers: LCCN 2017028253 (print) | LCCN 2017029094 (ebook) | ISBN
   9781509505340 (Epub) | ISBN 9781509505333 (mobi) | ISBN 9781509505302
   (hardback) | ISBN 9781509505319 (pbk.)
Subjects: LCSH: Cultural industries. | Race. | Cultural pluralism in mass
   media.
Classification: LCC HD9999.C9472 (ebook) | LCC HD9999.C9472 S24 2017 (print)
   | DDC 338.4/70705--dc23
LC record available at https://lccn.loc.gov/2017028253

Typeset in 11.25/13 Dante by Servis Filmsetting Limited, Stockport, Cheshire
Printed and bound in the UK by CPI Group (UK) Ltd, Croydon, CR0 4YY

For further information on Polity, visit our website: politybooks.com

Contents

Preface and Acknowledgements

As I was writing this book, the UK voted to leave the European Union. Five months later, Donald Trump won the US presidential election. Both the 'Brexit' and the Trump campaigns were controversial in their tactics, and in their loose use of 'facts' in particular. But what they have strongly in common is that they both exploited strong racial discourses that have intensified in their circulation in and around Western nation-states – the threat of terrorism, the crisis of multiculturalism, the 'swarms' of refugees and immigrants flooding the nation, black lives and deaths, and a fundamental sense of 'Us' versus 'Them'. Living in a multicultural country like the UK, I believe there to be a huge disconnect between people's actual experience of multiculture – which is mostly undramatic, mundane and indeed, ordinary – and their overall attitudes to others of a different hue, captured in the two aforementioned election victories for the populist right. While anti-immigrant sentiment can be explained in terms of economic inequalities (where racism is regarded as a form of scapegoating during times of scarcity), this focus can neglect the profound role the media has in shaping society's attitudes to race (including those of the haves as well as of the have-nots). While it seems rather banal to say that we live in highly mediated times, the fact is that even in a cosmopolitan city like London, from where I write this, people's encounters with difference occur mostly through the media.

Research into race and the media is dominated by studies of representation, invariably highlighting the destructive and devisive ways that racial and ethnic minorities appear in the news and popular culture. Such studies have shown that when not rendered invisible, minorities are persistently demonized, stereotyped, mocked, exoticized, dehumanized. These findings are indisputable, but I nonetheless find two troubling tendencies in a solely textual approach to race and the media. First, it does not always fully account for contradiction. On a very basic level, if the media were so deeply racist, I, personally speaking, would not consume so much of it. The fact is, the media enriches my life, in keeping me entertained and informed, but also in helping me understand my own sense of self (including racial identity) and the world around me. As I write this, I have been enjoying much media produced by people of colour, including the TV series *Atlanta* written by and starring Donald Glover (broadcast on Rupert Murdoch-owned channel FX, no less), the music of Solange and the Swet Shop Boys (featuring British Pakistani rapper and actor Riz Ahmed, who also appeared in *Star Wars* spin-off movie *Rogue One*), the novels of Jumpa Lahiri, and the columns of Gary Younge in the *Guardian*. I am currently excited about seeing upcoming horror movie *Get Out*, directed by comedian Jordan Peele, about a young black man meeting his middle-class white girlfriend's family (a truly terrifying experience). With their diverse and at times radical depiction of black and brown lives, these cultural texts can seem like exceptions to the rule, sneaking into the (white) mainstream against all odds. But what if, rather than aberrations, we understand them as constituted by the very logic of the cultural industries and industrial cultural production itself? How might this shed new light on the ideological role of the media?

The second problem I have with research focused solely on the text is that it struggles to offer forms of praxis – other than to argue that we need to counter negative representations of minorities with more positive ones. Sometimes scholars articulate a need for better representation of minorities in the creative workforce itself, based on an assumption that more racial and ethnic minorities working in the media will stop misrepresentation and will diversify the images of nonwhite folk in media content. But is this enough to tackle either the complexity of the politics of representation or the entrenched nature of racist ideologies in the cultural industries? In my research into British South Asian cultural production, I frequently encountered media workers who defined their very practice in terms of wanting to reverse the reductive representations of Asian communities, but then I would look at their film, their television documentary, their play or book, and find that they had reproduced the very racialized representations that they had set out to challenge. Why then is this the case? Were these individuals being disingenuous in the first instance, or are there greater forces at play?

In order to answer these questions, this book argues that we need a greater emphasis on cultural production itself: a focus on how representations of race are made. This entails looking closely at the experience of industrial cultural production, its mechanics and processes and the creative workers involved, but also a broader consideration of how the cultural industries are shaped by capitalism and legacies of empire. While research into race and cultural production is relatively minor in the broad field of race and media studies, there is nonetheless a growing body of work examining this topic, though it currently feels like a disparate field. The aim of this book is to pull this research together in order to build a fuller and more complete picture of the making of race in the cultural industries. Its primary interest is to uncover why race continues to be represented according to particular, seemingly immutable, tropes rooted in colonial times. But its also emphasizes ambivalence and contradiction in production in the cultural industries, which can account for those moments when we encounter a cultural good that disrupts common-sense understandings of racial difference. Recognizing that these two apparently different phenomena are in fact part of the same dynamic is crucial to deepening our understanding of how cultural industries *make* race. Moreover, this awareness is crucial for the formulation of generative counter-political interventions in the media – a way of making race that contributes to its undoing.

This book is based on ideas that have been developing over a long time, mostly through conversations and interactions, both formal and informal, with many colleagues and friends, whom I want to acknowledge here. The book's core arguments started taking form during my PhD studies, for which I need to thank my supervisors Michael Keith and Ben Gidley for helping to give sense to what was a muddle of ideas. Both David Hesmondhalgh and Les Back (separately, though occasionally at the same time) have been inspiring teachers, mentors, colleagues and now friends. I have learnt so much from them, and need to thank them for the amazing opportunities they have given me – and also for reading drafts of chapters in this book. For also providing comments on drafts, I need to thank my fantastic colleagues Des Freedman and Gholam Khiabany; David O'Brien, who, in the relatively short time I've known him, has been an excellent and generous collaborator; and the anonymous reviewers who also provided valuable feedback that has helped strengthen the book. (I of course take sole responsibility for any mistakes or inaccuracies.) So much of the book's arguments were honed following conversations with colleagues on conference panels, seminars and various colloquia, in the pub after those colloquia and, of course, social media. In this category I need to thank (in no particular order) Helen Kim, Georgina Born, Kate Oakley, Kim Allen, Sanjay Sharma, Ash Sharma, Mark Banks, Tim Havens, Nabeel Zuberi, Jo Littler, Angela McRobbie, Dhiraj Murthy, Vivek Bald, Vijay Prashad, Paul Gilroy, Parminder Bhachu, Caspar Melville, James Curran, Sarah Kember, Sarita Malik, Clive Nwonka, Gavan Titley, Nisha Kapoor, Sivamohan Valluvan, Malcolm James, Jonathan Gray, Shilpa Davé, Orson Nava,

Charlton McIlwain and Roopali Mukherjee. Most of this book was written during term time while I was teaching and administrating, so I need to thank all my colleagues in the Department of Media and Communications at Goldsmiths who provided – and continue to provide – support and good cheer on a daily basis. Special thanks go to my brilliant bosses both old and new who have all been tremendously supportive – Natalie Fenton, Julian Henriques, Sean Cubitt and Lisa Blackman – and those colleagues who have had to put up with me the most, including Clea Bourne, Liz Moor, Aeron Davis, Wendy Jordan, Edwina Peart, Brett St Louis and Yasmin Gunaratnam. Thanks also to the amazingly patient admin staff, especially Zehra Arabadji, Amanda Gallant, Leanne Benford, Sarah Jackson and Bridget Ward. Special mention goes to Bethany Klein, who has been a brilliant, supportive (ex-)colleague and friend, while also telling me *how it is* when necessary. Sorry for messing up your house.

I need to send my gratitude to those people who supported the writing of the book, probably without them even realizing they were doing so. This was either through exchanging ideas, or just sending out positive vibes in general. I am thinking of Yasmeen Narayan, Nirmal Puwar, Hannah Jones, Milly Williamson, Bev Skeggs, Daniel Burdsey, Kimberly Keith, Eric Woods, Toussaint Nothias, Melissa Fernandez, Eithne Quinn, Shamea Mia, Bradford Bailey, Sophie Watson, Rachael Gilmour, Thomas Zacharias and Rajeev Balasubramanyam. I salute also my musical academics-in-arms: Isaac Marrero-Guillamon (lead guitar), Hilde Stephansen (bass/backing vocals), Chris Moffat (bass) and Rahul Desai (drums). I want to thank too my friends beyond the campus who have not only been so encouraging (or at least feigned interest very convincingly), but have also contributed to the book, whether through dissecting popular culture together, or providing me with insights into their careers in the cultural industries. This includes Sara Bivigou, Andy Lee, Andrew Philip, John Nolan, Gwyneth Holland, Adey Lobb, Geraldine Smith, Sarah Wayman, Jon Raznick, Kat Wong, Paul Thomas, Erin King, Nora Allen-Wiles, Rowan Cope, Jon Butler, Stephen Dumughn, Ilona Jasiewicz and Ewa Jasiewicz. I want to acknowledge also the Amersham Group – my reading group (also the name of the pub where we meet) featuring Alex Rhys-Taylor, Will Davies and Emma Jackson. I feel very lucky not only to have studied with these folk, but also to work with them now. A special mention must go to Emma, who has been such a brilliant colleague and friend over the years (and also a musical comrade) and who is at the centre of the 'circle of niceness' for so many of us.

All my family have been so supportive during the writing of this book.

I must mention the ever-expanding Collins clan, especially Stevie and Ray for purchasing the academic books that I would put on my Christmas lists during my PhD studies (many of which are cited in this book). My sister Paromita continues to influence my career and work – and cultural tastes – more than she probably realizes, and has been an important source for exchanging ideas (and was of particular help with chapter 2). My parents have *always* encouraged and supported me even when not quite sure what I am doing: 'culture something. . .'. I owe them everything. Watching my daughters Latika and Uma grow up is easily the most fulfilling and joyful thing in my life. Now I've finished this book I look forward to having more time to play *My Little Pony* Top Trumps with them. And all my gratitude and love goes to Kara, my wonderful partner. Kara gives me the time and space to immerse myself in work when I need it, but, thankfully, ensures that I balance this with the really important stuff like spending time with our family. She also keeps me on my intellectual toes and does not tolerate long sentences. I owe her everything too.

Part I

Framework

1

Race and the Cultural Industries

Introduction

Very few would argue with the notion that the cultural industries shape society's ideas about race. Yet there remains relatively little sustained analysis of the production and circulation of racial discourses by the media. Why is the media considered a relatively trivial issue by scholars of race and racism? Similarly, why does the study of race take a marginal status in critical media studies? On the other hand, why in light of the very real material effects of racism – whether racial violence or forms of economic and social exclusion – should we even care about the media, especially in relation to popular culture? One way of opening up this discussion is by briefly uncovering a neglected aspect of the work of Frantz Fanon, the Caribbean psychiatrist, philosopher and revolutionary, who has become one of the key figures in postcolonial theory.

Fanon is eulogized for his writing on the psychosocial trauma of racism and anticolonial struggle, but he is less known for his interest in the media, popular culture and representation.[1] Yet in *Black Skin White Masks* (1986[1952]), Fanon's analysis of the psychological devastation caused by racism is littered with references from cinema and literature, and even supposedly benign forms of popular culture such as children's songs and comics. For Fanon, the inherent Eurocentricity of the narratives contained within these cultural commodities contribute to the alienation experienced by the Negro subject. This is powerfully illustrated in the following quote, which describes his experience watching the Hollywood war film *Home of the Brave* in a French cinema hall among a white audience:

> The Negro is a toy in the white man's hands; so, in order to shatter the hellish cycle, he explodes. I cannot go to a film without seeing myself. I wait for me. In the interval, just before the film starts, I wait for me. The

---

[1] Though his work has had an influence on film studies, particularly from a psychoanalytical perspective; see Kaplan (1999).

3

people in the theatre are watching me, examine me, waiting for me. A Negro groom is going to appear. My heart makes my head swim.

The crippled veteran of the Pacific war says to my brother, 'Resign yourself to your colour the way I got used to my stump; we're both victims'. (Fanon, 1986: 140)

Fanon here describes the damaging effects of Western cultural goods upon the black psyche. For Fanon, texts such as popular literature, film or indeed Mickey Mouse comics perform the role of providing a 'collective catharsis' (Fanon, 1986: 145) for the population; a safety valve where the fears/desires/aggression that accumulate in a society can be safely released. But in the West only the dominant white subject experiences catharsis, which plays on racial fears (and desires). Meanwhile, the products of Western culture industries flood into colonial societies where young black children learn invariably to identify with the white heroes who feature in the imported comics and storybooks. Growing up in this environment, Fanon, like his fellow colonial subjects from the Antilles and other Francophone nations, subconsciously identifies as white and French. But entering European society, and surrounded by the white people in the cinema hall, he suddenly feels the weight of his ascribed race, forced to identify with the 'Negro' protagonist who is about to come onscreen. As the quote vividly captures, this produces a disorienting and debilitating and, indeed, disassembling affect for Fanon, such that his heart makes his head 'swim' – and his body and mind eventually 'explode'.

In the last part of the quote, Fanon refers to the final scene from the film *Home of the Brave*, released in 1949 (Robson, 1949). In it, an African American soldier called Mossy experiences a double trauma: of witnessing the death of his white best friend during a small US reconnaissance mission into a Japanese-held Pacific Island, and of experiencing racism, back home in America and within his company. Unable to deal with this dual burden, Mossy has a mental and physical breakdown, becoming paralysed from the waist down. A sympathetic psychiatrist eventually cures him by helping him face up to his victimhood. In this final scene, the white sergeant who has lost his arm on the same mission exhorts Mossy to treat his race like the sergeant treats his missing limb, an affliction that he will need to learn to deal with despite the disadvantages and prejudice he will face in the outside world. With its representation of psychiatry and black subjectivity, *Home of the Brave* uncannily encapsulates Fanon's own concerns regarding the psychosocial effects of racism and also psychiatry as a means through which individuals of colour are suppressed/assimilated (see Bergner, 1999: 226). It provides a vivid scene for Fanon to explore the experience of being racialized in a white world.

There are two reasons for opening this book with this passage from Fanon. First, it evocatively illustrates the scarring and disfiguring impact of media on racialized minorities. Even the pleasures that black folk seem to experience in watching Hollywood films is regarded as a form of dissimulation for Fanon (1986: 152). Perhaps more than any other scholar, Fanon captures the sheer visceral brutality of racism in its physical and psychosocial manifestations, and, as suggested, an unrecognized element of his work is his attribution to the role of media texts in producing this affect. With particular pertinence for this book, in light of the psychological damage brought about by white cultural objects upon the Negro subject, Fanon considers the potential of black cultural production – using the examples of magazines and songs conceived specifically for black children – as constituting an integral part of a decolonizing project designed to counter the alienation of the Negro (1986: 146–148).

Second, underlining how Fanon's emphasis on popular culture is a neglected aspect of his work allows me to open up to a broader point: that the study of the media and race as a whole is a relatively marginal area of research and scholarship. As I have suggested, in sociologies of race and racism the study of the media appears on the margins of the discipline. Inversely, in media and communications studies the study of race takes up a similar peripheral status. This is a point shared by Darnell Hunt (2005: 3–9), who describes the sociology of race and critical media studies as 'two neighbours' who rarely meet.

This was not always the case, however. The impact of cultural studies on both aforementioned disciplines, when inflected by postcolonial theory, for a moment turned our attention to the question of representation and the way in which ideologies of race take hold in society through the media. The idea that popular culture was something to be taken seriously, as well as news media, was a particularly important intervention. Yet this discussion has somewhat stalled in recent times – what Herman Gray (2013: 771) describes as a '"waning" in what a cultural politics of representation can yield' – and has subsequently been dismissed as part of the *culturalist* turn in the social sciences, which, in the context of the sociology of race and racism, deflected attention from the very real experiences of racial violence, exclusion and marginalization. While the charge of cultural reductionism is unfair – the best media studies of race framed their approach explicitly in terms of structural racism and social injustice – this field ultimately was unable to translate its complex theoretical ruminations on the politics of representation into meaningful forms of social action.

Race and the Cultural Industries aims to reinvigorate research into race and the media. Studies of 'race' and ethnicity in the media are nearly always textual in focus. Such research exposes the ways that media representations shape our understandings of cultural difference, either reinforcing or challenging certain ideas around ethnicity and race at specific times and in specific contexts. Yet the tendency of these studies is to treat the text – whether a film, a book, a television programme or a piece of music – in isolation, as though it sprung directly out of the imagination of the author. That is, there is a lack of recognition of how such texts are a product of the cultural industries and also of rationalized and standardized industrial processes that determine the way that the text appears at the point of consumption. Put more simply, cultural industries shape the media products that we consume and, in turn, ideas about racial and ethnic difference as embodied in these texts. This point has immediate political ramifications. As critical political economist Nicholas Garnham (1990: 44) states, as long as we remain transfixed on just 'the ideological content of the mass media it will be difficult to develop coherent political strategies for resisting the underlying dynamics of development in the cultural sphere in general which rest firmly and increasingly upon the logic of generalised commodity production'. While textual analyses can highlight the discourses and ideologies that underpin racialized representations of difference, they cannot tell us how and why these representations come to be made in the first place – and crucially, what strategies can be employed to disrupt their spread. In response, this book seeks to explore the complex ways in which race and ethnicity are experienced and operate in cultural production. It asks a very simple yet hitherto neglected question: *how do cultural industries make race?*[2]

The book's central argument is that we need a new theory of race and ethnicity in cultural production, which foregrounds the cultural industries context in the making and circulation of symbolic goods. This entails an equal emphasis on macro questions that deal with power, history and structure, and micro issues dealing with labour, agency and texts in order to help understand why representations of race and ethnicity take the shape that they do. More specifically, it involves a deep engagement with cultural commodification and, again, its macro and micro dimensions, and

---

[2] This notion of 'making race' is adapted from Herman Gray (2016: 249), who is describing how the discourse of 'diversity' in the media effectively 'makes race', that is, it constructs industry and public understandings of race. In this regard, Gray describes the production of cultural commodities that articulate race in some way as 'race-making practices', a form of 'power/knowledge that operates as a logic of production' (2016: 249).

how this process shapes racial discourse as embodied in cultural commodities. In other words, what I am proposing is a production analysis of race and the media.

The purpose of this opening chapter is to make the case for why we need to focus on production and, more precisely, frame the discussion on media representations of race within the cultural industries. To do so, it highlights the ways in which the study of the media and race have featured, and ultimately have become peripheral, in what I broadly describe as critical racial and ethnic studies, as well as media/cultural studies. As stated, after making an important intervention in drawing attention to the cultural forms of racism, media analyses of race and representation have been reduced to a marginal status and the purpose of this opening part of the chapter is to consider why that is the case. By highlighting the possibilities and limitations of textual approaches to race and the media, I then make the case for an interdisciplinary approach that situates the critical reading of media texts with an analysis of cultural production. Paying closer attention to the dynamic of cultural production, incorporating an analysis of changes and continuities in the political economy of the cultural industries, the cultures of production that emerge and the way that creative workers operate within, but in turn influence and shape the processes of production, deepens our understanding of how media discourses of race are physically made – or, indeed, *how race itself is made*. This subsequently reveals how the counter narratives of difference are governed within capitalism, and how racialized governmentalities, as I put it, can then be challenged and resisted. The paradox of living with racism in advanced capitalism is in how, on the one hand, racialized communities continue to be oppressed and their experiences and histories disavowed and, on the other, racial and ethnic differences become qualities used to distinguish products within a hypercompetitive market. The cultural industries provide the exemplary site in which to explore this contradiction of capital.

Race, racism and racialization in the twenty-first century

In the *Forethought* of *The Souls of Black Folk*, W.E.B. Du Bois (1994[1903]) declared that 'the problem of the Twentieth Century is the problem of the colour line'. A hundred years later, Stuart Hall (1993: 361) echoes Du Bois in prognosticating that 'the capacity to live with difference is, in my view, the coming question of the twenty-first century'. As the uneven flows of globalization intensify – not least the movement of people –

demographics change, sometimes radically, producing anxiety, tension and fear in the national consciousness of Western states. (As global capitalism and free trade render national borders increasingly insignificant, one of the remaining places where borders still have very real, physical effects is in the regulation of the flow of people.) Hall highlights the slow, incremental and quiet, yet profoundly transformative, nature of the 'multicultural drift' that occurs in countries like the UK. But he also notes the 'archaic forms of nationalism' that are activated in reaction to the irreversible change that globalization brings.

Deep into the twenty-first century and we find racist histories repeating themselves in the West. Moral panics over 'migrant crises', 'bogus asylum seekers' or the clandestine entry of 'swarms' of 'illegal immigrants' still persist, with politicians from the left and the right of the political spectrum cynically unleashing anti-immigration rhetoric at moments of social unrest, while implementing policies designed to make countries a purposefully hostile place for migrants. Within the nation-state, urban governance produces formal and informal forms of segregation along the lines of class, race and ethnicity. The ghettoes that result are blighted by poor housing and schooling, a lack of healthcare provision, limited employment opportunities and significantly higher levels of incarceration that are the inevitable consequence of these forms of social deprivation. Moreover, these communities are physically brutalized, whether at the hands of the police or white vigilantes, such that racialized communities are still having to assert that black lives matter. Meanwhile, geopolitical developments and Western excursions into the Middle East have produced so-called home-grown terrorists, resulting in the use of biopolitical technologies and surveillance tools to monitor the nation's Muslim, Arab and South Asian populations, both on and offline. Politicians shrug their shoulders and disingenuously lament a situation where they have no choice but to exercise undemocratic practices such as the indefinite detention of citizens suspected of terrorism and the enacting of rendition (coupled with illegal forms of torture) for the safety of the nation. Across Europe far right parties gain positions of power even in the social democratic Nordic nations, and deep-rooted antisemitism still finds expression, all playing out alongside 'the routine acts of racist commentary and violence' that constitute contemporary 'digitalia' (Gilroy, 2012: 381). David Theo Goldberg (n.d.) goes as far as suggesting that 'public racist expression has generally grown more virulent and vicious than it has been since the 1960s'. Ash Amin (2010: 3) similarly comments how 'the steady achievements of multiculturalism and the politics of diversity in general in the last decades of the 20th century have melted away'. The inauguration of the first black American president in 2009 supposedly ushered in a 'post-race' era, but his replacement, whose election campaign was avowedly racist, shows we are anywhere but.

Thus, how we live with difference remains the key issue of our time. Yet there is still a tendency, born of a lingering economic reductionism in the social sciences, to think of racism as an epiphenomenon of capitalism and modernity rather than as intrinsic to it. The discipline of sociology has traditionally been the most attuned to the dynamics of multiculture, yet it still appears reluctant to bring issues of race and racism into the centre of its research agenda. The fact is that the study of race and ethnicity remains of relative minor interest in a discipline that Gurminder Bhambra (2014) describes as hegemonically white, despite the critical contributions of collections such as *The Empire Strikes Back* and *The Death of White Sociology* (see Back and Tate, 2015). As part of her argument that American sociology still experiences a type of institutional and epistemological segregation whereby 'black sociology' is marginalized from the core of the discipline, Bhambra (2014: 473) underlines how colonialism was 'a feature of the very rise of nation-states that typically provide the focus for dominant national sociologies . . . the nation-state form itself can be regarded as a product of colonialism and not just a product of nationalism'. As Ali Rattansi (2005: 284) states, 'conceptions of race (and whiteness) have in the modern period been central to the formation of Western states and even of the ideologies of liberalism that have underpinned the formation of the liberal democratic parliamentary polity'. Indeed, for Stuart Hall (2011: 17) neoliberal governments (speaking in the UK context) gain consensus through the appeal to a conservative nationalism rather than the espousal of free market rationality. My argument is not just that the study of race and ethnicity is a neglected area, but that centralizing these issues can be immensely generative in producing new knowledges about the operations of modernity and the nature of the current neoliberal conjuncture.

Scholars working in critical studies of race and ethnicity, in the intersections between sociology, geography, anthropology, cultural and media studies, philosophy, postcolonial theory and literary studies, have made an important contribution in this regard. Research in this field has exposed the workings of racialized governmentalities in its structural and vernacular forms, from outlining the neoliberal governance of race in terms of policy, both foreign and domestic (Goldberg, 2009; Kapoor, 2013; Jones, 2013) to shedding light on the ambivalence of multicultural drift and everyday encounters with difference (Wise and Velayutham, 2009; Watson and Saha, 2013; Jones and Jackson, 2014; Valluvan, 2016; Rhys-Taylor, 2017).

This critical approach, often empirically grounded, is sensitive to how categories of race and ethnicity are socially constructed, while committed to the project of exposing how race still structures experience and the persistence of phenotypical racism.[3] 'Racialization' in this context is a particularly key concept for many critical scholars of race and ethnicity, and is, indeed, a central concept for this book. It seems a little facetious to suggest that the term effectively performs the same role as putting 'race' in scare quotes, but in some ways this is quite correct. Racialization refers to the process through which meanings derived from race-thinking are ascribed to people and their supposedly physical characteristics (see Murji and Solomos, 2005). But many scholars have broadened its use beyond the question of the somatic, referring also to practices, objects and discourses. This slight shift has received criticism from scholars who argue that racialization in this way can be applied to anything and everything and is consequently theoretically ambiguous and far too casually deployed (Goldberg, 2005). Michael Banton (2005), who originally coined the concept in the context of British sociology at least, complains that his original definition of racialization – which refers specifically to moments when race is evoked in terms of its status as a biological category – has been expanded to such an extent that it encompasses nonracial categories such as ethnicity and religion, which for him is semantically incorrect, and as a result loses its specificity. I reject this rather pedantic critique and follow Nasar Meer and Tariq Modood's (2009: 344) defence of the broadening out of racialization in a way that deliberately challenges the characterization of racism as a form of single 'inherentism' or 'biological determinism' that leaves little space to conceive of the ways in which cultural racism draws on physical appearance as one marker among others, and is not solely premised on conceptions of biology in a way that ignores religion, culture and so forth.

Meer and Modood in this instance are making a case for how discourses of antisemitism and Islamophobia need to be understood as forms of racialization, and this is an approach I apply in this book, which draws from case studies from a range of international Western contexts – specifically, the United States, Canada, the UK and Europe, and Australasia – involving different racial, religious, ethnic and indigenous groups. While it is paramount to acknowledge the regional and historical particularities of these individual cases, and the different forms of racism that they may entail in the way that Goldberg (2005; 2009) rightly insists, the very strength of

---

[3] There is also a self-reflexive understanding of how social research is itself implicated in the reinforcement of racial categories (Alexander, 2006).

the concept of racialization, as Meer (2013: 389) argues, is how it acts as 'a meta-concept that is nimble enough to host a number of potentially competing concerns'. In light of this, I also work with Nikhil Singh's (2005: 223) definition of racialization as a 'technology of race' that is something more than skin colour or biophysical essence, but rather 'those historic repertoires and cultural, spatial and signifying systems that stigmatize and depreciate one form of humanity for the purpose of another's health, development, safety, profit or pleasure'. In the context of the media, we can think of the powerful effects of representations that in Fanon's terms 'amputate' the humanity of its object and supplant it with a racialized figure on screen. Thus, it is through the concept of racialization, as a process whereby people and objects – and, indeed, cultural commodities – come to be inscribed with ideas from race-thinking, that I switch the question from how cultural industries *represent* race, to how cultural industries *make* race. Indeed, with this emphasis on production, one of the central arguments of this book is that we need to shift from a notion of the commodification of race (which is the way that the relationship between race, culture and capitalism often gets made sense of), to a new notion of the racialization of the cultural commodity.

Locating the 'politics' in the 'politics of representation'

Singh's reference to signifying systems that transform race into a source of 'profit or pleasure' draws attention to the issue of commodification and the role of the cultural industries in racializing processes. Yet, to reiterate, in critical studies of race and ethnicity the issue of the media remains a peripheral area of study. The aim of this section is to unravel why this is the case. In doing so, the need to tackle the question of race and representation more explicitly in terms of production and the cultural industries becomes more apparent.

While I maintain that the subject of the media in critical racial and ethnic studies is marginal, that is not to say that scholars working in this field do not take the question of media representation seriously. News journalism is one aspect of the media that has featured fairly regularly in sociological and cultural studies of race and racism. As John Downing and Charles Husband (2005: 5) state, news media is probably the best place to start in thinking through the media's role in racialization processes, '[f]or it is precisely in the definition of the situation offered by news media that a racialization of events may be transmitted more or less uncritically to audience'. For Ronald Jacobs (2014), it was Hall et al.'s (2013[1983]) *Policing the Crisis*, about the British moral panic over 'mugging' in the 1970s, that showed sociologists in particular how racial consciousness can be shaped by media representations.[4] The importance of this seminal study was not just in drawing attention to how news stories on mugging were racialized to the extent that the word 'mugger' became synonymous with 'young black male'; in addition, Hall and colleagues, adopting a Gramscian framework, exposed how such news stories subsequently formed a consensus for the British state to enact policies that allowed for the greater policing of Britain's urban black populations, provoking the civil unrest and the race riots of the 1980s and, significantly, the rise of Thatcherism, which was the backdrop against which *Policing the Crisis* was being written.

Studies of representations and race in the news remain the predominant way in which race and the media are studied (Campbell et al., 2012). In more recent times, post-9/11 and beyond, there has been a spike of research into Islamophobia in the media, which invariably has had to tackle the news and the representation of Muslims within it (Semati, 2010; Saeed, 2007; Poole, 2002; Poole and Richardson, 2006). Indeed, this particular area of research has seen contributions from sociologists who are not usually engaged with questions of the media, but the rampant nature of Islamophobic discourse in news and current affairs is such that the study of factual media cannot possibly be avoided. In this regard, of note is Meer et al. (2010), who examine the nature of the inclusion of Muslim commentators in the British press following then-Labour MP Jack Straw's controversial comments regarding the hijab. While the further racialization of Muslims is the clear outcome, the authors nonetheless acknowledge the proliferation of a broader range of Muslim voices, seen as a potentially important intervention in British politics, opening up the previously narrow, secular, racially focused multicultural policies of the state. Indeed, Meer at al.'s approach exemplifies what Jacobs (2014) sees as the value of sociological approaches to representation with its emphasis on intertextuality; that is, looking at how representations operate in the wider social world not just in terms of how people consume texts and what meanings they get out of them, but of how meanings circulate in society at large. As

---

[4] Interestingly, Robert Park of the Chicago School, who is famous for his work into race and black urban experience, is also recognized as the founding figure in media sociology (Jacobs, 2009), especially for his research into press and power. Surprisingly, however, issues of race are very rarely touched upon in his research on the news and the formation of public opinion.

Jacobs (2014: 174) states in relation to the study of race and representation, '[w]e cannot only study texts themselves; we must also explore how media texts become objects of commentary and critique in a variety of multiple yet overlapping publics'.

Thus, news media is considered an important object of study, but, outside media and communication studies at least, less attention has been paid to popular culture. This was not always the case, as we shall shortly see, but one suspects that for scholars interested in race and racism, the issue of popular culture can be seen as rather trivial, or at least should not be our primary concern when this 'post-race' age has, if anything, intensified the urgency for dealing with escalating racial violence and worsening material realities for racialized groups. A quote from Claire Alexander (2008: 8) is illustrative in this regard, as she questions the fascination in what she disparagingly labels 'culturalist' approaches to race and ethnicity with issues of 'cultural commodification, production and consumption at the expense of people and the structures of power and material contexts within which "culture" takes shape'. She adds: '*I wonder whether, in the current climate, this is a luxury we can afford?*' (my emphasis).

In the introduction to a special issue of the journal *Cultural Studies* on Stuart Hall, Alexander (2009), in light of her criticism of this 'broader trend' in cultural studies, bemoans the loose and shallow ways in which Hall's work has been taken up by cultural studies theorists – used more as 'a store cupboard than a toolbox' (2009: 459). As she acknowledges, it was Hall's work on cultural identity that helped initially to drive the cultural turn in the social sciences in the 1980s, which brought questions of media, culture and representation into the centre of the growing field of critical race and ethnic studies. Hall's work on cultural identity and diaspora was itself inspired by the expressive culture of the second and third generations of Black and Asian Britons, particularly in the fields of visual culture including art, photography and cinema; as Hall states in an interview with Laurie Taylor, 'I was writing about identity and they were practising it' (quoted in Alexander, 2009: 468).

This field, initially at least, marked an important intervention in the study of race and racism in drawing attention to racism's cultural forms, furthering our understanding of the complex spectrums of racism that characterize contemporary racial politics (Back and Solomos, 2000). Popular culture and other forms of cultural representation became legitimate areas of study in revealing how meaning is attached to race and ethnicity within modern formations of national identity and globalized subjectivities. Furthermore, it allowed scholars to explore and articulate 'new ethnicities'

(Hall, 1996a[1988]; see also Gilroy, 1993b; Mercer, 1994; Brah, 1996; Back, 1996) that exploded absolutist versions of race and ethnicity, recognizing the plurality and heterogeneity of racial and ethnic groupings as intersected by class, gender, sexuality, region and so on, but nonetheless held together not by an essential biological core, but by the common experiences of oppression and shared histories of colonialism and slavery. This predominantly British scholarship had a parallel movement in the United States. As Cornel West (1990: 19) writes in his inimitable style, the purpose of the 'new cultural politics of difference', then, is 'to trash the monolithic and homogeneous in the name of diversity, multiplicity and heterogeneity; to reject the abstract, general and universal in light of the concrete, specific and particular; and to historicise, contextualise and pluralise by highlighting the contingent, provisional, variable, tentative, shifting and changing'. In this way, for Hall (1981: 239), popular culture is a battleground, 'where this struggle for and against a culture of the powerful is engaged' – which, he states, is the only reason he in fact gives a *'damn about it'* (my emphasis).

Scholars working in this new critical cultural approach to race and racism thus began to study popular culture in all its forms, particularly in music (Gilroy, 1993a; 1993b; Lipsitz, 1994; Rose, 1994; Back, 1995), television (Gray 1995; Malik, 2002) and film (Mercer, 1994; Ross, 1995). Yet following this initial wave of vital scholarly work, cultural studies loses its way, provoking an exasperated response from Hall (1996a: 271):

> [W]hat in God's name is the point of cultural studies? At that point, I think anybody who is into cultural studies seriously as an intellectual practice must feel, on their pulse, its ephemerality, its insubstantiality, how little it registers, how little we've been able to change anything or get anybody to do anything.

As Alexander alludes to above, what Hall is referring to here is the slipping away of the 'politics' in the 'politics of representation'.[5] Heavily influenced by postcolonial criticism, but coinciding with the rise in postmodern thought, textual studies of race and representation and popular culture as a whole would too easily slip into uncritical and celebratory accounts of media texts (perhaps as a long-overdue reaction to the dismissive way that popular culture was and still is regarded in political economy and critical theory). Certainly, in weaker versions of the study of popular culture and

---

[5] This specific quote emerges out of Hall's reflection on the AIDS epidemic. As a matter of life and death, the epidemic makes stark for Hall the marginality of intellectuals and how little effect they have on the real world; see Nelson et al. (1992: 6–7).

representation, issues of inequality and social justice are neglected, and the realities of racism and discrimination that minorities face in the everyday are side-tracked. Drawing strongly on poststructuralist ideas, this type of scholarship would slip easily into esotericism, and would, as it adopted increasingly elaborate and sophisticated techniques of deconstruction, taking on ever more abstract theories of culture and identity, find itself further removed from the actual lived experience of the minorities whose images were being studied (Sivanandan, 1990).

Yet, this criticism of the field is short-sighted, since the very best research into race and popular culture never lost sight of issues of racism in the everyday and structural level. The strongest studies were very clear in their motivation for studying media texts, in what they reveal about the nature of contemporary race formations and racism under neoliberalism. Gray (1995; 2005; 2013) is one of the most important and consistent con-tributors to the cultural politics of race debate and provides a nuanced take on the politics of representation, deconstructing simplistic binaries of posi-tive/negative, truthful/biased, stereotypical/authentic that frame weaker studies of media depictions of race and ethnicity. Like Hall, he too makes a persuasive argument for the importance of situating the cultural as 'a political terrain that matters' (Gray, 2005: 10). As he continues: 'Discourses about race in the United States are not just the products of structuring influences and regulatory technologies. They are produced in the represen-tations and logic of commonsense racial knowledge constituted in media such as television news and entertainment' (2005: 22). Like Gray, Evelyn Alsultany (2012), in her research into representations of Arabs and Muslims on US network television, draws attention to the complexity of represen-tational politics, where she considers the ideological work being done as seen in the surprising regularity, post-9/11, of 'sympathetic' Muslim and Arab characters in popular television drama series. Drawing attention to the affective responses such 'simplified complex' representations induce, Alsultany argues that their ideological purpose is 'to project the United States as an enlightened country that has entered a post-racial era' (2012: 16). In doing so, these narratives deny how 'the severity of the persistence of institutionalised racism becomes possible' (2012: 28), while allowing the state to enact racist policies towards its Arab and Muslim populations. There are strong echoes also of *Policing the Crisis* when Alsultany argues that media discourses help legitimate domestic and foreign US policies. Media discourses – both news and entertainment – come together, interact and contribute to a 'hegemonic field of meaning' (2012: 7) through which racist state policies and everyday discrimination take place.

My argument here is that popular culture still matters. Alexander is cautious about an excessive focus on issues of representation that becomes untethered from the material realities of racism, and this is precisely the challenge for those of us interested in popular culture: to ensure that our analyses can make a meaningful contribution to a discussion on structural racisms and social injustice. Yet, as much as I have referred to weaker textual studies of race, I believe in turn that critics of 'culturalism' in race research misunderstand what is at stake in a study of culture and representation that is alert to the economy or politics as exemplified in the work of Gray and Alsultany. What denouncements of culturalism are at risk of underestimating are the powerful psychosocial effects of racist discourses produced through the popular cultural texts circulated by the cultural industries. We can make this point again through the work of Fanon (1986: 152) when he describes how 'every neurosis, every abnormal manifestation, every affective erethism' in the racialized subject is produced 'slowly and subtly – with the help of books, newspapers, schools and their texts, advertisements, films, radio – [that] work their way into one's mind and shape one's view of the world of the group to which one belongs'. Quite simply, popular culture alongside news and current affairs determine – in terms of exerting pressure, as Raymond Williams defines it[6] – social understandings of race and difference, which in turn have powerful affects upon both dominant and minority groups.[7] I agree that the study of popular culture has been impeded by overly celebratory accounts (as much as overly critical ones) that can find political agency in any and all expressions of vernacular culture. But it is a grave mistake to regard the subject of media representation as embodied in mass commodities as a frivolous area of study. Indeed, Fanon appears to anticipate his analysis of children's comics being dismissed as trivial when he says, 'I shall be told that this is hardly important; but only because those who say it have not given much thought to the role of such magazines' (Fanon, 1986: 146). Coming from a figure who is a true radical intellectual, Fanon's comment suggests that the analysis of cultural texts, far from being a 'luxury' area of interest, is an

[6] Following Raymond Williams (1973: 4), I use the word 'determine' in terms of 'setting limits, exerting pressures', rather than as a definition that means totally controlling an outcome in its entirety.

[7] As Gilroy notes, Fanon described how both the oppressor and the oppressed are alienated by racism, where common humanity is amputated and 'authentic interaction between people becomes impossible' (Gilroy, 2010: 157). The psychological well-being of both parties is damaged by racism, to differing extents obviously, but the losses felt on both sides are significant.

absolutely critical object to consider, not just in the context of the intellectual study of race and racism, but in antiracist struggle itself.

Introducing race and the cultural industries

How then to analyse and write about race and the media in a way that is not insubstantial and ephemeral, and is able to contribute to meaningful social action / transformation in some way? In short: we need a new, stronger and more sustained emphasis on production. Textual studies of race in media representations – which is the stock method for exploring these issues – expose the ideologies and discourses about race contained within media texts, factual and fictional, that then feed into, help legitimate and are themselves shaped by the regulatory and political dimensions of white / European racism (Hesse, 2000). Goldberg (2012: 126), drawing upon Amin, characterizes the new 'machinic architecture' of racist states as the interaction of vernacular and biopolitical regimes, 'between everyday expression and newly fashioned modes of racially ordered securitisation and dispersed control', and the very best textual accounts of media representation consider how media texts literally mediate these interactions (as Alsultany's research into the representation and policing of Arab and Muslim bodies illustrates). The problem then for scholars of race and media is what to do with these insights. If we agree that media representations matter, how can research contribute to a radical politics in a way that does more than merely demand 'better', or 'positive', or 'truthful' depiction of racialized groups?

First, we need to go beyond these dualisms of positive / negative, truthful / biased, stereotypical / authentic, and think about instead, as Rattansi (2005: 292) puts it, the '*opening* up of representational practices' (my emphasis). Which brings us on to the issue of production. The reason I put the stress on 'opening' in Rattansi's quote is because it draws attention to cultural production, which, it is implied, in its industrial form narrows and reduces the range of narratives on marginality and being marginal in relation to race and ethnicity. Returning to Garnham's comment, cited above, on the lack of praxis involved in the deconstruction of media texts, his argument is that a radical political strategy in the context of the cultural sphere entails resisting and transforming the underlying dynamics of industrialized and capitalistic symbol production that increasingly shape it (1990: 44). In other words, following Garnham, I argue that attention must be paid to the cultural industries context within which representations of race get made. Put another way, we need to shift the discussion from the politics of representation, to the politics of production. As Garnham (1990: 6) explains, all mediated forms of communication involve the use of scarce material resources, and thus 'the understanding we have of the world, and thus our ability to change it, will be in their turn determined by the ways in which access to and control over those scarce resources is structured'. In specific relation to race, Downing and Husband (2005: 20) add that 'a political economy of the media that addresses the institutional dynamics of ethnic representation is a necessary adjunct to any study of the ethnic specificities of media content'. To reiterate: what is required is a theory of race and cultural production that illuminates the complex ways that the material shapes the symbolic – in other words, how the cultural industries make race – and that can explain both why particular representations of race persist and, crucially, why contradictions invariably occur. This is what a focus on production and the cultural industries specifically can bring.

Yet the cultural industries and cultural production comprise an area that, until now at least, has received little attention in critical studies of race and media (Hesmondhalgh and Saha, 2013). As stated, the emphasis of scholars in this area is nearly always on texts, though there has been some Birmingham School-inspired work on audiences (Jhally and Lewis, 1992; Gillespie, 1995; Hunt, 1997). For Downing and Husband the emphasis on the textual is a natural consequence of the primarily symbolic nature of the media, but, as the above quote suggests, they recognize the value of incorporating a political economy analysis into studies of representation of race, 'given the transposition of the demographics of ethnic diversity into the commercial imperatives of economically viable media audiences' (Downing and Husband, 2005: 22). In other words, representations of race and ethnicity are shaped by the commercial rationales of industrial production. Therefore, understanding and intervening in the politics of representation must pay due attention to production and the industrial context in which symbolic goods are made.

For Downing and Husband, the lack of research on production in this context is simply because it is such a tricky area to study, in terms of the logistics of gaining access to the sites of media and cultural production. This is certainly true (see Paterson et al., 2015), but I would add that this neglect is part of a broader trend in social sciences. Simon Cottle (2000: 15), for instance, alludes to the dominance of 'theoretical frameworks disposed to privilege the "moment" of the text'. Delving deeper, David Hesmondhalgh (2008) explains the lack of interest in production as following the cultural turn in the 1980s/1990s, which in itself was a reaction to the excessive 'productivism' of Marxism and critical theory that dominated social research and media and communication studies. This backlash brought with it a demand for texts and audiences/consumers to be taken seriously, and in the process media production research fell out of favour, and was even deemed out-dated (Hesmondhalgh, 2008). Considering that critical studies of race and ethnicity arrived as part of this cultural turn (and, indeed, helped drive it), then this explains the emphasis on text and, though to a lesser extent, audiences, in studies of race and the media.

Such was the impact of this shift that it is only until very recently that a critical interest in race, ethnicity and cultural production has emerged. Yet any researcher who wants to work on this issue has to immediately deal with certain caveats set by cultural studies scholars. One such quali-fication is to stress that a focus on production does not presuppose that the meanings that audiences consume from a media text is automatically determined by the producer. In 'Encoding/Decoding', Hall (1980[1973]) argues that audiences do not necessarily consume messages in the way that media producers intended, and in fact can produce their own oppositional readings. It is a mistake, however, to assume that the audience studies that 'Encoding/Decoding' spawned took this to mean that media producers are insignificant, or that audiences hold all the power. Rather, it was when postmodernism came into prominence that the question of ideology and the mass media fell by the wayside (see Garnham, 1990: 1–2), and to this day scholars interested in a production perspective can immediately expect to be challenged on the grounds that they are assuming the passivity of audiences. The most astute research being done in critical studies of race in cultural production – and production studies as a whole in fact – do not merely acknowledge the agency of audiences, but build issues of audience reception into their argument. Gray (1995; 2005) and Timothy Havens (2013), for instance, underline the impact of global audiences on the pro-duction of black US television. Havens draws attention to the myriad ways in which these shows are received in different geographical and social contexts, and how the attempts of executives to interpret the particular consumption patterns of foreign audiences produce 'industry lore' that influences production and network decisions at home.[8]

There is still a danger that we afford too much agency to the audience – or, rather, interpret all cultural meaning as relative – and in the process downplay the influence of the cultural industries, particularly in relation

[8] Havens is working explicitly in the new paradigm of cultural studies of media produc-tion, which perhaps explains his sensitivity to audiences (since culture in the everyday is a key area of concern in cultural studies of media) as well as production dynamics.

to representations of race and ethnicity. To counter this, Downing and Husband (2005) produce a deeper reading of Hall's theory of representation, which, they argue, as Alexander does, has been deployed somewhat lethargically by researchers. Working within a poststructuralist framework, Hall argues that all representations are socially constructed (that is, they are never a 'mirror' of society), and that all meaning relating to representation is constructed within history and culture. In other words, representations are produced through discourse, which defines how we represent others and ourselves. Moreover, these discursive frameworks allocate us 'subject-positions'. We of course have the power to move out of these positions, but we nonetheless tend to adopt the 'line of least resistance to our being discursively placed' (Downing and Husband, 2005: 43); as Downing and Husband suggest, although we can reject these subject-positions, we rarely in fact do. Hall thus uses the term representation not in the reductive terms of presence/absence or constructive/unconstructive that feature in weaker cultural studies (and policy accounts), but in relation to how such representations are received – part of a more complete circuit of production and reception. As Hall (1996a: 447) himself states:

> The cultural industries do have the power constantly to rework and reshape what they represent; and, by repetition and selection, to impose and implant such definitions of ourselves as fit more easily the descriptions of the dominant or preferred culture. That is what the concentration of cultural power – the means of culture-making in the hands of the few – actually means. These definitions don't have the power to occupy our minds; they don't function on us as if we are blank screens. But they do occupy and rework the interior contradictions of feeling and perception in the dominated classes; they do find or clear a space of recognition in those who respond to them.

Hall's reference to the 'concentration of cultural power' once again brings us back to political economy concerns (which, as I shall show in the following chapter, only receives fleeting attention in Hall's analysis), but also, echoing Fanon, to the psychosocial effects of representation, reflecting as they do the 'interior contradictions of feeling and perception in the dominated classes'. Herman Gray is not a political economist, and would probably not even describe himself as a production theorist (even though he produced an exemplary form of production research in his empirical study of an independent jazz record label; see Gray, 1988). Yet his interest on the cultural politics of black cultural production makes a strong case for a contextual account of the reading and evaluation of cultural texts. For Gray (1995; 2005), the conditions of production (in its institutional and noninstitutional contexts) are critical to understanding the new cultural politics of blackness. As he states, 'black cultural expression is shaped by flexible conditions of production, new technologies of communication and circulation, regulatory state policies, expanding means and sites of representation, competing claims of ownership and authenticity, and contested discourses of judgement and evaluation' (2005: 18). Particularly pertinent in terms of this book is one of Gray's (1995) most cited case studies on commercial network television in the United States and how governmental deregulation and industrial reorganization in the 1980s contributed 'to the enabling conditions (and constraints) within which the black television market/audience [was] constructed as a profitable (or ignored as unprofitable) commodity by the television industry' (1995: 20). It is worth underlining the dialectical fashion in which he unpacks this particular case of cultural production – and the reference to enabling/ constraining forces in particular – which, as we shall see, resonates strongly with cultural industries scholars' conceptualization of commodification. Gray is interested in the strategies that black cultural producers employ to 'negotiate the contemporary cultural and institutional landscape' (1995: 15). Accordingly, in order to develop a keener sense of how blackness operates culturally and politically in certain temporal and spatial contexts, the method must be a mapping of 'the discursive, political, and social conditions that structure the cultural and social spaces of black cultural production' (1995: 15).

A focus on cultural production not only deepens our understanding and awareness of how media discourses of race and ethnicity circulate within capitalism, but also helps us consider and formulate potential cultural political interventions. Such an approach is effectively a conscious way of injecting the 'politics' back into the 'politics of representation'. It demands more than a question of how we can convert negative representations of race into positive ones; it also requires thinking through new practices and strategies that can open up representational politics, leading to, as Gray (2005: 10) puts it, 'vibrant black cultural manoeuvres and practices that see, imagine and engage the world differently, in all of its complexity and myriad possibilities'. This resembles the multiple ways that critical race and postcolonial scholars have addressed the issue of cultural politics.[9] And when coupled with a politics of redistribution, it amounts to effective and meaningful antiracist politics, in what I consider a Fanonian sense. (After

---

[9] I am thinking of Barnor Hesse (2000) on *cultural transruptions*, Homi Bhabha (1997) on the *minoritization of the arts* and Michael Keith (2005) on *new cosmopolitan imaginaries*.

all, Fanon argued that the colonial subject 'must wage war on both levels' – that is, the levels of subjectivity and individual psychology, and social-economic structure; see Chen, 1998: 10.[10])

The one thing lacking in Gray's account, however, is that he does not in fact pay that much attention to the specificities of production in the cultural industries. It is perhaps because he is attending to multiple institutional and industrial settings, from US network television, to art galleries and cultural centres, to the Internet, that he discusses black cultural production in more general terms,[11] but when I use the term cultural production I am specifically referring to industrial or semi-industrial forms of symbol creation and circulation in modern societies that relate directly to the media, rather than to the general creation of vernacular culture. As will be developed further in the following chapter, this book, which deals predominantly with what Hesmondhalgh (2013) defines as the 'core' cultural industries – television, music, film and publishing – but also includes discussion of other cultural sectors such as the theatre and the arts, is explicitly concerned with the political economy of the media and its emergent 'cultures of production' (Negus, 1997) through which representations of race and ethnicity get made.[12]

The central premise of this book is that the persistence and churn of particular media discourses of race can be explained by a deep engagement with the very distinctive nature of the cultural industries, particularly in relation to the issue of commodification. Commodification is at the core of the work that the cultural industries do, transforming an aesthetic expression of culture into a commodity to be bought and sold – for instance, a song into a record, a script into a TV programme or film, a manuscript into

[10] Echoing an earlier point made in the chapter, for Fanon racism is not just an element of the superstructure, but instead has 'a substantive capacity to structure the character of social relations' (Coulthard, 2007).

[11] There have been some powerful studies of cultural production in this broader sense, particularly from feminist critical race studies/anthropology, that are global in outlook and examine the making of vernacular culture, unravelling the complex interactions between the global and the local, the macro and the everyday; see Clarke and Thomas (2006), Zhao and Chakravartty (2007), Tsing (2011).

[12] One sector that receives less attention in this book is the promotional industries – advertising, PR and marketing. While they can be broadly considered part of the creative industries, they work according to their own distinct and very specific rationales and logics. That is not to say that there is not any overlap, but for the purpose of this book I have chosen to focus on cultural production in the context of the cultural industries only. Two exemplary production studies that relate to race in advertising and marketing specifically are Dávila (2012) and McClintock (1995).

a book. I will argue that it is the process of commodification that steers the work of cultural producers into reproducing historical constructions of Otherness.

Understanding commodification's role in the governance of race entails a macro perspective that unpacks cultural commodification in relation to capitalism and legacies of empire. It also entails a micro perspective that explores the specific stages of production in the cultural industries that constitute commodification in order to see how the cultural text comes to be racialized during the production phase. In this way, I will argue that commodification acts as a technology of racialized governmentalities in that it consists of an assemblage of rationalized processes, apparatus, rationales and logics; and that these are embodied in each stage of cultural production that governs the representation of race and racism in very specific ways, which mostly, though not always, lead to the reproduction of historical constructions of Otherness. There are two further key arguments that will be developed in relation to this. First, the logics behind rationalization in industrial cultural production are so dominant and persuasive that it can be seen why even apparently enlightened minority producers end up producing racialized tropes in their work (such that I argue that diversifying the media workforce alone will have little effect on the diversity of representations emanating from the cultural industries). Second, that being said, commodification needs to be understood as a fundamentally ambivalent process, which has both enabling and constraining tendencies. While it exploits labour and oversupplies certain types of commodities over others, it has also resulted in a vast proliferation of symbolic goods that have (whether we like it or not) enriched our lives. Moreover, as much as audiences rely on familiarity, they also crave difference and novelty. As such, while reductive representations of race dominate in the media, there are still moments and opportunities where the enabling properties of commodification can be harnessed by producers in order to make race in radical and subversive ways that contribute to its undoing.

The structure of the book

This book explores the representation of race and racism in the cultural industries of the West. It deals mostly with the UK and the US, but also Europe, Canada and Australasia. This is out of necessity; with the book's interest in race and cultural production, the relatively small field of production studies engaged with questions of race come mostly from British or North American contexts. While these Western nations share their roots in the Enlightenment from which modern ideas about race are effectively derived, there is a danger in banding together countries with very specific histories of colonialism and migration that have shaped their relationships to multiculture. Consequently, when necessary I will situate the case studies of race in cultural production from which I draw upon within their particular (trans)national sociocultural and historical contexts. This focus on just the West admittedly leaves this book open to charges of Eurocentrism (Zhao and Chakravartty, 2007). But while its contribution to the important project of de-Westernizing media/communication studies appears limited, it is my belief that the interdisciplinary framework that I conceptualize for this book – a sociological approach to cultural production informed by cultural industries research and postcolonial/critical race studies – can be applied to studies of how the media makes racialized, gendered, classed and sexualized identities that go beyond the 'Occident'.

Having introduced the book's main themes and the rationale behind it, in chapter 2, I outline a theory of race and cultural production that frames the analysis that follows in the rest of the book. As discussed, production studies of race are generally lacking in media and sociology. However, the chapter critically examines two fields where studies of this kind do exist: journalism/newsroom studies and cultural studies of production. While I highlight the strengths of these fields, I also argue that they would benefit from an underpinning in a more robust theory of cultural production that adequately integrates race and ethnicity, combining analyses of the macro and micro, structure and agency, and change and continuity in the cultural industries. In response, I outline this book's particular interdisciplinary approach that combines the 'cultural industries' tradition of critical political economy with postcolonial/critical race studies, which, I argue, can best explain how capitalism and legacies of empire shape the production of representations. Ending Part I, the purpose of chapter 2 is to provide the theoretical and conceptual framework for what is to follow.

The remainder of the book is split into two further parts consisting of two chapters each, with Part II exploring the macro dimensions of race and the cultural industries. Chapter 3 situates issues of race and ethnicity in cultural production within the context of the global shift towards neoliberalism. While I draw from some historical case studies (and advocate a historical approach), I focus very much on the contemporary, which entails a discussion of the neoliberal incarnation of capitalism that has grown in ascendency in the UK and US in particular since the late 1980s. I work with Zhao and Chakravaryty's (2007: 4) definition of neoliberalism as a political philosophy 'rooted in a claim that the market is more rational than the state in the redistribution of public resources and is based on a "return" to individualism animated by modern consumer sovereignty'. One of the chapter's tasks is to tie together two dimensions of neoliberalism that are nearly always analysed separately: first, neoliberalism, in terms of the 'post-racial' moment, as representing a new form of racialized governance, and, second, neoliberalism in relation to the increasing commercialization and marketization of the media industries, particularly in the West, where deregulation has intensified media concentration, arguably leading to less diversity in output as well as ownership. One attempt by scholars to think through the economic and racial effects of advanced capitalism has been through the notion of the 'commodification of race'. According to this radical cultural studies perspective, the repetition of reductive representations of race in the media is the inevitable consequence when the expressive cultures of minority groups are co-opted by capitalism and transformed into a commodity. But I want to problematize this narrative by drawing from the work of cultural industries theorists such as David Hesmondhalgh and Nicholas Garnham, who underline how commodification is in fact an ambivalent process that is both enabling and constraining. In response, the chapter argues for a shift from the notion of the commodification of race to a more discursive notion of the racialization of the cultural commodity. This perspective provides a further case for focusing our attention on cultural production itself, at the same time developing a more complex and nuanced understanding of how the counter narratives of difference are managed within capitalism.

In chapter 4, I tackle the issue of policy and, specifically, diversity discourse. One critical issue that the commodification of race narrative fails to recognize is how minority cultural producers are often supported by media and cultural policy, based on national and local, civic and multicultural rationales rather than commercial ones. As such, this chapter critically examines the policies behind public service media, arts funding and diversity initiatives in particular, each of which attempts to address the 'problem' of race and multiculturalism in the media, in terms of both portrayal and participation. Drawing from critical policy studies as well as cultural industries research, feminist studies and critical legal theory, the chapter examines race and ethnicity in cultural and media policy in different Western contexts. Such policy has attempted to enable the work of minorities in the media, whether through public service remits or subsidies, seemingly designed to protect cultural production from market forces. But this chapter argues that cultural policy in contemporary Western societies follows neoliberal logics that govern difference in a way that amounts to what Hall (1996b: 471) calls 'segregated visibility'. It explores how discourses around multiculturalism and diversity are shaped by wider ideological and economic forces, where it is argued that recent trends in policy have been shaped by and have facilitated the shift towards neoliberalism, acting as a form of racialized governance. Moreover, the chapter discusses how policy has constructed particular cultures of production in the cultural industries, which steer the work of those involved in the production of popular cultural representations of race and ethnicity in very specific ways.

Having fleshed out the macro dimensions of race and cultural production, in Part III of the book, I zoom in and focus on the dynamics of cultural production at the micro level. The subject of chapter 4 is how cultural goods come to be racialized during the process of cultural production. After a brief discussion of the issue of authorship, I begin the chapter proper by critically assessing a field of cultural studies research that has attempted to explain the reductive making of race through empirical research. Such studies demonstrate how individual creative workers bring with them socially derived common-sense understandings of race that manifest through implicit bias during the production process. While there is something very persuasive about this argument, it cannot explain those all-too frequent moments when minority cultural producers (who, if you asked them, would be adamant they hold no such racial bias) also reproduce the same reductive tropes of race, gender, class and sexuality. As such, through applying a cultural industries approach, I demonstrate how specific stages of production contain within them particular rationalizing logics that constrain the practices of minority cultural producers. So, for instance, I will demonstrate how it is through rationalized processes such as formatting, packaging and marketing that historical constructions of Otherness (in its racial and gendered forms in particular) are reproduced, despite the motivations of individual actors to do the opposite. I call this the rationalizing/racializing logic of capital and I argue that it is how race is governed in the cultural industries.

One of the key aims of *Race and the Cultural Industries* is to highlight the ambivalence of commodification and popular culture. That is, while the cultural industries of overdeveloped, industrial modernity have a tendency towards homogeneity and standardization, cultural production should nonetheless be understood as complex, contested and ambivalent. In chapter 6, I explore how cultural producers have harnessed the enabling capacities of commodification and managed to produce progressive forms of multiculture. The chapter draws from a number of case studies, which explore different types of enabling spaces for minorities, including minority ethnic media, independent media, the new forms of digital production, public service media and even corporate media. Despite this, in the book's conclusion I argue that commodification is a mostly constraining process and that the cultural industries need significant transformation in order to contribute meaningfully to social justice and minority empowerment. However, I will add that, through shrewd industry practice, cultural producers can build more successful cultural political interventions. Put another way, it is argued that a radical cultural political programme is absolutely contingent upon production strategies – that is, an effective 'politics of production'. Situating the politics of representation explicitly within the cultural industries and industrial cultural production gives us a more nuanced and complex understanding of the ideological role of the media in the making of race, which in turn leads to a broader understanding of the governance of racial and ethnic identities under neoliberalism.

Coda

Home of the Brave, the film that was referenced in the quote from Fanon that opened this chapter, was based on a 1946 play written by Arthur Laurents. In the original production, the main protagonist was Jewish and the central theme was about antisemitism rather than racism. However, when it came to adapting the play for the cinema, the main character was turned into a black soldier, since, Laurents was told, 'Jews have been done' (Deane, 2009: 17). How to make sense of this comment from the film's producer Stanley Kramer? Film studies on this period of cinema draw attention to how *Home of the Brave* and other films like it are reflective of the new liberal attitudes towards race as part of the postwar reconstruction of the United States (Nickel, 2004). Indeed, films dramatizing specifically African American experiences became a subgenre within the form of the social issue film, dubbed 'Negro Pix' (Nickel, 2004: 25). The filming of *Home of the Brave* in fact was conducted in total secrecy, which Kramer explained in terms of wanting to evade the attention of racist groups (and the potential meddling of black organizations for that matter). But also motivating his decision was Kramer's desire to make this the first film on this issue, as he was aware of several other films in production at the same time that were carrying a similar racial theme (Deane, 2009: 21–22). In other words, he wanted to get his film featuring a black lead out first, before anyone else.

What this short anecdote demonstrates is that there is a cultural industrial context to Fanon's alienating and traumatic experience in the cinema.

In order to get onto the big screen, the experience of the black character is filtered through issues of formatting and what Georgina Born (2010: 192) describes as 'genre-in-process', and formed through the dialectical tension that characterizes cultural production between the need for novelty and difference, on the one hand (where the social margins are seen as fertile ground for mining), and the inherent tendency of capitalistic production towards standardization and homogenization on the other. The media-scape has changed dramatically since Fanon's time; the cultural industries are as diverse as ever, with some people of colour even holding senior positions in key institutions. Yet this has not translated into a more varied, diverse range of depictions of human life. As the dominant domestic/global cultural industries shift ever more towards neoliberal market modes, this has impacted upon the representation of racialized groups and the media discourses that circulate about them. The aim of the book is to understand how.

2

Approaching Race and Cultural Production

Introduction

To better grasp and then transform the nature of industrial cultural production so that it opens up representational practices rather than constrains them demands a more nuanced understanding of the structure of the media industries, its relation to capitalism, nation and empire, and the nature of production within it. This needs to be based on a theoretical foundation that captures and can explain fully the complexities, contradictions and contestations of symbol production under capitalistic conditions. Essentially, we are searching for a framework that pulls together the political economic and the sociocultural dimensions of industrial cultural production, that incorporates an analysis of structure, agency and text. This is certainly an ambitious task but, as I will outline, focusing our attention on the distinctiveness of symbol creation via the cultural industries approach (Hesmondhalgh, 2008; 2013) is a useful starting point for untangling this complex web of macro and micro variables. The aim of this chapter, then, is to formulate a theory of race, ethnicity and cultural production, which provides the framework for the rest of the book.

Before outlining the structure of this chapter, I want to open up the discussion regarding the need for a more systematic theory by briefly returning to Hall et al.'s *Policing the Crisis*, this time focusing on some of the criticism it received. The book is acknowledged as marking a key moment in the study of race and racism. As Jacobs (2014) points out, before this intervention sociologists were focused on the social factors that constituted racial consciousness without recognizing the media's role in such processes. Taking the moral panic around mugging in Britain in the 1970s as their subject, Hall et al. adopted a Gramscian framework to argue that the racialization of urban youth that resulted was the product of a crisis of hegemony, born out of postwar cultural rupture and economic decline, which in turn paved the way for Thatcherism and a more authoritarian state. Central to Hall et al.'s analysis was the role of the media, and specifically the press, in the creation of this moral panic and its overreaction to the 'problem' of black youth. They find that police and politicians, acting as 'primary definers', effectively framed the media's response to black criminality, which in turn created a consensus for the state to apply policies that worked in its favour rather than deal with the problem of youth unemployment, let alone racism.

For its complex account of media, ideology and race, *Policing the Crisis* is rightly regarded as an important piece of work. However, it is not without its critics, especially in the field of political economy/communications studies. While it is recognized that Hall and his collaborators produce a remarkably sophisticated and nuanced account of ideology, one that manages to counter the functionalist tendencies associated with French philosopher Louis Althusser (who was a key influence for Hall), political economists and media sociologists have both argued that a major oversight of the book is critical engagement with the media itself. A clear intervention of Hall's work in general is in underlining the polysemic nature of cultural meaning and, as such, his interest is in the production and consumption of ideology – and the mass media's implication in this – conceptualized as a site of ongoing struggle. Yet, what is missing in his account is how exactly ideology is produced by and through the media. This is a criticism articulated most strongly by Nick Stevenson (2002: 35), who argues that Hall's 'over-concentration on the theme of ideology means that other determinant levels, such as the ownership and control of the mass media, drop out of the analysis'.[1] Stevenson claims that although mass communication is a core object of focus for Hall, he is surprisingly uninterested in media institutions. This is a slightly unfair criticism, especially if we consider Hall's (1993; 1995) contributions to debates on the BBC and public service broadcasting in particular. But Stevenson is correct in pointing out that, for someone who underlines the centrality of culture in political, economic and social processes, Hall in fact shows little interest in the dynamics of (industrial) cultural production itself. While *Policing the Crisis* does pay attention to news production, the main focus is on the level of semiotic meaning; what is ignored are the internal and external dynamics of news production and an account of the political economy of the media. As Stevenson (2002: 40) states, Hall et al. in general fail 'to trace back cultural production to institutional levels of analysis'. Cottle (2000: 11) adds that the authors' 'explanation of the exact mechanisms linking

---

[1] For a critical political economy critique of the perceived over-emphasis on ideology in communications scholarship, see also Mosco (1996) and Garnham (2011).

media institutions, professional practices and cultural representations to political forces of change may now appear under- (or over-)theorised and in need of empirical support'. And of particular relevance to what is to follow in this chapter, Stevenson concludes that although Hall offers an incredibly sophisticated critique of how ideology is diffused and received in society, in doing so he 'severs the determinate relation between the *material structures and symbolic forms*' (Stevenson, 2002: 43; my emphasis).

As we shall see in chapter 3, this is a criticism that can be levelled at some of the most important theorists of race, culture and the media, from Stuart Hall to bell hooks to Edward Said: that their complex theories of white supremacist capitalist patriarchy, as hooks (1992) memorably put it, lack an empirical understanding of how such ideologies are actually produced by the media. This does not in my view undermine their arguments (as I shall certainly underline chapter 3), but rather, their accounts could do with being augmented by a critical account of media production, not just to deepen our understanding of how media texts are encoded with racialized meanings, but as the initial and crucial step towards the formulation of counter-hegemonic, counter-discursive strategies of difference. As Elfriede Fürsich (2002: 66) argues in the context of news production, while Hall suggests a strategy that contests the dominant regime of representation as 'located within the complexities and ambivalence of representations itself, [his] strategy is difficult to implement as an actual journalistic strategy'. To reiterate: Hall offers the most complex and sophisticated critique of how media representations impact upon the social, but, like Fürsich, I question whether this is enough to build a concrete counter politics of difference.

What *Policing the Crisis* lacks is an account of news/cultural production. An analysis of cultural production is central to understanding how media texts come to constitute particular discursive formations of race and ethnicity and how and where necessary interventions to disrupt/strengthen these knowledge formations need to be mounted. Moreover, such an analysis needs to be able to cover the full macro and micro contexts of production in the cultural industries. The aim of this chapter, then, is to put forward a theory of cultural production that is attuned to the dynamics between the political economy of the cultural industries, cultural production 'on the ground' and representations of race as they appear in cultural texts. In other words, it seeks to formulate a theory of race, ethnicity and cultural production that incorporates an analysis and explanation of structure–labour–text.

As stated in the previous chapter, the relative lack of attention paid to issues of production is a product of the cultural turn in media and cultural studies that rejected the productivism of the Marxist accounts that dominated the study of the (mass) media. That is not to say that studies of race in media production are totally absent, and in this chapter I critically examine two fields of research that have been most attuned to these issues: (1) production studies of news (including newsroom studies), and (2) cultural studies of production. While these two broad approaches have produced many valuable insights – and, indeed, will provide many of the case studies that I draw upon in the following chapters – I will be highlighting their limitations as well as strengths in order to shed light upon what a more systematic theory of race and cultural production needs to look like. In the second half of this chapter, I put forward such a theory, which, as stated, is heavily influenced by the cultural industries approach to the media. This includes an analysis of cultural production under capitalism, an analysis of creative labour and an analysis of cultural texts, in order to unpack the determinate relation between material structures and symbolic forms, as Stevenson puts it. This provides the conceptual framework that structures the remainder of the book.

Newsroom studies of race

As the author of the one of the few book-length empirical studies of race and ethnicity in media production, Simon Cottle makes the strongest case for the importance of a contextual analysis of race and representation. In his research into the production of 'minority ethnic programmes' in the BBC and independent sector, Cottle (1997) begins by critiquing the type of textual analysis that dominates studies of race and ethnicity in the media, stating that:

> Without a full appreciation of the different institutional contexts and programme-making regimes shaping programme production across the television industry, as well as the diverse professional aims and cultural politics of representation enacted by different producers, critics are poor placed to understand the parameters and constraints shaping those programmes later subjected to analysis and (often heated) debate. (1997: 1)

Cottle is arguing, as I do, that one cannot fully appreciate, evaluate or explain a text without understanding the various forces of production (from the macro to the micro) that have shaped how it appears at the point of consumption. Moreover, Cottle alludes to the political potential of such an approach – though it is only hinted at in parentheses – when he goes on to say that critical engagement with media output by itself 'remains insufficient if we want to understand better (and possibly intervene to realign) the forces currently shaping programme representations' (1997: 1).

The subjects of Cottle's book are producers working on current affairs programmes and, as a result, he situates his research within scholarship on news production. For Cottle, sociological studies of news production and journalism are 'by far the most developed area of research into media professionals and media production' (1997: 12). Certainly, if we look at those journalism studies focused on the newsroom and production dynamics in terms of the sheer body of work it has generated, it is hard to argue with Cottle's assertion that this type of research is at the forefront of production research as a whole. As such, while this book's focus is on popular culture, I want to consider whether production studies of news can provide a potential framework for a theory of race and cultural production.

What I refer to as production studies of the news, encompassing newsroom and journalism studies, broadly describes research interested in the everyday production of news texts. The development of the field reflects the evolution of the industry, shifting from a focus on the bureaucratic routines of news organizations, where such institutions were once cohesive, singular sites ripe for ethnographic immersion, to a multifaceted, multi-method approach that has had to adapt to the temporal and spatial fragmentation of a news ecosystem transformed by the Internet (Paterson et al., 2015). Although the industry has transformed, the questions remain the same, with scholars interested in journalistic practices in relation to routines, norms, news values, use of sources and objectivity, as well as questions of power, influence and ideology, particularly in relation to technological change. The field can crudely be split into two types. One is the media sociology approach that Cottle alludes to, with a strong emphasis on ethnographic studies of the newsroom. The other is a communications studies approach to news production, which, coming from a more positivist tradition, deploys content analysis and qualitative interviews (and to some degree, participant observation) to think through why news stories take the form that they do. On the specific study of race, ethnicity and the news, the latter approach has provided the most studies (mostly from the US), often coupling strong empirical material with theoretical insights drawn from critical race studies.

Studies of representations of race have provided damning evidence of the way that racialized minorities are treated in the Western news media. It exposes how people of colour are either invisible or stereotyped (as law-breakers, on welfare, drug addicts or dealers), how refugees/asylum seekers/migrants are portrayed as at best a drain on resources and at worst a contamination of the nation's body politic, and how Muslims are presented as having beliefs and values that are irreconcilably different, incompatible with and a literal threat to the West. In the rare instances that we see positive news stories, these tend to be framed using Orientalist tropes: the 'steel bands, saris and somosas' approach (see Troyna and Carrington, 2011: 79) that characterizes 'boutique multiculturalism' (Fish, 1997). There are exceptions, and the best textual studies of the news demonstrate how representations of Otherness are ambivalent (Fürsich, 2002) and conceptualize the news landscape as a site of struggle over meaning (Jacobs, 2014). But if such research suffers from the same limitations as textual analyses of representation that I described in chapter 1, production studies of news makes an important intervention by drawing attention to how the diversity and dynamics of the newsroom shape stories involving racialized minorities.

In terms of issues of diversity – or, rather, the lack thereof – researchers find a clear correlation between the negative representation of people of colour and the lack of people of colour in the newsroom. Studies of diversity from a production perspective focus on the overwhelming whiteness of news sources (Poindexter et al., 2003; Grabe et al., 1999); the whiteness of newsrooms with very few minorities in senior editorial roles (Johnston and Flamiano, 2007); and the lack of trust between minority reporters and white senior editorial staff (Rivas-Rodriguez et al., 2004). Pease et al. (2001) acknowledge, albeit cautiously and with some caveats, that in those instances when there has been an increase in the number of minorities working as full-time journalists in a newsroom setting, this has had some positive impact upon the representation of racial and ethnic groups.

Implicit in these production studies of newsroom diversity – as well as in policy accounts, as we shall see in chapter 4 – is the assumption that a more diverse workforce will automatically improve the representation of minorities in the news. But this is called into question by scholars who choose to focus more on the dynamics of news gathering and news making than on just the ethnic and racial constitution of newsrooms, and who expose how increasingly commercial imperatives as well as journalistic routines and norms place constraints on reporters (particularly those from minority backgrounds) and their ability to tell stories in the way that they want to.

For instance, this approach draws attention to the effects of commercialization and tabloidization on the industry and the pressures that a 24-hour news cycle has placed on reporters, who do not have time or the resources to properly research and write meaningful or nuanced stories about race (Heider, 2000). It also exposes the racialized nature of journalistic norms, where news values of objectivity, accuracy, balance and fairness place a sort of negative burden of representation on minority journalists who are wary of appearing as advocates for their groups (Nishikawa et al., 2009). In a similar vein, scholars reveal a form of 'racial profiling' that occurs in the newsroom itself, where minority reporters are expected to cover minority stories and rarely little else; thus news production amounts to a 'hegemony of whiteness' (Pritchard et al., 2007: 232), through which diversity initiatives that appear progressive 'actually privileges whiteness and marginalises the very journalists of colour whom it purports to welcome into the fold' (Mellinger quoted in Pritchard et al., 2007: 244). Journalistic practices and norms in effect produce conformity, such that the efforts to increase the numbers of black journalists actually has little impact on the nature of news (Wilson, 2000).

If we zoom out and focus on the theoretical/political/methodological underpinnings of production studies of news in a broad sense, we could characterize the field as predominantly focused on agency, taking individual subjects as its starting point. This can be read as a response to economic determinist and functionalist accounts of news production that typify certain forms of political economy research. Emily Drew (2011), for instance, frames her production study of the news explicitly against Althusserian accounts of ideology that she argues leave no gaps for contestation. Instead, she wants to concentrate on the 'human agency of journalists' (2011: 356). Interviewing white journalists contributing to a special series of articles dedicated to understanding racism in the post-Civil Rights era, Drew produces an optimistic take on the transformative effects that writing these in-depth 'treatment' pieces had on her subjects. In particular, she looks at how producing these features in turn generated critical self-reflection in the journalists, who were forced to address difficult questions of content, norms and diversity in newsrooms. Mark Deuze (2005: 452–454) similarly sees multiculturalism as a potential challenge to journalists and their understanding of their responsibilities as journalists to (multicultural) society.

However, other than the issue of interview-based research, where the white respondents were perhaps always going to produce celebratory accounts of the effects of working on these treatments,[2] the problem with Drew's account is that the sole focus on production means that the issue of content and representation slips away and it is assumed that the treatments in questions are immediately progressive/radical. In contrast, Peter Parisi's

---

[2] For a critique of interview-based methodologies, see Jerolmack and Khan (2014: 178).

(1998) study of the type of lengthy, extensively reported pieces on race and racism produced by Drew's subjects finds something more ambivalent. Focusing on the textual features of the *New York Times* series, 'Another America: Life on 129th Street', but contextualized within news production, Parisi finds that the adoption of a certain kind of narrative style that characterizes this type of journalism has troubling epistemological effects. As he explains, 'the aestheticism of the photos and of the writing emerges as a sort of domestic "orientalism," projecting the residents into an exotic but profoundly alien culture'. Thus, this journalistic norm produces an effect that undermines the (genuine) intentions of the editor and the black journalist working on the story: 'his desire to present a "compelling," "riveting" story may also animate the focus on personal lives in "Another America" [but] this [narrative] framework grievously misrepresented the neighborhood's social vitality, human inventiveness and significant civility' (1998: 249).

Fürsich (2002) also produces a more complex take on the politics of representation, which is grounded in questions related to production. She adopts a normative approach tackling head on what it will take to transform representations of Otherness. Fürsich draws inspiration from visual anthropology, which is most concerned with the question of how to represent the Other. Like Parisi, and indeed like Drew, Fürsich puts the onus on the producer to reflect more on their practice in order to transform it. Thus, production is a site of struggle, where the emphasis needs to be on journalists and cultural producers creating their own 'alternative narrative frameworks' and formulating new 'narrative and ideological strategies' (Parisi, 1998: 249). The problem of representation depends on intervening in and transforming the nature of representation itself.

Yet I believe that the authors cited have too much faith in the agency of the author. The interest in narrative frameworks in both Fürsich's and Parisi's accounts ignore how such frameworks are formed through commercial imperatives and broader political economic (and socialcultural) forces, and that attempting to change the nature of representation will necessitate transforming the structures of production themselves. This is by no means easy; as Parisi (1998: 250) himself admits, 'attempts to revise journalistic narrative strategies are likely to face severe resistance'. If there is too much onus on individual agency in production studies of news, then Simon Cottle's (1997; 2000) important intervention is in swinging the emphasis back the other way and focusing more on the way that institutions (and their political economies) constrain journalistic practice. Cottle identifies four forces that shape production of ethnic minority production, including sociohistorical and technological forces as well as political economic ones: (1) the changing regulatory context of broadcasting and institutional responses to this; (2) development of new technologies; (3) intensified commercial imperatives and effects of this upon programme commissioning; and (4) changing cultural politics of 'race' and multiculturalism (1997: 7–8). Cottle later goes on to draw attention to wider 'geopolitical realities' (2000: 17) as a key structural determinant that shapes news production, a dimension that tends to be neglected in journalism studies. His main argument is that too much explanatory burden can be placed on journalists; that is, their agency can be overstated. Referring to production studies research, Cottle demonstrates that racism or racialized storytelling is not simply down to the individual journalist's personal prejudices, stating that 'these studies collectively point to the fallacy of singling out journalists and their attitudes as sufficient means of understanding the nature, routines and forms of journalism'. Put another way, institutional contexts and professional practices themselves constrain the work of cultural producers that impacts upon representation. The framing of racial and ethnic minorities within racialized tropes in news reporting cannot always be explained in terms of racism, or institutional racism. Or rather, it is much more complex than that. But as I have shown in the examples above, the problem for many production studies of news is that they are so concerned with challenging a functionalist interpretation of news production that there is a danger that too much autonomy is afforded to the individual journalist. Consequently, I appreciate Cottle's attempt to tip our attention back towards issues of structure. As he states, 'complex institutional arrangements and economic processes, themselves often shaped by and shaping of surrounding social, cultural and political forces, rarely grant individuals an entirely free hand – even if the professional ideology of journalism suggests otherwise' (1997: 12).

In this way Cottle, has the most sophisticated account of race in news production, taking on political economy, institutions and newsroom dynamics, and the varying effects that these have on the journalist, and, albeit to a lesser extent, the text itself. There is also an acknowledgement of historical factors and the changing politics of multiculturalism, though these too are underdeveloped in his analysis. Indeed, this brings me on to the problem with Cottle's approach. While it touches on all the right variables that shape news production, it lacks a coherent theoretical grounding that can build these different issues into a full explanatory and evaluative framework. Cottle's work, in my view, despite his efforts, faces the same problems as production studies does as a whole: in rejecting the economic determinism and functionalism of political economy approaches, there is a tendency to lose sight of questions of capitalism and power – precisely the issues that critical political economy is interested in the most. In response, all that can be proposed as potential solutions is self-reform in terms of codes of practice: more effective monitoring, greater resourcing, greater cultural awareness and better recruitment. But this does not do nearly enough to attend to the entrenched ways in which racism operates in contemporary societies, and how it manifests in cultural production and symbol creation in very particular ways.

While studies such as Cottle's provide valuable micro studies of cultural work, when it comes to questions of race and ethnicity, production studies of news have too often failed to ground themselves adequately in social theory in a way that would explain why certain patterns of discrimination and marginalization recur. Moreover, a greater social theoretical grounding would help explain the dynamics of news production in a more sophisticated and fuller way, explaining why they take the form they do, and why contradictions can occur. Production studies draw attention to the lack of diversity in the newsroom and how this impacts on the news reporting on minorities, but also the dynamics of news production itself, which constrains the ability for reporters to tell the stories that they want to tell. The question remains, however, of how to explain such underrepresentation – and the failure of diversity policies – beyond merely making the obvious point that racism permeates society. This is the kind of gap that a more systematic approach to race, ethnicity and cultural production, which incorporates social theory as well as empirical work, may help to provide.

Cultural studies of production and race

In terms of this book's interest in race and cultural production, the strongest forms of production studies of news and race are those that fold into their analysis a serious consideration of the news text itself in order to think through how the dynamics of news gathering, and, increasingly, the constraints placed on it, shape the way that racialized minorities appear (or do not appear) in the news. In addition, the most productive studies are ones that, drawing strongly from cultural studies, emphasize the ambivalence of representation. Yet, in a field shaped by its roots in a positivist tradition of social science, research that is sensitive to the complexity of representational politics is lacking. However, within the discipline of cultural studies itself, we have seen a relatively new interest in cultural production that offers a different way of approaching race, representation and the media, not least with its broader focus on popular culture, which is a comparably neglected area in production studies as a whole.

The recent spike of production research from a cultural studies perspective feels new in a discipline that is generally associated with studies of texts and audiences. Yet as Havens (2014) highlights, the cultural studies approach to production has a lineage that goes back to the work of one of its founding figures, Raymond Williams. Havens refers to Williams's (1973) critical dissection of the base–superstructure relationship using the case of television production, where Williams argues against the tendency to focus exclusively on articulations between audiences and texts, espousing instead the idea that greater attention be paid to the production of the media text as a cultural practice that occurs within and to the economic base. What Williams is effectively calling for, as Havens (2014: 106) puts it, is 'a sociology of cultural production that attends to both how cultural works are created and their aesthetics and meanings'. This is the foundation for cultural studies of production, and when grounded in social theory in this way it potentially offers a route to a more systematic theory of race and cultural production than the type of production research that characterizes the study of the news.

Cultural studies of production comprise a diverse field consisting of a variety of conceptual and methodological approaches and research objects. Nonetheless, research in this field shares two core characteristics. First of these is an interest in power. Studies in this area either explicitly or implicitly adopt a Gramscian framework that conceptualizes the production and reception of ideology as a site of struggle. Putting forward the agenda for their own form of cultural studies-inflected production research, which they call 'critical media industry studies', Havens et al. (2009: 235) stress its emphasis on 'the complex and ambivalent operations of power as exercised through the struggle for hegemony'. In this way, cultural studies of production contrast sharply with the neutral tone of the 'production of culture' approach, which is more concerned with how organizations work, featuring less emphasis on questions of social power, conflict in production and how organizational dynamics influence what is produced (Havens 2014; Hesmondhalgh, 2010). Cultural studies of production also counter a crude Marxian form of political economy accused of having an economically determinist – or certainly less nuanced – approach to ideology, which sees media industries as a direct extension of capital/state power.[3]

---

[3] Indeed, Havens et al.'s (2009) agenda-setting piece on critical media industry studies provoked a rather defensive response from Wasko and Meehan (2013) who believe

This leads on to the second core characteristic of cultural studies of production: an interest in day-to-day practices, through a mid-level approach (Havens et al., 2009). Thus, it represents a challenge to political economy and its apathy towards empirical studies of producers themselves (and media genres other than news and current affairs). Instead, cultural studies-influenced scholars working in this subfield engage with the very culture of production, or, as Mayer et al. (2009: 2) put it, 'production as culture'. This involves deconstructing the codes and rituals of cultural production 'to understand how people work through professional organizations and informal networks to form communities and shared practices, languages and cultural understandings of the world' (Mayer et al., 2009: 2). Consequently, the predominant focus of this scholarship is on constructing empirical studies of producers 'in action', whether through interviews or participant observation. However, research may also include textual analysis of trade and worker artefacts (Caldwell, 2008; Saha, 2016) or even media representations of creative work (Mayer et al., 2009). The purpose then, as Havens et al. state (2009: 249), is to think through 'the myriad ways in which specific discourses are constructed and articulated at various institutional sites including policy, regulation, production practices, distribution, and marketing and how such discourses are incorporated or resisted in the practices of cultural workers'. This presents cultural production as a messy, complex and unpredictable process, a point that is emphasized much more than in production studies of news. As Havens (2014: 106) adds, 'this strain of cultural studies scholarship shares an emphasis on understanding the particularities, complexities and contradictions inherent in cultural production and cultural representation, as well as the ways these two fields are articulated to produce specific cultural practices'.

As stated, scholars conducting cultural studies of production use an array of conceptual framings and methodological approaches. But broadly speaking, as Jennifer Holt and Alisa Perren (2009) state, the general interest is in how the media industries impact three aspects of media texts: (1) style, (2) authorship and (3) genre. Havens adds a fourth topic into the mix, which is particularly relevant to the discussion in this chapter: the relationship between industrial practices and representations of social difference, including gender, race and sexuality, with the focus on the 'articulations between the worldview of a wide range of industry executives and creative

that the authors have misrepresented political economy approaches to media, asserting a form of 'contextual' critical political economy which effectively does, and has been doing, what Havens et al. argue for.

workers, and the representational politics of the texts they produce' (2014: 107). This is indeed a potentially important contribution made by cultural studies, but the fact remains that, in this relatively new field, research into racial and ethnic difference is severely lacking.

There are some exceptions however. Aymar Jean Christian (2011) examines the production of a web series in relation to issues of race, gender and sexuality, but framed within a fandom perspective. His subject is the web series *A Real Girl's Guide to Everything Else*, and is based on interviews with those involved in its production, including executive and associate producers, the writer, the director and actors. Christian uses the series as a case study to examine how 'industry workers, driven, as many web producers are, by fandom, respond to mainstream texts and practices in ways that are both political and industrial in nature' (2011: 1.2). For Christian, what is most interesting about this particular web series is how it attempts to produce a more radical representation of race, gender and sexuality but not necessarily in opposition to corporate power, even though 'independent production as fan practice' (2011: 1.2) is often framed in this way. Rather, he demonstrates a much more complex relationship; *A Real Girls Guide to Everything* is in fact very commercial in terms of its narrative form and style. Unpicking the reflections of the producers themselves, Christian demonstrates how they are attempting to 'formulate a way to think about marketing content as artistic, progressive, and at the same time commercial' (2011: 4.6). Thus, in this example, a production perspective draws attention to how the opening of representational politics that new technologies potentially offer (now that barriers to entry are lowered) does not necessarily run counter to the commercial objectives of the 'traditional' core media industries. This study effectively offers a more nuanced take on the potentiality of fan industries practices, and what Hesmondhalgh (2013: 28–29) calls the 'commerce-creativity dialectic'.

While the issue of representational politics is a key aspect to his paper, Christian's predominant interest is in fan industry practices, and so there is relatively less analysis of the actual text itself. Alfred L. Martin, Jr (2015), in contrast, offers a more in-depth analysis of representation framed in terms of the concept of authorship in the context of industrial production (see Gray and Johnson, 2013). Martin's study is based on interviews with African American writers working on black-cast sitcoms who have written episodes on issues of sexuality – specifically, one gay man and two heterosexual women. While acknowledging that these episodes represent important moments in recognizing the black gay experience, Martin is ambivalent about the way that they are nearly always framed within a 'coming-out-of-the-closet' trope. This in a way is a product of the episodic structure of sitcoms, where recurring characters are limited, and thus coming-out stories are perfect for a single episode arc. But as Martin notes, issues of sexuality very rarely feature again. Consequently, wanting to explore the 'industrial logics that shape black gay representation from within the writers' room' (2015: 650), Martin uses Hall's concept of transcoding to explore how African American writers can 'impact the complexity of representations of black characters and black culture' (Martin, 2015: 649) in terms of bringing their own positionality, experience and subjectivity into their scripts and characterizations. Framing his study in terms of authorship is significant, since, while industry processes are cited by interviewees as constraints upon their practice, Martin argues that the individual biographies of authors are a greater determining force in how the stories take shape (though still mediated through and struggled over within the writer's room) and, in fact, may be the source of the very heterocentrism of the storylines. As he states 'it is the writers, not necessarily the showrunners, who have a possessive investment in coming-out narratives' (2015: 660). Martin's case study thus adds to the literature on how industrial cultural production is best understood as a site of struggle. But his original contribution is in drawing attention to the influence of autobiography and individual subjectivity in production, which exposes the burden of representation experienced by authors within themselves, whereby writers might, in this particular example, 'exercise caution in attempting to break down long-held tropes about black homosexuality' (2015: 661).

In these two studies Christian and Martin demonstrate the value of the contextual textual analysis offered by a cultural studies approach to production. Together, this work stresses how it is not enough to look at the text by itself if we want to develop a fuller understanding of how racial meaning is produced through the media. Providing a more in-depth study that factors in structural concerns as well as a critical interest in representational politics is Havens's (2013) study of the social life of African American television. Grounded in the work of Stuart Hall, Herman Gray and Raymond Williams, Havens's contribution is noteworthy for managing to build into his analysis a discussion of texts, audiences, institutions and the global marketplace of the television industry. This is a truly cultural studies approach to understanding media production, in thinking through each node of the 'circuit of culture' (du Gay et al., 1997).

Like Martin and Christian, Havens is interested in how cultural representations are shaped by industrial forces. Yet in sharp contrast to production studies as a whole, there is a greater emphasis on audiences. Focusing on the international syndication of African American television, Havens is interested in how such programming is received and interpreted in different national contexts. This is important for, as he argues, the way specific programmes are consumed abroad (or rather, how they are believed to be consumed) shapes the nature of production at home. Havens uses the concept of 'industry lore' to describe the understanding that executives use to make decisions about the production and distribution of African American programmes. Industry lore is the knowledge that informs programming executives' strategies and decision-making regarding the international distribution of television, and which consequently decides the types of programmes that get made, or, in more precise terms, informs what gets bought and sold. This knowledge is produced through a complex web of factors, including commercial, technological and regulatory dimensions, as well as the individual cultural and social values of media professionals. As such, industry lore around African American programming is a distinct form of power/knowledge through which racial knowledge circulates globally.

Thus, Havens presents a detailed and complex account of the circuit of culture, fully operationalized, which takes into account the political economy of television syndication, the dynamics of production and consumption, framed within issues of representational politics. As an example of the cultural studies approach to production, Havens's work exemplifies its strengths: grounded in questions of power and attuned to the contradictions and messiness of cultural production. Moreover, alongside the studies on race and ethnicity cited, what Havens bring to this scholarship is an emphasis on how material structures shape the symbolic (and vice versa), which, as I have stressed, is a neglected area in production studies as a whole.

I still have some misgivings about the cultural studies of production approach, however. Perhaps because it consciously sets out to challenge the economically determinist and functionalist tendencies of political economy approaches, critical questions that political economy brings to the fore – particularly concerning ownership, regulation, policy and concentration – tend to be omitted, something that I shall address more in the following two chapters. In addition, while Havens's work is, as I have shown, consciously grounded in social theory, this is not always the case for cultural studies of production, which, while empirically and conceptually innovative, can lack a more concrete – and historical – explanation for the (at times, contradictory) relations between culture and industry in the context of capitalism (Hesmondhalgh, 2010). As a result, while these approaches can effectively describe and produce new understandings about the dynamics of cultural production, they are less likely to be framed in terms of normative questions. This is Hesmondhalgh's (2013) particular critique of this scholarship. In light of the emphasis on the discourses that constitute production or representations of cultural work that typify cultural studies approaches to production, he asks how 'we are ultimately supposed to evaluate what is being observed' (2013: 56). The type of normative questions that he is referring to relate to power, social justice and inequality – again, issues that are particularly high on the agenda for critical political economy. That is not to say that cultural studies scholars are not interested in these questions, but it is the lack of social theoretical base (or perhaps the non-foundationalist nature of the neo-Foucauldian approach that can characterize this scholarship) that Hesmondhalgh suggests makes questions such as these slightly trickier to address within this research. As he states, 'while culture, representation and discourse are vital for analysis of the social, systemic and structural factors still need to be considered in order to provide the kind of explanatory and normative orientations vital for any critical social science worthy of the name' (2013: 155).

A related critique, which is particularly apposite for production studies on race, is that cultural studies approaches are in danger of slipping into a far too relativist account of representational politics. Gray, Havens and Hall all produce exemplary complex accounts of the ambivalence of representation and the polysemic nature of media texts, in the process deconstructing monolithic conceptions of racist ideology.[4] But what can we do with this knowledge, especially in terms of formulating a cultural politics of difference founded upon representational strategies? If we understand that media representations can be interpreted in a number of ways, how then are we supposed to critically evaluate these texts? How can we decide what types of representations are more productive or generative, or indeed better than other representations?

This will be addressed again later in the chapter, but for now we can return to Cottle's argument that any effective critical discussion of media texts cannot take place without a consideration of how the text was made in the first place. This in turn entails a normative orientation, as Hesmondhalgh puts it, that can explain and evaluate production itself, which as I have suggested is what cultural studies of production arguably lacks.

---

[4] See Gray (1993), where he argues that Jhally and Lewis's critique of *The Cosby Show* simplifies the nature of racist ideology.

I should stress that, despite these criticisms, generally I see much potential in the cultural studies-influenced approach to production for the study of race and the media. Yet I am drawn to another approach, which is grounded in social theory and a critique of capitalism, and which provides a fuller framework for explaining and evaluating the relationship between capitalism and the industrial production of culture. When coupled with an analysis of empire and representation, a more robust theory of race and ethnicity in cultural production begins to emerge.

A cultural industries approach to production

Despite the limitations that I highlight, the fields that I refer to broadly as production studies of the news and cultural studies of production both make a valuable contribution to scholarship on the media and race by drawing attention to the production process and how this shapes representations of race and ethnicity. Research within both these subfields has exposed a number of dynamics that affect the representation of racialized minorities. These include issues of diversity in the workplace (and the lack thereof), the inherently racialized nature of professional codes and practices, stifling institutional work cultures, and the tension between the largely commercial objectives of the media industries and the political, social and cultural values of individual actors. However, as I have argued, this research would benefit from the underpinning of a fuller theoretical framework that can pull together these different strands into an overall critique of capitalism and its governance of race. In the remainder of the chapter I propose a more systematic theory of race in cultural production that incorporates an analysis of the political economy of the media, the dynamics of cultural production, and the text/cultural commodity itself to produce a more coherent and singular account of the relationship between the material and the symbolic with regard to the media's treatment of race.

The basis for such a theory comes from grounding the discussion of media texts and representations within the cultural industries. The term 'cultural industries' is obviously a descriptive term for the media and the industries within it. It also can refer to a form of public policy that originated from a 1982 UNESCO paper (see Hesmondhalgh, 2008: 554–557). But in this instance 'cultural industries' refers specifically to a tradition of critical political economy, and, more precisely, a particular theoretical approach within the field known as the 'political economy of culture' (Hesmondhalgh, 2008).

With the centrality of culture in its analysis, there are many similarities with cultural studies of production, but the cultural industries tradition has its own separate genealogy. As Hesmondhalgh (2002: 15–18) outlines, the cultural industries approach originates from the work of French sociologists Edgar Morin and Bernard Miège who rejected Theodor Adorno and Max Horkheimer's version of a unified 'culture industry' based on a uniform logic, instead preferring a plural notion of the cultural industries that immediately highlights different forms of cultural production each with their own unique qualities. Moreover, while Adorno and Horkheimer conceptualized commodification as a blanket process where culture had already been subsumed by capital, the French sociologists argued that this spread was actually uneven and incomplete, and that the production of culture is always contested. 'Cultural industries' is a thoroughly political economy tradition in that it is grounded in ethical and normative questions regarding media power. However, what distinguishes it from other types of political economy are its sociological roots and the complex account of power and ideology that follows, which recognizes the contradictions inherent in capitalism. As Hesmondhalgh (2008: 556) states, the cultural industries approach is in fact derived from a 'properly sophisticated reading of Marx, of the ambivalence of markets'. A further distinction is the interest of cultural industries scholars in popular culture – a neglected topic within the broad field of political economy. Drawing from cultural studies and social theory, the cultural industries approach argues that commercially produced culture needs to be taken seriously, and not dismissed as the product of a 'culture industry'. In addition, again similar to cultural studies of production, it sees production itself as a thoroughly cultural process, shaped by the meanings and values of producers, as well as the structures of the media and perceived audience demand.

But if cultural studies of production can be recognized for its diversity, in terms of its concern with a wide range of issues, the cultural industries approach has a more singular objective: to explain recurring dynamics in culture under capitalism. In doing so, the focus is often on what makes cultural industries distinct from other industries. Researchers in this tradition have focused on, for instance, the unique nature of cultural commodities (their symbolic quality as well as their peculiar status as a semi-public good), how production in this sector is inherently unpredictable, which produces a number of risk-minimizing responses from media organizations, and the tension between commerce and creativity in cultural production, specifically the tensions between symbol creators and their aesthetic, political aims, and the commercial objectives of executives and shareholders (and the symbol creators themselves of course) (Garnham, 1990; Ryan, 1992; Hesmondhalgh, 2013). In more recent times, driven by its commitment to social justice and equality, cultural industries research has moved into thinking through the particularities of creative labour (Banks, 2007; Oakley, 2014; McRobbie, 2016) and, in the normative spirit of political economy, the extent to which it can be considered 'good' or 'bad' work (Hesmondhalgh and Baker, 2011). The critical point that needs stressing is that this focus on the distinctiveness of cultural industries is not just a scholastic exercise. Rather, in carefully (and empirically) unpacking what makes cultural industries and the labour within it unique, it deepens our understanding of the complex relation between culture and industry as well as the nature of capitalism itself. This is the broad insight that a cultural industries approach brings, which, as we shall see, has particular pertinence for the study of race, representation and the media.

Unpacking the dynamics of the industrial production of culture from the cultural industries perspective highlights three dialectical tensions that can directly inform a more robust theory of race and cultural production. First is the tension between structure and agency. Rejecting the functionalism and economic determinism of certain political economy approaches, the cultural industries approach emphasizes the role of human agency in cultural production. A central observation of the cultural industries approach is how symbol creators are given a relatively large amount of autonomy compared to workers in other industries. This is because the products of the cultural commodities cannot be standardized in the same way as noncultural commodities (despite cultural industries' inclination to do so), as they rely on difference, originality and novelty as much as familiarity. Moreover, in these literatures there is an emphasis on the role of 'cultural intermediaries' (Negus, 1999), who literally mediate between media owners, symbol creators and audiences. The stress here is on uncertainty and the way that cultural workers negotiate attempts to rationalize cultural production in order to control the unpredictability of the market (Ryan, 1992; Negus, 1997; Hesmondhalgh and Baker, 2011; Saha, 2016). More broadly, in the political economy of culture we see a shift from a 'production of culture' perspective (which is interested in the organizational formation of cultural production) to a focus on the 'cultures of production' (du Gay et al., 1997; Negus, 1997); that is, 'how structures are produced through particular human actions and how economic relationships simultaneously involve the production of cultural meanings' (Negus, 1997: 84). According to this perspective, cultural production is not just economic activity, but is enacted through the 'messy, informal world of human actions' (Negus, 1997: 94). But if there is a danger that this type of analysis goes too far the other way, affording the cultural worker too much autonomy, the strength of the cultural industries approach is that it retains questions of power and control. As I shall describe in the following two chapters, the cultural industries have seen an increasing shift towards marketization in terms of the adoption of neoliberal models in both the commercial and subsidized sectors, and this a crucial contextual feature for those researching the cultural industries (Galperin, 1999; McRobbie, 2004; Born, 2004; Banks, 2007; Hesmondhalgh, 2008). The question then for researchers is how such a structural shift impacts upon the practices – and agency – of symbol creators and cultural intermediaries.

The second tension related to cultural production that a cultural indus-tries approach highlights concerns change and continuity. Countering in particular a version of the evolution of cultural production as driven by technological innovation, the emphasis of cultural industries research is as much on what aspects of the industry persist over time as on what has radi-cally changed. Thus, a cultural industries approach emphasizes a historical analysis – albeit not in terms of presenting historical case studies. Rather, it is based upon an understanding that at different moments in time, pro-duction is shaped by different historical forces – or that certain historical forces produce different arrangements of production. So, for instance, cultural industries scholars have drawn attention to the shift under 'capi-talist modernity' from a patronage system of production to what Williams (1981) describes as the 'corporate professional era' (see Hesmondhalgh, 2013: 66–67). However, a theory of cultural production needs to be under-stood as marked by multiple temporalities – which prevents simplistic, binaristic models of change such as the idea that digitalization marks a shift from industrial forms of cultural production to an information society.

The third tension that cultural industries scholarship highlights is between macro and micro forces. In contrast to political economy tradi-tions, and in particular the Schiller–McChesney model (see Mosco, 1996; Hesmondhalgh, 2013), that tend to focus solely on macro level concerns such as ownership, concentration and the influence of corporate and political interests, the cultural industries tradition of political economy is multifaceted and attempts to unravel the relations between micro pro-cesses of cultural work and its broader economic, political and cultural context.[5] As such, it is shaped by a more critical approach to the politi-

---

[5] Mosco (1996) and Hesmondhalgh (2013) delineate the various forms of political economy, from a neo-classical model, to the Schiller–McChesney tradition, to a

cal economy (see Golding, 1978; Murdock, 1982; Garnham, 1990; 2000), which is sensitive to the contradictions and ambivalence of capitalism in a 'properly' Marxist sense, and a sociological approach to industrialized production (see Ryan, 1992; Negus, 1999; McRobbie, 2004), which is similarly attuned to the oscillating dynamics between structure and agency. While certain cultural studies of production advocate a 'mid-level' analysis, the cultural industries approach can be characterized as zooming in and out between macro and micro perspectives.

Staying on the issue of the micro dimensions of cultural production, when it comes to the analysis of the text itself the cultural industries approach is, however, lacking. As a tradition of political economy, textual analysis features rarely in this type of research, though examples can be found in the work of scholars more strongly influenced by cultural studies (Hesmondhalgh, 2000; Saha, 2013a). The strength of the cultural industries approach is in its explanation, grounded in social theory, of how material structures shape cultures of production and vice versa, and how the cultural commodity is produced through this dynamic relation, but it would benefit from a more detailed account of how the material shapes the symbolic. One route towards developing a more concrete and fuller theory of the material and aesthetics is found in the work of Georgina Born, who represents a link between production studies (her 2004 book *Uncertain Vision* is regarded as one of the seminal studies in this field) and the sociology of art as the study of the practices and institutions of artistic production. In a highly complex essay, Born (2010) critiques the production of culture perspective that dominates sociological approaches to art for deliberately untethering the question of the production of art from the question of aesthetics. She subsequently attempts to tie it back, via a discussion of the strengths and weaknesses of the work of Bourdieu. To do this, she argues that a sociology of art needs to become a (post-Bourdieuian) sociology of cultural production. Drawing on Janet Wolff, Born argues

European critical sociological approach. Despite its political commitment and the centrality of questions of power and ideology (and in fact, the frequency to which references to 'cultural imperialism' and 'colonialism' appear in critical political economy accounts, would suggest a convenient overlap with postcolonial studies), its lack of interest in the media text is just one reason why its use to my analysis is immediately limited. In fact, Hesmondhalgh (2013: 44–47) has noted that it has a rather dismissive attitude towards the products of popular culture. However, there will still be references to certain political economy theories throughout this research; in fact, a dose of political economy is often needed to balance the readiness to overstate the autonomy of the symbol creator.

that the aesthetic is autonomous (and not just a tool of domination, as Bourdieu argues) and that the study of aesthetics, as Wolff puts it, 'necessarily involves the study of aesthetic conventions' (Wolff quoted in Born, 2010: 175) as well as the institutions of artistic production. In other words, aesthetics can only be understood and critiqued within the context of production. In terms of what this means empirically, Born (2010: 176) calls for

> the need, when analysing any case of cultural production, for the researcher not only to endeavour to be reflexive about her own aesthetic prejudices, but, on this basis and informed by producers' and critics' exegeses on the art object in question, as well as by an understanding of its social mediations and historical conditions, to offer a critical interpretation of the object.

Born is stressing the need to situate a study of aesthetics within the historical development of aesthetic codes and genres-in-progress, which in turn are shaped by industrial forms of cultural production.

Born's argument effectively echoes Williams's (1973) point on how a sociology of cultural production needs to attend to how cultural works are created, as well as their aesthetics and meanings. And this is what I argue is desperately needed in the study of race, representation and the media. While this book is more concerned with discourse and representation than with art and aesthetics (though Born applies her theory to core cultural industries such as television), the argument still stands: in order to understand media texts, we need to understand how these texts are shaped by production. I am not necessarily suggesting that representation as embodied in cultural commodities can only be critiqued in terms of their production, but, less contentiously, that a study of how representations are physically made helps us explain and evaluate them. And Born's particular articulation of a sociology of cultural production helps provide a normative framework from which to deconstruct representations of race (for an example, see Saha, 2013a). It is worth adding that while Born's work is not strictly a part of the cultural industries tradition, not least since it is not a political economy analysis, its sociological grounding slots neatly within the cultural industries framework.

Thus, the cultural industries approach defines cultural production as characterized by tensions between structure and agency, macro and micro forces, and change and continuity. This is a much more nuanced take on production than less critical forms of political economy. But as significant, the cultural industries approach does not conceptualize cultural production as simply messy, random and unpredictable, a conclusion you could draw from some cultural studies accounts of production. Rather, as mentioned earlier, the cultural industries approach, based on a deeper engagement with Marxist theory, stresses the ambivalence of markets; that is, it has enabling and constraining features. As Hesmondhalgh (2013: 68–71) explains, commodification is enabling in that it has resulted in a vast proliferation of symbolic goods that can enrich our lives. But it is constraining too in terms of the exploitation of labour within cultural production, and the tendency to oversupply some types of commodities over others. In light of this, Hesmondhalgh stresses commodification as a complex, contested and ambivalent process. In contrast to the Schiller–McChesney version of political economy, the cultural industries approach is therefore able to 'offer explanation of certain recurring dynamics, rather than polemically bemoaning the processes of concentration and integration that are a feature of capitalist production – including media production' (Hesmondhalgh, 2002: 553). This is an advancement too on cultural studies of production, which, while reaching similar conclusions as cultural industries scholars, would benefit from this social theoretical grounding that can, again, explain and evaluate why certain dynamics of cultural production recur over time.

A theory of race and cultural production[6]

Curiously, with the emphasis on social justice and equality, research into cultural industries and creative labour generally lacks engagement with issues of race and ethnicity (see Balaji, 2009).[7] Nonetheless, I argue that the cultural industries approach offers the most productive route to a systematic theory of race and cultural production – one coupled with an engagement with issues of empire and postcoloniality as shall be made clear in the following chapter. To conclude this chapter I want to highlight how a grounding in cultural industries, and attendant theories of macro/micro, structure/agency, and change/continuity, informs a theory of race and cultural production.

First, a theory of race and cultural production recognizes that racism is a powerful structural force but there is always the potential for contestation and disruption. It understands that a lack of diversity in cultural industries – especially in the upper echelons – has deep historical roots. But

---

[6] Portions of this section originally appeared in Hesmondhalgh and Saha (2013).
[7] One exception is Banks et al.'s (2014) study of the working lives of Black British jazz musicians.

crucially, it rejects an economic determinist or functionalist approach to understanding racism in relation to the state and capitalism (which believes that racist ideologies are a product of state and capital's needs for labour migration) even though racism is so deep-rooted (I shall unpack this more in the following chapter). So emphasizing the dialectical tension between macro and micro forces, structure and agency, a theory of race and cultural production explains the production of popular culture and news with regard to race as complex, ambivalent and contested. Gray provides an illustration of this approach by highlighting how black expressive culture is structured by three elements: social conditions, political struggles and cultural discourses. Thus Gray, as I do, emphasizes complexity, contestedness and a number of determining factors, including discourse. Yet the multiplicity of different forces that shape representations of race does not mean that cultural production should be understood as a haphazard and unpredictable process. Rather, as the cultural industries approach attests, the making of representations of race and difference is better understood as mediated through several dialectical tensions that take certain forms at certain conjunctural moments.

Second, a more systematic theory of race and cultural production recognizes the complexity and contradiction of black expressive culture itself. When consumed as commodities, the marginalized position of subordinated racial and ethnic groups often makes them the object of projections and fantasies concerning pleasure, sociability and vitality, which then can become highly desirable entities. But they do not always lose their meaning or magic because they are commodified. As Paul Gilroy (1993a) stresses, black Atlantic culture is itself a counterculture to modernity; it has a doubleness that is a product of and a challenge to Western modernity. So again, a theory of race and cultural production involves an analysis that includes the political economic as well as the cultural and the discursive, and seeks to integrate them while recognizing their heuristic separateness.

Third, further elaborating on the first point, a theory of cultural production takes agency as well as structure seriously. This entails recognizing the ability of oppressed peoples to exercise agency in producing cultural forms that provide pleasure, entertainment, and fecund meanings that may not be apparent to the outside observer. This emphasis on agency is linked to the need for richer strategies of aesthetic and cultural evaluation than have been apparent in some of the research literature. So it means that we do not dismiss those instances when minorities interact with commerce as necessarily aesthetic or political vitiation. But then we shouldn't celebrate all minority cultural productions as evidence of their resilience. A more helpful and theoretically informed way of understanding the production of (popular) culture comes from Hall, who characterizes popular culture as the 'double movement of containment and resistance, which is already inevitably inside it' (1981: 228). Cultural domination is neither all-powerful nor all-inclusive; rather, 'there is a continuous and necessarily uneven and unequal struggle, by the dominant culture, constantly to disorganize and reorganize popular culture' (1981: 228). As such, Hall conceptualizes the production of popular culture as a site of ongoing struggle, neither the pure product of the dominant class or capital, nor authentic culture of the heroic masses. Instead, he paints the production of popular culture as 'the dialectic of cultural struggle' (1981: 228). This emphasis on the dialectics of popular culture neatly maps onto the cultural industries approach to cultural production and is the foundation for this book. Recognizing that cultural production in relation to race is complex, contested and ambivalent doesn't make it any easier to evaluate and critique. But it at least provides a normative positioning for approaching and explaining why media discourses of race and ethnicity take the form that they do.

Thus, a theory of race and ethnicity in cultural production benefits from being rooted in the cultural industries tradition outlined. It means situating the study of cultural production within political economy and postcolonial concerns with power and empire to prevent a slip into the kind of culturalist reductionism that can afflict research into race and ethnicity that has followed the cultural turn in social sciences. It entails recognizing that the global cultural economy through which cultural production takes place is an uneven, heterogeneous, unpredictable terrain, but nonetheless 'structured in dominance', that manages the shifting hierarchies of racial difference (Hall, 2000). It necessitates marrying an approach that combines questions of political and economic power, ownership and control with one concerned with notions of textuality and representation, and being equipped for the complex ways in which such a relation is played out (through cultural production itself). Furthermore, it demands empirical data that challenges the form of 'epochal theorising' that renders micro level relationships and contextual details banal and insignificant (du Gay and Pryke, 2002), but also grounds the 'messy, informal world of human actions' (Negus, 1997: 94) within larger structures, themselves mediated through political economic and social cultural determinants.

Conclusion

In the remainder of the book I will operationalize my theory of race and cultural production in addressing why historical constructions of race persist in the media. It is organized according to the broad framework I have outlined in this chapter, specifically in terms of the macro and micro dimensions of cultural production. In the chapters that constitute Part II, I am going to adopt a macro approach that looks at broader structural issues relating to capitalism and empire and how the role of the cultural industries can be understood as shaped by the dynamic between these two historical forces. Part III will examine the micro context of how race is made during cultural production. It will also pay close attention to the forms of rationalization and bureaucratization employed in the corporate form of production that characterizes contemporary cultural industries (Ryan, 1992).

As explained, my analysis will draw from case studies, many coming from the fields of production studies of news and cultural studies of production that I have delineated in this chapter. The aim is to use these studies to piece together and flesh out the existence of race and racism in the cultural industries. Using the framework outlined in this chapter, I write against determinist and functionalist understandings of the media, ideology and race, stressing ambivalence, contradiction and tensions between structure and agency. But to reiterate, this will be explained in a way that prevents a slip into a purely relativist account of cultural production that regards it as wholly unpredictable. As I will demonstrate, the particular patterns that characterize race-making in the cultural industries can be explained by understanding how capitalism and legacies of empire dovetail during cultural commodification and how racial ideologies manifest themselves, invisibly, via the processes of rationalization embedded in industrial cultural production. Moreover, the more nuanced account of commodification that the cultural industries approach entails recognizes how it has both enabling and constraining tendencies that can explain those moments when minorities have managed to subvert, undermine and transgress racist discourses in the media. This issue of commodification in relation to race is the subject of the following chapter.

Part II

Media, Race and Power

Capitalism, Race and the Ambivalence of Commodification

Introduction

This book revolves around a central question: how do the cultural industries make race? That is, how do they work to reproduce particular discourses of race and ethnicity? Its primary concern is to explain the persistence of historical constructions of Otherness that characterize contemporary media in the West. But the question is framed in a way that allows for the ambivalence of representation.

Echoing du Bois and Hall, how we live with difference is the key issue of our times, and the role of cultural industries in shaping consciousness around race is pivotal. Through repetition of certain symbolic and narrative tropes, cultural industries rework and reshape, implant and impose definitions of race that reinforce the status of the (unraced) dominant culture. The seriousness of this situation is made more urgent by the fact that most people's encounters with Othered groups is enacted through the media – even for those living in diverse cosmopolitan metropolitan cities – through their consumption of television sitcoms, newspapers, movies, MP3s, popular fiction, and so on. The inescapable yet slow and incremental transformative effects of multicultural drift are not enough to counter the overwhelming scale of negative discourse around race in the media (as reflected in the gains made by recent populist right-wing and far right political movements in Europe and the US).

Yet it is important to acknowledge that Hall's argument regarding popular culture is better understood as a dialectical struggle. Traces of a crude fatalistic version of the Frankfurt School's early work on the mass media can still be felt in race scholarship that too readily dismisses the products of the 'culture industry'. But the media is the space where social understandings about race are challenged as well as reinforced. Moreover, discourses of race as embodied in cultural commodities take on different meanings in different spatial and temporal, historical and political contexts as they circulate throughout the global cultural economy. A material culture perspective such as this immediately challenges a functionalist understanding of the media, which sees it as a pawn of the capital that determines its production.

The creative consumption of cultural commodities that either explicitly or implicitly contain ideas about race and difference is important to track for what it reveals about how Other(ed) groups and cultures are made sense of (Pitcher, 2014); this point is clear. But as I have argued, there is less awareness of the context around and experience of cultural production and how this shapes consumption, let alone the form of the commodity in question. Attentiveness to these issues deepens our understanding of how discourses of race come to take the shape that they do, as embodied in the representations that constitute symbolic goods. As I have stressed, such knowledge is critical to the formulation of effective cultural political interventions that can disrupt and even transform common-sense understandings of race.

In this and the next chapter, I analyse the macro context of race making in the cultural industries. I broadly consider two structuring forces. The first is historical, referring to how legacies of empire and colonialism shape the present. The second is political economic, and relates to the nature of industrial cultural production under advanced capitalism, entailing a discussion of the shift of the cultural industries towards neoliberalism. The micro dynamics of these issues will be unpacked in Part III.

While chapter 4 tackles the question of media and cultural policy, this chapter focuses on the cultural industries and marketization, and specifically the issue of commodification. Commodification is an important concept in that it helps us think through the relationship between race, empire and capitalism. Moreover, the way commodification is taken up in both cultural studies and political economy research helps stitch together the potentially awkward marriage between postcolonial and cultural industries approaches that informs the theoretical framework of this and following chapters.

The first section of the chapter begins with a brief discussion of why representation still matters, entailing a brief discussion of postcolonial theory, before focusing on critical cultural studies scholars who have challenged over-celebratory accounts of race in popular culture, which, in their eyes, neglect the context of 'racial capitalism' within which popular culture is made. In these critiques, the notion of the 'commodification of race' is used to describe capitalism's co-option and exploitation of racial difference for both profit and the reinforcement of white supremacy. While I acknowledge the value of this approach for grounding the discussion of representation within the context of capitalistic production, these accounts, without a proper analysis of the media itself, can too easily slip into a functionalist and economically determinist reading of the cultural industries. To counter this tendency, the second part of the chapter considers critical political economic approaches to the media, particularly those made by scholars whose analysis of the media is grounded in social theory and who stress the contradictory nature of media power. This is a dialectical approach, evident in the 'properly sophisticated reading of Marx', as Hesmondhalgh (2008: 556) puts it, that understands commodification as complex, contested and ambivalent. However, I will argue that critical political economy, with its call for a greater focus on labour exploitation and copyright law, mistakenly downsizes the ideological dimensions of commodification to which the critical race scholars referenced earlier draw attention. To resolve this, in the final section of the chapter I argue for a shift from the notion of commodification of race to a notion of the racialization of the cultural commodity. This is a much more discursive take on cultural production and the politics of representation, which crucially can explain contradictions as well as the dominant versions of race that appear in the media. In other words, it is able to explain the persistence of historical constructions of Otherness, while stressing the ambivalence of representation as a whole.

Racial neoliberalism and the commodification of race

As mentioned in chapter 1, for Herman Gray (2013: 771), there is currently a '"waning" in what a cultural politics of representation can yield'. Gray argues that the new technologies of self-representation and self-making – where racial difference often takes centre stage – are more likely to reflect a neoliberal, entrepreneurial and individualistic subjectivity rather than represent a politics of recognition based on solidarity, community and social alliance – the product of the ascendency of what Gilroy (2013) calls 'black vernacular neoliberalism'. But I find a similar waning in critical race scholarship too, albeit for different reasons, in the conviction regarding the potentialities and possibilities of representation. Yet we should not interpret the diminished interest in race in relation to representational issues as meaning that representation no longer matters.

Edward Said makes the strongest case for the centrality of representational practices and technologies to empire. For Said, it is through representation that the Other is controlled and suppressed; as he states, 'the power to narrate, or to block other narratives from forming and emerging, is very important to culture and imperialism, and constitutes one of the main connections between them' (Said, 1994: xiii). He describes representation in this context as an act of symbolic violence that reduces others, all the while exuding a 'calm exterior' (2004: 40). Empire relied on the management of the Other through representation, 'put to use in the domestic economy of an imperial society' (2004: 41). Said argues that when a system of representation absolutely defines the other epistemologically as radically inferior to the imperial Self, then an intervention is necessary. Articulating a necessary political response he (2004: 42) suggests that 'we must identify those social–cultural–political formations which would allow for a reduction of authority and increased participation in the *production of representations*, and proceed from there' (my emphasis). Said goes as far as to say that such cultural political strategies represent a radical form of resistance – more so than the oppositional work of governments, whether socialist, Third World, etc.

Said's point about taking control of the mode of production of representations is something I shall come back to in chapters 5 and 6. For now my interest is in how Said's historical analysis of representation in colonial times informs contemporary understandings of race and racism. Postcolonial theory makes three claims about how legacies of empire shape the present. First, it states that decolonization is actually an incomplete process that has merely led to a reconfiguration in the relationship between the (displaced) centre and the periphery, while actual power relations remain intact (Spivak, 1993: 156–157). Second, it argues that the text cannot be divorced from the past and the Imperial/postcolonial context (Said, 1991[1978]; Spivak, 1993). And third, it understands that (post) colonialism relies on the consistent maintenance of a binary system that constructs the absolute distinction between the Imperial Self and the colonized Other (which, as Anne McClintock (1995) underlines, has gendered, class and sexual dimensions as well as racial ones) in order to preserve its domination (Bhabha, 1994). This is an argument developed further by Gilroy, who describes one of Great Britain's responses to its own unshakable 'postcolonial melancholia' as the infliction of a culturalist form of racism (replacing the biological forms of racism found in the earlier parts of the twentieth century) based on an ideology of ethnic absolutism that demands a 'culturally bleached' and pure nation (2004: 156). When Gilroy argues that 'the imperilled integrity of national states are being communicated through the language and symbols of absolute ethnicity and racialized difference' (2004: 155), he is alluding to the 'language and symbols' found in, as one of multiple sites, vernacular culture.

Cultural racism, as a product of histories of empire and colonialism, explains to an extent contemporary racial discourse that circulates through the media. Yet this narrative is incomplete until we properly account for the capitalistic – and increasingly industrial – form of the production of representation. One of the limitations of postcolonial criticism's approach to representation is, with its roots in literary studies, that there is a tendency to focus on 'high art' (such as literary fiction or world cinema), and, as a consequence, it assumes that these texts exist outside the commodity system or are immune to commodification. But my argument begins with the notion that there are epistemological issues at stake when capitalism spreads into the field of postcolonial cultural production – when the 'third space' becomes a commodified space.

Before we get to the specifics of the implications of the industrial and commodified production of representation,[1] I want to think more broadly about the relationship between capitalism and race. In the Western capitalist societies that are the focus of this book, racial and ethnic minorities are economically and socially disadvantaged, with particular racialized groups the most worst off in society, forming what Rex (1970) describes as an 'underclass'. Those communities that fare better economically still suffer in other respects in relation to their white counterparts, generally receiving fewer opportunities in employment, education, housing, and so on. In addition to the economic realities of racism under capitalism, there are also the psychosocial – and physical – repercussions of a nationalist discourse that asserts who belongs (the unraced white) and who does not (the raced Other) (Gilroy, 2004).

The crux of the issue for researchers and theorists of race and racism is whether race and the experience of race should be linked to economics, or whether they should be treated as distinct phenomena, independent of the political economy of capitalism (and class relations). The former camp is defined by a neo-Marxist position that, in its most orthodox form, claims that race represents false consciousness (see Back and Solomos, 2000). More nuanced historical materialist accounts argue that racism should be understood as a social relation of oppression rather than an ideology in itself (Toynbee, 2013; Camfield, 2016) so that an effective antiracist

---

[1] It is important to distinguish between 'industrialization' and 'commodification'. As Hesmondhalgh (2013: 68–69) outlines, commodification is a broad term that refers to the conversion of something into a commodity. Industrialization, on the other hand, refers specifically to industrial forms of production including mechanized processes, a division of labour and capital investment.

programme entails a class-based politics (Miles, 1989; Sivanandan, 1990). Opposing this view is a critical cultural approach (exemplified by the contributors to the seminal collection *The Empire Strikes Back*), which argues that 'race' is not determined by state and regulation; rather, it is an open construct that is struggled over, where racial (as well as gender and sexual) categories can be used productively in the struggle against political oppression. Essentially, they challenge a Marxist argument that treats racism as epiphenomenal to capitalism. One of the most robust examples of this challenge comes from Cedric Robinson (2000[1983]) in his conceptualization of 'racial capitalism', where he denounces Marxist and other Western thought for imposing class through its analysis, consigning 'race, gender, culture and history to the dustbin'. Robinson instead argues that the oppression of racial minorities was central to Western civilization and the birth of the modern nation-state, and that 'racialism' is a material force in itself (2000: 2). For Robinson, racism is not a by-product of capitalism, but intrinsic to its very development.

There remains a stand-off between historical materialist and culturalist accounts of the relationship between race and capitalism (and what form a counter politics of race should take). But I believe that we can take something from both approaches, as Chakravartty and Silva (2012) do. Critical of a cultural approach that can leave out questions of the economic, and also of historical materialism for its inability to account for the ways in which capitalism has lived off colonial/racial expropriation, Chakravartty and Silva argue that race under capitalism entails both economic exploitation *and* racial subjection. They argue that these dimensions exist in a dynamic relation rather than with the one determining the other (which, it has to be said, has much in common with Jason Toynbee's (2013) critical realist approach too). Similarly, in her historical study of imperialism and 'commodity racism' (a form of cultural racism that supplants scientific racism), McClintock (1995) finds that the creation of race in the imperial context had both an economic and an ideological objective. Through analysing the Victorian representation of the colonial Other prevalent in soap adverts in particular, she argues that 'the Victorian obsession with cotton and cleanliness was not simply a mechanical reflex of economic surplus . . . [T]he middle class Victorian fascination with clean, white bodies and clean, white clothing stemmed not only from the rampant profiteering of the imperial economy but also from the realms of ritual and fetish' (1995: 211). McClintock is arguing that while the use of the Other in the aestheticization of commodities had clear profitable benefits, it had a symbolic value too in the normalization of a superior (and gendered) European identity.

Thus, what I take from her argument, alongside that of Chakravartty and Silva, is that racism is central to capitalism both economically and ideologically. It entails the economic exploitation of race that has been integral to the expansion of capitalism. Moreover, it is central to the construction of a cohesive – that is, unflinchingly white – national identity upon which the modern nation-state relies. In relation to this book's specific interest in the cultural industries, what this suggests is that, quite simply, there is more at stake in the production of representation than just the mere extraction of surplus value.

What does 'racial capitalism' in the context of the West look like today?[2] For Nisha Kapoor (2013), recognizing the nature of racism in the contemporary context entails grounding such an examination within the operations and advancement of the neoliberal state. For Kapoor, neoliberalism has ushered in a new racial moment, where 'race has become increasingly de-politicised as the state has more vehemently attempted to separate it from structure' (2013: 1030). In other words, what Goldberg calls 'racial neoliberalism' in this context amounts to a new form of racial governance under capitalism.

Following Goldberg (2009; 2012) and Kapoor (2013), there are three aspects of 'racial neoliberalism' that distinguish it as a new form of racism. First is the ascendancy of the discourse of 'post-race'. Such a discourse suggests that race has finally been transcended, and that we live in a post-racial society no longer defined by racial disharmony let alone oppression.[3] On the contrary, race critical scholars expose the ideological function of post-race as a way of disavowing racism while pursuing racist politics; a shift from antiracism to antiracialism (Kapoor, 2013). Moreover, for Goldberg (2012: 121), 'any attempt to characterize and criticize such expression as racist itself is reversed, and itself quickly becomes charged as racist'. Alana Lentin and Gavan Titley (2011) think through the so-called 'failure

---

[2] Goldberg (2009) argues persuasively that it is a mistake not to address the specificity of racism and racial histories in particular nations. In other words, racial capitalism (or racial neoliberalism, as he puts it) takes different forms in different states. For my purposes, I work with the notion of the 'West', referring specifically to European, North American and Australasian advanced capitalist societies. Though nations within these continents have their own particular historical relationships with race, they nonetheless broadly share an experience of empire and colonialism that shapes modern formations of race.

[3] It's too early to tell whether the new post-Trump, post-Brexit era has ushered in a new discourse around race, though what is clear is that the 'post' prefix in 'post-race' is looking increasingly redundant, if it was not so already.

of multiculturalism' in terms of racial neoliberalism, arguing that such rhetoric is less about actual statist multicultural policies (which amount to nothing more than a 'a patchwork of initiatives, rhetoric and aspirations') and more an expression of an exasperation over race. In effect, the declaration of the 'failure of multiculturalism' exemplifies a post-race discourse in that it is actually fundamentally about race, while denying it in the same stroke.

A second dimension of racial neoliberalism is what Kapoor (2013) describes as the privatization of race. This regards policy and 'the protection of the private from state interference' (Kapoor 2013: 7). Goldberg (n.d.) highlights how, despite the disproportionate number of minority men who are hassled, stopped and searched, incarcerated, etc., politicians still argue that race can be removed from legal processes – since justice should be colour-blind; a further iteration of the racialized character of meritocracy (Littler, 2017). In addition, for Goldberg (2009), under 'racial neoliberalism' the onus is on the racialized subject to manage and be responsible for their own integration into society, rather than it being a duty of the state.[4]

This brings us to a third dimension of racial neoliberalism: the implementation of biopolitical technologies to govern racialized segments of the population. This is a new form of governance that operates on the tension between the neoliberal state's imperial and domestic (economic) goals. Essentially, biopolitical governance – typified in the state policies carried out in the name of the 'War on Terror' – is a method for policing and regulating the Oriental Other as the neoliberal state opened up its borders to trade and the flow of finance and commodities (and people). It is 'a way of legitimising the policing of bodies where the formalism of equality law would not allow it' (Kapoor, 2013: 3). It includes a range of technologies that are enacted on racialized bodies either directly (indefinite detention, rendition, use of torture, undercover entrapment) or indirectly (online and offline surveillance, special registration of travellers from Arab and Muslim majority nations) (Medovoi, 2012: 43–44) and represents a broader 'regime of discipline' (Amin, 2010: 9) that 'defines the norms of personhood, citizenship and integration, the demarcations of home, nation and

---

[4] Of course, this aspect of neoliberalism is not exclusive to racialized minorities, and is felt by the disabled, by single mothers, by the working class and so on. I would add that racial neoliberalism is one of multiple neoliberalisms that governs different populations and sections of societies in both similar and distinct ways. See Cornwall et al. (2008) for a useful overview of discussions of neoliberalism and gender, for instance.

the outside, the contours of who counts for what'. To sum up, the supposed utopianism around 'post-race' is not naive, or even disingenuous, but is in fact deeply ideological; as Goldberg (2012: 121) states, speaking of racial neoliberalism in the United States, 'we are nowhere near the promise of a raceless America, or of a post-racial one'. The same certainly applies to other supposedly post-racial nations in the West.

These accounts make for a compelling and deeply troubling reading of racial politics within the current neoliberal conjuncture. Yet there is one aspect of racial neoliberalism that is missing in the work I have cited, but has been taken up by scholars more engaged with questions of culture. What I am referring to is something I have alluded to earlier, that is, the contradiction between how, on the one hand, racial minorities are oppressed and brutalized in real life, and how, on the other, as Herman Gray states (2013: 780), 'racial neoliberalism willingly concedes, even celebrates difference'.[5] This has been explored in terms of a 'corporate multiculturalism' (Hall, 2000) or 'boutique multiculturalism' (Fish, 1997) and can be summed up by Hall's (1996b: 470) sardonic comment that the West loves nothing more than 'a bit of the Other'. But there is something to be said about this condition within the specifics of neoliberalism and advanced capitalism. Paul Gilroy, for instance, laments how under neoliberalism consumer rights have replaced civil rights, where 'racial differences not only became integral to the processes of selling and advertising things – they helped to make and to fix various products in an elaborate system of racial symbols' (2010: 8). Both Gilroy (2013) and Herman Gray (2013) describe the emergence of the neoliberal racial subject, described by Gray as a 'self-crafting entrepreneurial subject whose racial difference is the source of brand value celebrated and marketed as diversity; a subject whose very visibility and recognition at the level of representation affirms a freedom realised by applying a market calculus to social relations' (2013: 771). Under racial neoliberalism, race in fact can carry a value, as long as it is explicitly in terms of market goals and is compatible with continued upward redistribution of resources (Duggan, 2003: xii).

These arguments allude to a blindspot in the literature on neoliberalism and race as a whole: the role of the cultural industries. It is worth reminding ourselves again of Gray's (2005) comment that discourses about race are produced in the representations and logic of common-sense racial knowledge constituted in the media, whether news or entertainment.

---

[5] This dynamic between racism and exoticism is unpacked more by Toynbee (2013) in his social-historical account of the experience of black British jazz musicians.

The forms of racial exploitation and domination under racial neoliberalism outlined above amount to just one half of the equation. As Howard Winant (1994: 113) recognizes, the other half is the 'processes of subjection and representation, that is . . . struggles over meaning and identity'. If biopolitical forms of racism depend on an assemblage of technologies used to govern raced groups and bodies, what I propose later on in this chapter is that we similarly conceive of commodification – specifically cultural commodification – as a technology of 'racialized forms of governmentality' (Hesse, 2000: 2). That is, commodification acts as a form of governance of race; a way of managing the production of racial epistemologies as embodied in media representations.

Commodification refers to the conversion of a thing, a culture, or an aspect of life that does not have an intrinsic economic value into a commodity to be bought and sold. In Marxist theory, the concept of commodification has a more precise definition and specific implications that I shall unpack shortly. But the term has been taken up by cultural theorists of race and ethnicity in a looser, though no less critical, way. I am referring here to a body of work that has explored the governance of race specifically in the context of the cultural industries and popular culture in terms of the 'commodification of race'.

The commodification of race argument is best exemplified by bell hooks, and is summed up by her provocative remark that 'within commodity culture, ethnicity becomes spice, seasoning that can liven up the dull dish that is mainstream white culture' (1992: 21). Here, hooks is unravelling how the West's fascination and desire for the Other plays out in commodity fetishism – 'fetishism' being literally taken in this instance. This fetishism is based on sexual desire for the Other, which itself is tied up in an 'imperialist nostalgia' (1992: 25) – again, a case of how empire still shapes the present. Echoing Gilroy's notion of postcolonial melancholia, hooks argues that 'the desire to make contact with those bodies deemed Other, with no apparent will to dominate, assuages the guilt of the past, even takes the form of a defiant gesture where one denies accountability and historical connection' (1992: 25). As shall be explored in chapters 5 and 6, this has a double effect, as the Othered subject is 'seduced by the emphasis on Otherness, by its commodification, because it offers the promise of recognition and reconciliation' (1992: 26). Critically then, for hooks, the exploitation of this desire 'reinscribes and maintains the status quo' (1992: 22). Moreover, commodification subsumes any political potential of black expressive culture. Talking of symbols of black identity, as embodied in cultural forms such as rap music, hooks (1992: 33) claims, 'as signs, their power to ignite critical consciousness is diffused when they are commodified'.[6]

There are two ways in which scholars have developed the commodification of race argument. The first follows a subcultural studies approach, where commodification is the means through which capitalism co-opts black vernacular culture for its own profit-making needs; what Rupa Huq (2003b: 197) describes as the 'youth cultural-commercial incorporation cycle'. For instance, Ash Sharma, in his exploration of the cultural politics of the new British (South) Asian dance music that for a moment in the mid-1990s cocked the ears of cultural critics and academics alike, explains how 'the vital, independent cultures of socially subordinated groups are constantly mined for new ideas with which to energise the jaded and restless mainstream of a political and economic system based on the circulation of commodification' (1996: 17). A second route is less about subcultures and more generally about how race and ethnicity become symbols or markers used to differentiate products in an overcrowded market. This is particularly apposite for cultural commodities that have no discernible difference between them in terms of use value; in which case, symbols of race and ethnicity, especially when tapping into the fears and desires bound up in imperial nostalgia or postcolonial melancholia, are able to give commodities a competitive advantage (Huq, 2003a). Gilroy describes this as the 'cultural economy of "race" and nation' (2004: 124), referring to the activation of representations of blackness in relation to new kinds of commerce and capital, where racial difference is glamourized, and indeed seduces the Other into thinking that this represents an opportunity for cultural and economic recognition.[7]

The arguments I have referred to offer the more nuanced and sophisticated approaches to the subject of the commodification of race. Together, they highlight how symbols of race and ethnicity can represent value, or, as Nancy Leong (2012: 2190) states, 'racial capital', a concept I shall return to in chapter 4.[8] The commodification of race argument consequently provides a promising route to help think through how the products of

---

[6] It is in these terms that hooks controversially labelled Beyoncé a 'terrorist'. See http://jezebel.com/what-bell-hooks-really-means-when-she-calls-beyonce-a-t-1573991834.

[7] There is a separate literature produced by social geographers who have applied a cultural economy approach to the commodification of race; see Jackson (1999; 2002), Dwyer and Crang (2002), Crang et al. (2003).

[8] It is worth stressing that, for Leong, under racial capitalism it is white people who mostly derive the value from the racial identity of another person who actually holds that identity. This shall be developed more in the following chapters.

the cultural industries might serve racial capitalism. However, the above studies aside, when the concept of commodification is taken up in cultural studies as a whole, it generally lacks specifics, and slips into polemics. Too often, commodification is employed in a fleeting way, as short-hand to describe capitalism's co-option of potentially resistive subcultures, or, in the case of this book, the subsumption of the potentially disruptive nature of minority cultural production, and the production of its own form of corporate multiculture.

The main problem I have with certain forms of the commodification of race argument is that it too easily slips into a weak account of the media that is guilty of a determinist and functionalist interpretation of cultural production. It is determinist because it assumes that, once subsumed by capitalism, the vernacular culture of racialized minorities has no counter-hegemonic potential, and can only embody capital. It is functionalist because it assumes that capitalist imperialist ideology works through and spreads from the media in a frictionless fashion, allowing no room for complexity, contradiction or contestation. (Such an assumption is why so many sociologists of race and critical theorists are dismissive of popular culture, even though they no doubt consume and are enriched by these products themselves.) Essentially, I argue that the commodification of race argument lacks a concerted media analysis. The purpose of the next section is to outline such an analysis of the media that avoids the determinist and functionalist slippages just described.

Capitalism, contradiction and the cultural industries

While I am critical of some of the ways that the concept of commodification has been taken up in cultural studies of race and ethnicity, that is not to say that the concept does not hold value. After all, the production of representation in advanced capitalist societies *does* mostly take an industrial form, *is* based on commodity exchange and consequently involves the question of commodification. What I argue for is a more sustained and detailed examination of the concept of commodification, grounded in the specific dynamics of the cultural industries, in order to develop a keener sense of how material structures shape symbols of race and ethnicity.

As stated, having explored the ideological questions that relate to production of representations of race, this now needs to be augmented with a detailed media analysis. For this purpose, I draw specifically from critical political economy approaches (including cultural industries research outlined in the previous chapter), since this is the field most engaged with questions of capitalism, media and power and, by extension, the politics of commodification.

Jonathan Hardy (2014) broadly defines the critical political economy approach as primarily concerned with three issues: (1) media ownership and the influence over labour and production, and the strategies and operations of media organizations, (2) concentration of ownership within and across different media sectors (with a small number of companies controlling the majority of output) and (3) corporate dominance and the implications of a media system driven by profit-making imperatives (commercialism) and commodity exchange (commodification). Fundamentally, critical political economy is concerned with the nature of media power, dealt with at the macro, structural level.

The main narrative in political economy literatures is that the cultural industries in advanced capitalist nations – and beyond – are shifting towards marketization, where the production of symbolic goods is commercialized and commodified. The transition from a patronage model to a market economy has been accelerated by a period of liberalization (following the long downturn, service industries such as cultural industries suddenly became seen as investment opportunities). Policies of deregulation – or what Hesmondhalgh (2013) prefers to call re-regulation, since they involve active state involvement (examples include the US 1996 Telecommunication Act and the UK 2003 Communications Act) – facilitated further commercialization, merger activity (both horizontal and vertical) and internationalization and increasing convergence between telecommunication companies, computer companies, Internet companies and media companies (Hesmondhalgh, 2013; Golding and Murdock, 2000; Freedman, 2008; Hardy, 2014). This has political implications. Hardy (2014: 80) describes this trend as 'the corporate takeover' of places and practices once organized according to a different social logic based on universal access, social participation and citizenship.

In strong opposition to market advocates, who argue that a free market brings greater choice to audiences, critical political economists argue that media concentration is the inevitable result of a deregulated market that in turn leads to a narrowing in content (and political perspectives). Media concentration, then, is a threat to media plurality and cultural diversity (which is why, for political economy scholars, praxis comes in the form of more effective regulation needed to break up concentration). Although issues of race feature little in political economy literature,[9] this critique of

---

[9] One notable exception is Gandy (1998).

concentration is actually very relevant for the study of race and representation, as the opportunities for narratives dealing with racial identity or
experience in the media are hampered by a commercial environment that
favours profitable consumer markets, relies on advertising that demands
commercially friendly media content (that is, that reflects and targets the
dominant culture) and fundamentally is more interested in profit rather
than the 'principles of democratic participation, equality and universality'
(Hardy, 2014: 104–105). This will be expanded on in chapter 5.

While few of them would wholly disagree with this narrative, most
critical political economy theorists argue that the situation is nonetheless more complex. First, the actual scale of concentration itself is highly
contested, since it is so difficult to measure (Hesmondhalgh, 2013; Hardy,
2014). Certainly, discussions of media concentration can neglect the large
number of small firms that continue to operate in media markets and
can be significant players at certain moments – for example, the permanent presence (and cultural, artistic importance) of independent record
labels in the music industry (Toynbee, 2000). A further complication
in the picture is how the march to deregulated, free markets is hardly
smooth. For instance, there are numerous examples of failed mergers
or merger deals that have been contested by politicians and the public
alike. As much as the trend in the media industries has been towards
concentration, there has simultaneously been a great deal of de-merger
and de-conglomeration activity. Since media organizations are increasingly reliant on financialization, they are susceptible to boom–bust cycles
much like any other commercial organization (Winseck, 2011: 143). In
other words, while media corporations undoubtedly have tremendous
clout, they are still vulnerable to economic downturns. Moreover, they
are increasingly beholden to investors and their demands for high returns
(Fitzgerald, 2012). As Hesmondhalgh (2013: 199) sums up, 'cultural-
industry corporations are both powerful and yet also operate in a highly
uncertain environment'.

Speaking of uncertainty, it should be noted as well that the behaviour we associate with media corporations – such as increasing in size
through vertical and horizontal integration, lobbying for tighter copyright laws (which, critical political economists counter, work against the
public interest) – takes place not merely because of greed and a thirst for
dominance (though this no doubt is a factor), but because of the inherent
unpredictability of cultural production. Cultural commodities are unique
in several ways: they are semi-public goods, involve high production/
low reproduction costs, and their success is impossible to predict and, as

such, the corporate response of getting bigger or of tightening intellectual property is as much about dealing with insecurity and the inherent riskiness of cultural production as it is about hatching a Machiavellian plot to achieve power and greater influence over society (Garnham, 1990; Hesmondhalgh, 2013). Indeed, the danger with certain forms of political economy analysis is that they can slip into polemics[10] and a functionalist argument which states that, since the media is owned by rich and wealthy elites, media output reflects their interests and ideologies.[11] Hardy (2014) questions whether media concentration directly equates with media power, since actual power depends on how it is exercised and not merely on the number operating in and across media markets. Returning to the question of race and cultural production, while attempts to improve the representation of racialized minorities are hindered or, indeed, shut down by commercial (and racist) imperatives that perceive such narratives as 'niche-interest' and unprofitable (Gandy, 1998), the media nonetheless has produced and distributed at times radical depictions of race identities and lived experience that cut across the common-sense understandings of the groups in question, whether in music, film, book publishing or television.

The problem for political economy arguments – particularly those versions that lack grounding in social theory (Hesmondhalgh, 2009) – is that they are unable to account for the inherent contradictions of cultural production, as suggested in the previous chapter. A different approach is put forward by Des Freedman (2014), who conceptualizes a dialectical version of media power that aims to dismantle simplistic assertions over the media as an instrument wielded by powerful groups. Adopting a historical materialist approach, Freedman argues that in the same way that the base does not define the superstructure (see Williams, 1973), the economy does not determine the media; rather, they exist in a dialectal relationship. As Freedman (2014: 10) states, 'media power, according to this perspective, is structurally tied (but not subordinated) to wider patterns of privilege and control'.

---

[10] Hesmondhalgh (2013: 44–47) critiques a certain form of US political economy that he calls the 'Schiller–McChesney' approach (named after two of its most famous proponents) for its rather straightforward account of media power that lacks sufficient engagement with social theory and is unable to account for the contradictions and contestedness of media production.

[11] Post-Fordists, by contrast, argue that power has fully dispersed and has been decentralized through networks, though for Freedman (2014) this is a similarly exaggerated assertion.

Freedman's (2014: 15) aim is to reconcile two approaches: one that recognizes the media as 'symbolic practices and textual operations' that construct social reality, and a second that takes seriously the macro-economic side of the media (i.e., political economic concerns) in order to produce a fuller picture 'of the significance of communicative activity for the contemporary world'. His intervention conceptualizes a model of media power specifically in terms of contradiction and a close reading of Marx that recognizes contradiction and ambivalence as key features of capitalist society. He alludes to the enabling/constraining dynamics of capitalism outlined by cultural industries scholars when he draws attention to Marx's combining of an approach that acknowledges 'the revolution-ary achievements of capitalism with an analysis of why it is systematically unable to make available the full potential of these achievements to its subjects' (Freedman, 2014: 25). So the contradiction at the core of capital-ism lies in its dynamism and its simultaneous exploitation of the masses; something that drives capitalism, but will also ultimately drive it to its destruction.

This is the 'properly sophisticated reading of Marx' on the ambivalence of markets that Hesmondhalgh calls for. The cultural industries approach, as outlined in chapter 2, defines cultural production as 'ambivalent complex and contested' (Hesmondhalgh, 2013: 45), and commodification as both enabling and constraining. It is enabling in that it has resulted in a vast proliferation of cultural goods that enrich our lives. It is constraining because it oversupplies certain types of goods and undersupplies others (usually the goods that society would be better off consuming more of), while underrewarding and exploiting the labour that goes into the produc-tion of such goods. This is a dialectical way of understanding media power, and it begins to help us understand why representations of race can be so reductive, as well as why they are at times unsettling and disruptive in a productive way – and why, to paraphrase Stuart Hall, we should give a damn about them. Indeed, as Freedman (2014: 26) points out, the contra-dictions of capitalism 'are played out both at the level of institutions and ideas, material as well as symbolic practices'.

Yet some critical political economists would challenge Freedman's com-ments on the significance of the symbolic plane, and are dismissive more generally of the way ideology has been employed in media and film studies (as exemplified in the work of Stuart Hall), arguing that ideology is fre-quently overdetermined in media studies. Vincent Mosco (1996: 145–147), for instance, laments how there is too much emphasis on media content, with much less on the exploitative nature of labour processes within the communication industries.[12] Garnham similarly argues that there is an overemphasis on the ideological dimension of media production, diverting attention away from the economic base. He questions whether capitalism even shares or requires a singular ideology, let alone relies on one, arguing that capitalism will produce 'the very culturally enriched and educated workers and citizens necessary for its own suppression' (2011: 46). Garnham's and Mosco's main argument (though they express it in different ways and to varying degrees) is that the role of commodification in the exploitation of labour, in its absolute (i.e., extending the working day) or relative (intensification of the labour process) forms, has been neglected (Mosco, 1996: 146). This is the real issue at stake for a particular Marxist approach to media power rather than the ideological constitution of media content.

Yet, just as it would be short-sighted to minimize the importance of the exploitation of media/cultural labour, it would also be dangerous to downplay the role of ideology, particularly in relation to the media's role in the reproduction of racial hierarchies. As Hall (1985: 100–101) counters, why it is that media workers 'tend to reproduce, quite spontaneously, again and again, accounts of the world constructed within fundamentally the same ideological categories? How is it that they are driven again and again, to such a limited repertoire within the ideological field?' For Gwyneth Mellinger (2003: 145), precisely what makes newsrooms – though we can broaden this to cultural industries in general – distinct from other industries is how these spaces represent 'an entrenched apparatus of racialized normativity and interpolative power. Diversity in newsroom employment, then, is not primarily a problem of economic inequity and class exploitation, as it would be in other workplace contexts, but an issue of cultural valuation and recognition as well.' Even though the commodification of race argument cited in the previous section might not entail the technical understanding of commodification of critical political economy theorists, there is nonetheless something very persuasive and powerful about its description of how representations of race become commodities that in fact reinforce and reinscribe the power of the status quo. Ideology, like representation, matters for raciality, as well as for antiracism. How best to understand ideology that can factor in these different dimensions?

It is beneficial to look again at Freedman's analysis of media power

---

[12] Though the recent emergence in creative labour research would appear to address this. See Banks (2007); Hesmondhalgh and Baker (2011); Oakley (2014); O'Brien et al. (2016).

and the way in which it reconciles both political economy and cultural studies approaches to ideology. Resonating with the argument of Hall outlined in chapter 1, Freedman sees the production and reproduction of ideology as a site of struggle and driven by a dialectical tension. Drawing from Antonio Gramsci, he argues that media power produce, in the main, 'common sense' (i.e., ideology), but also at times 'good sense' (the formation of a more progressive set of ideas developed in the course of struggling against the capitalist class), 'albeit in fragile and temporary ways' (2014: 27). Following Raymond Williams, Freedman stresses how hegemony is never singular, unitary or fixed. Rather, it is highly complex and has to be continually 'renewed, recreated and defended' (2014: 27). This is particularly the case for when there is a crisis in hegemony and capitalism feels under threat, where media power works to legitimate and maintain its own authority. For Freedman, this is the nature of media power as enacted by commercial media organizations. It attempts to dominate but can never do so totally and will always leave space for opposing voices. This has specific ramifications for people of colour. For, even though the mainstream media is heavily implicated in the reproduction of power and existing social relations (including racial hierarchies), it is also the site where voices from the margins, whether related to class, gender, sexuality and race and ethnicity, have managed to be heard, providing at times 'critical or "magical" perspectives' (Freedman 2014: 28). As Freedman (2014: 28) states, one of the multiple contradictions at the heart of commercial media is the 'simultaneous desire for a narrow consensus and yet *a structural imperative for difference*' (my emphasis). The significance of this last part of the quote is in how it reminds us that, as Garnham (1990: 160) highlights, the use value of the cultural commodity is primarily 'novelty or difference'. Garnham uses this point to explain why the production costs of cultural production are so high (producing original product on an ongoing basis is an expensive enterprise), but I use it to underline how there is as inherent an imperative in media to resist homogenization as there is to reproduce it. This is where the potentiality for the cultural politics of difference is located. It is this 'structural imperative for difference' within media power that helps explain the dynamism of cultural production under racial capitalism.

From the commodification of race to the racialization of the cultural commodity

To reiterate: the cultural industries approach stresses how the business of cultural production is complex, ambivalent and contested. It is complex because it involves an interplay between political, economic and cultural forces that is enacted in very particular ways in particular organizational and historical contexts, which determine the experience of labour and the content and form of texts. It is contested because cultural industries are a site of struggle, and capitalism's attempts to dominate the production of culture is at times resisted, evaded and challenged through creative and organizational practices (for example, independent record labels committed to underground scenes that actively reject commercialism; or independent film companies that spurn Hollywood standards and norms both in terms of art form and business practices). It is ambivalent because, as shown, commodification is best characterized as having both enabling and constraining tendencies. Despite capitalism's attempts to fully extend into the realm of culture, to homogenize and standardize the production of culture (in the way that Adorno and Horkheimer provide the best account for), the unpredictability of audience behaviour means that cultural production is fundamentally a negotiation with risk and uncertainty, which cultural industries respond to with vertical and horizontal integration, and rationalizing strategies and other forms of 'tight control' (Hesmondhalgh, 2013: 32–33), as we shall see in chapter 5. I argue that it is these terms – complex, ambivalent, contested – that best describe the experience of race in the cultural industries, not only because they encapsulate the specific dynamics of cultural production, but also because, as I shall show in this final section of the chapter, they can be applied to explain the nature of the cultural politics of race within capitalist society.

I am suggesting that those critical political economy accounts that can explain the inherent contradictions of media power and cultural production mirror the most nuanced takes on race and cultural politics. In fact, the enabling/constraining dynamics of commodification – what Garnham (1990: 164) describes as 'a complex hegemonic dialectic of liberation and control' – lead to the same dialectical tension that Hall (1981: 228) identifies in popular culture, what he refers to as the 'double movement of containment and resistance'. This quote from Hall is taken from his essay 'Deconstructing "the Popular",' where he discusses popular culture rather than race specifically. But, as I shall demonstrate, Hall's emphasis on the dialectical nature of the politics of the popular maps on to how others have explored the inherent ambivalence of the cultural politics of difference and the production of representation.

In his excavation of the unshakeable resoluteness of race-thinking (despite the supposed rejection of spurious claims regarding the biological basis of race), Amin (2010) exposes the inherent instability and ambivalence of raciality. By unravelling the 'temporal logic of race' (2010: 3), he outlines three 'dynamics of race' that interplay over time:

> first, a restless impulse of variety and novelty, always disrupting and challenging settled patterns of racial formation and behaviour; second, the potential to return sameness if the forces of repetition are strong, perhaps organized and channelled; and, third, the potentiality of accumulated racial debris, variegated and dormant from different eras, ready to be instantiated in unknown ways. (2010: 5)

Amin argues that there is an 'evolutionary dynamic that maintains racial legacies close enough to the surface to spring back with force' (2010: 3), which governs and quashes the unseen novelties of difference. Yet the 'impulse of variety and novelty' is always lingering, always present and, at particular moments, bursts through 'nicks in time', disturbing existing settlements of race. Attempting to shift the sediments of race-thinking that accumulate over time is a colossal task, but Amin, as one strategy, sees potential in cultural production and the practices of a 'counter-culture that visualises the racial past and present in novel ways, exposing the harms and injustices as clear outrages (e.g. by photography during the American Civil Rights and Black Power struggles), showing the absurdities of reducing the raced other to biology/culture/phenotype' (2010: 14). What I take from Amin's argument, then, is a version of an antiracist cultural politics that highlights the possibilities of technologies of representation, that demands more than merely producing the inverse of negative racial stereotype, that pays attention to temporality, and lays open the very inherent instability of raciality.

The intrinsic precarity of race-thinking echoes Homi Bhabha's (1994) notion of the ambivalence at the heart of colonial discourse, where the existence of the colonized Other within the colonial framework opens a space that potentially acts as a site of resistance through representational strategies, including mimicry, repetition and hybridity. Fast forward to the postcolonial nation, and we see that legacies of empire and neocolonial ideologies remain inscribed on the bodies of the racialized Other, but so too, as Gilroy (2004: 110) highlights, are its ambivalences, which these 'unwanted settlers' project 'into the unhappy consciousness of their fearful and anxious hosts and neighbours'. Gilroy adds: '[T]he incomers may be unwanted and feared precisely because they are the unwitting bearers of the imperial and colonial past.' It is based upon these uncertainties within the national consciousness that cultural political interventions can be made. Updating his analysis to contemporary times, Bhabha (1997) helps develop the inherent countercultural nature of race highlighted by Amin, demonstrating how:

> the (relative) sovereignty of the nation-state and the assumed 'unity' of national cultures, upon which such a perspective is based, are both fundamentally disturbed when the 'core' areas turn into multivalent, multivocal and ambivalent networks that project the periphery 'internally' within central societies, turning the authoritative mirror of national sovereignty into the split-screen of projective identification.

Thus national cultures are never coherent or stable, and are easily disturbed by those moments when the periphery collapses into the core, undermining the authority of national sovereignty. For Bhabha, minorities are never full members of a nation; they are only ever partially recognized, but such a status can become the very resource for cultural interventions, which he calls a form of 'minoritization': 'a way of trying to think of different – not necessarily transcendent – but different interventionist measures' (quoted in Sheng, 2009). In a similar vein, Banor Hesse (2000) refers to the destabilizing presence of multiculture using the concepts of cultural entanglements and 'transruption', which represent those moments when the multicultural interrogates – at times unwittingly – the ontological status of the nation's imagined communities. As Goldberg (2012: 125) puts it, the attempt to objectify/subjectify, dominate and subjugate the Other always ends in disappointment: 'Their targets ultimately refuse, resist, rise up. Raciality accordingly fails as it succeeds. It takes away as it provides. In undercutting the values and virtues of heterogeneities, it projects easiness, simplicity, predictability, and profitability. But it produces always difficulty, complexity, fear, and fabricated danger; ultimately social loss.' Thus, the critical race scholars cited here highlight the ambivalence embodied in the very presence of the Other – that dismantles racism as racism tries to oppress it. And in these arguments there is an allusion to the potentialities of the expressive culture of the postcolonial subject in destabilizing the nation-state from within.

Situating the discussion of cultural politics more explicitly within the political economic context of global capital, and how it attempts to spread into the cultural realm, Hall also stresses the inherent ambivalence at the heart of the capitalism's governance of difference. He argues that while the neoliberal character of globalization tends towards cultural homogenization, it is more accurately characterized as a process marked by contestations. This is elaborated in a passage worth quoting in full:

> [Globalization] is a hegemonising process, in the proper Gramscian sense. It is 'structured in dominance', but it cannot control or saturate

everything within its orbit. Indeed, it produces as one of its unintended effects subaltern formations and emergent tendencies which it cannot control but must try to 'hegemonise' or harness to its wider purposes. It's a system for conforming difference, rather than a convenient synonym for the obliteration of difference. This argument is critical if we are to take account of how and where resistances and counter-strategies are likely successfully to develop. This perspective entails a more discursive model of power in the new global environment than is common among the 'hyper-globalisers'. (2000: 215)

Here, Hall is intervening in a debate on globalization and (multi)culture. He rejects the simplistic dichotomies of the 'hyper-globalizers' and describes how the new world system is marked by *différance*: not a scale between total uniformity and total difference but, rather, a weave of differences and similarities that refuse to split into binary oppositions. Hence, Hall suggests that within the very 'shadow' of globalization (2000: 216), sites of resistance and intervention emerge. This echoes Bhabha's notion of the colonial system marked by ambivalence; an ambivalence that destabilizes its claim for absolute authority or unquestionable authenticity. Therefore, rather than equating globalization to cultural imperialism or, inversely, an absolutely hetereogenizing force, a more accurate reframing sees the new global system as structured in dominance, striving for uniformity, but marked by an ambivalence that creates sites of contestation in its wake.

What I take from these literatures is the way in which they highlight the complexity, ambivalence and contestedness of cultural politics of race under capitalism, particularly in relation to the production of representation. This is more than just saying that representational politics is complicated, and it certainly is not saying that it is simply relative. The production of representation is characterized by a dialectical tension. As capitalism attempts to expand into the cultural sphere through the process of commodification, it leaves tears or fissures where its integrity is weakened, which become the locations where cultural political interventions – or 'transruptions' – can destabilize the patterns of racial settlements. The nation in turn responds by activating archaic forms of nationalism, what Hesse (2000) refers to as a highly dubious race relations narrative of governance that is structured discursively around a perception of the problem of national identity and the presence and proximity of racialized bodies.

The notion of what Hesse (2000: 29) describes as 'racialized forms of governmentality' is an important component of my argument. Hesse is using Foucault's concept of governmentality to 'convey the political, regulatory and representational dimensions of European/white racism in the West' and the 'relation between power and knowledge that is used to sustain and govern' the racialized distinction between European and non-white (2000: 29). This echoes Edward Said's (1991[1978]: 3) engagement with Foucault's work, where he reconceptualizes Orientalism as a discourse (rather than an objective scholarly approach) that leads to an understanding of 'the enormously systematic discipline by which European culture was able to manage – and even produce – the Orient politically, sociologically, militarily, ideologically, scientifically, and imaginatively'. In this instance, Said is referring specifically to the post-Enlightenment period, but, following Hesse, his argument extends to the manner in which racial and Orientalist discourses operate in contemporary (postcolonial) Western states. As a representational sphere, where the Other is managed, or indeed produced ideologically and imaginatively, the cultural industries comprise an arena where these racialized governmentalities are enacted (and also challenged). I want to add that Nikolas Rose's (1999: 3) definition of governmentality, as the 'invention, contestation, operationalisation and transformation of more or less rationalised schemes, programmes, techniques and devices which seek to shape conduct so as to achieve certain ends', has particular resonances with this book's interest in industrial cultural production, as it is the supposedly neutral processes of bureaucratization and rationalization that I argue shape the making of race in ways that reproduce neocolonial ideologies.[13] This is the subject of chapter 5 in particular, where I explore how racialized governmentalities operate in the production of cultural commodities that involve an articulation of race.

Returning to the issue of commodification, the discussion of the cultural politics of race that I have just presented stresses the ambivalence of the production of representation that I argue reflects – or, in fact,

---

[13] I want to stress that while I conceptualize commodification as a form of racialized governmentalities, this is shaped more by Said's and Hesse's adaption rather than Foucault himself. I have reservations about the value of Foucault to my argument, including the question of relativism (Fraser, 1989: 33) and his later disinterest in oppositional forces in society, especially in relation to colonialism (Said, 1994: 29). Indeed, I think it is significant that Said thinks through discourse in terms of hegemony, whereby he describes the relationship between the Occident and the Orient as a relationship of power and domination and 'varying degrees of a complex hegemony'; for Said, it is hegemony that gives the imperial discourse 'durability and strength' (1991: 5). This is particularly important to our understanding of the work that media discourses of race perform.

is – the same ambivalence that cultural industries and critical political economy theorists see as characterizing cultural production under capitalism. The challenge now is how to combine these two approaches to produce a complex account of the production of representations of race within the cultural industries, which explains why historical constructions of Otherness persist, but can also simultaneously incorporate into its analysis an explanation for the inevitable contradictions, ambivalences and contestations, thus avoiding the pitfalls of economic determinism and functionalism that the commodification of race argument frequently slips into.

We can look once again to the work of Herman Gray (2005) for a more nuanced interpretation of commodification. The commodification of race arguments that I covered earlier present a rather pessimistic account of the cultural political potential of media texts, suggesting that once culture has been commodified, it has been subsumed by capital and subsequently can only serve capitalism. In contrast, writing against the tendency towards 'polemics about the commodification of blackness' (2005: 15), Gray sees commodification as one of several social forces that structures 'the conditions of possibility within which black cultural politics are enacted, constrained and mediated' (2005: 3–4). For Gray, bitter pronouncements on the symbolic violence enacted by commodification are part of the same entrenched language that reduces cultural politics in the media to discussions around positive / negative, authentic / stereotypical representations. Commodification is not just something that is imposed from above on pure authentic culture, but, as Michael Keith (2005: 131) puts it in the context of urban culture, *'just is'* (original emphasis). Thus, for Gray (2005: 4), recognizing commodification as a mere social fact allows for a more discursive understanding of the politics of representation, which stresses 'how blackness is commodified and circulates, disrupting and threatening, domesticating and reorganizing social and cultural relations, as it touches down, is taken up, disarticulated, and redeployed in different locations'. Here, Gray is making a point about the variation in the consumption of blackness across different temporal and spatial contexts, but equally important for his analysis (and this book) are the 'structuring conditions' of the production of representation. As he adds (2005: 20), 'there is much at stake in how representations are produced, framed, and potentially deployed to construct political projects' not least in the way that 'different sectors of the communication industry (e.g., music, television, and cinema) are constantly packing, arranging, and vying to extend and exert control over the terms and circumstances in which their products circulate and take on value'. These notions of how cultural commodities are packaged, arranged and controlled (and the embedded complexities, ambivalences and contestations that these processes inevitably entail) are key themes in chapter 5.

Gray's analysis is a deliberate challenge to, as he puts it, polemics about the commodification of race. But nonetheless, there is still something valuable to be found in those arguments regarding the ideological dimension of commodification, which acts as a technology of racialized governmentalities. Commodification just is (albeit as a historical process and taking different forms in different conjunctural moments), but it is also mostly a constraining and deeply damaging process, whether in terms of the exploitation of labour that goes into it, or in terms of its tendency to reduce cultures as part of a process that transforms something with no inherent exchange value into something profitable (the point is, it *oversupplies* these type of representations of racial and ethnic minorities). Consequently, we need an analysis of the media that, as Downing and Husband (2005: 5) outline, can 'sustain an appropriate sophistication in tracking the penetration of race thinking into media institutions and media products'. This notion of how race-thinking and raciality penetrate the production of cultural commodities as well as the cultural industries is precisely what I attempt to do. Indeed, in light of Downing and Husband's call, I argue for a reframing of the terms of the argument: from the commodification of race, to the racialization of the cultural commodity.

In other words, our focus needs to be on how cultural commodities come to be racialized, on how cultural industries make race. This is a rejection of economic determinist accounts of commodification and a call for a more discursive take on how commodities get racialized – by which I mean imbued with racial meaning. As I showed in chapter 1, there is some contestation over the concept of racialization, which some critics have argued has been overused and applied to such a wide range of scenarios that it loses its conceptual specificity and usefulness (Goldberg, 2005; Banton, 2005). (Indeed, this criticism mirrors the way that I have argued the concept of commodification has been lethargically deployed.) Nonetheless, I believe that racialization has value in describing the social, economic and cultural processes through which texts/ideas/issues – and, specifically, cultural commodities – become suffused with reductive racial thinking. I conceive racialization as the ideological process by which minority groups are constructed in ways that, as Gilroy puts it (1993b: 110–111), 'rely absolutely on an absolute sense of ethnic difference'. As I have already argued, my definition of racialization is formed in relation to the question of commodification, in terms of how cultural commodities become racialized.[14]

I believe there are two advantages of reconceptualizing the commodification of race argument in this way. First, it stresses the ambivalence of representation and allows for contradiction. If the limitation with the commodification of race argument is in how it immediately forecloses the cultural political value of the cultural commodity, then the racialization of the cultural commodity accommodates possibilities as well as closures – producing a much more discursive account of racial meaning in the way that Gray suggests. As I will demonstrate in chapter 6, processes of racialization can be resisted or subverted and transformed into something productive, dependent on time and place and the political economic / sociocultural context. Second, it focuses our attention on the cultural industries and the actual processes of cultural production in the way that Downing and Husband propose, so that we can think through how race-thinking permeates cultural commodities and the labour that goes into making those commodities. Again, how this actually happens will be explored in chapters 5 and 6 when I zoom in on the experience of cultural production.

This last point offers a route towards thinking about the impact of marketization on the production of representation, and a way to reconcile political economic and postcolonial / critical race approaches to media culture, which opens up to the remainder of the book. Marketization has led to media concentration, and although the scale of this concentration is contested, critical political economy accounts of the media nonetheless maintain that it results in less plurality and cultural diversity. As Hesmondhalgh (2013: 200) explains, market concentration 'reinforces the power of the oligopolies dominating the cultural industries and promotes commercial imperatives at the expense of artistic values (in fiction and entertainment) and objectivity, independence and professionalism (in journalism)'. Here, Hesmondhalgh gets to the specifics of how concentration impacts upon cultural production, in terms of the dominance of commercial goals over artistic ones, and an undermining of journalistic norms and ideals. While Hardy (2014) rightly questions the tendency to lazily equate media concen-

---

[14] Rather than the 'racialization of the cultural commodity', it might be more accurate to describe the process to which I am referring as the 'racialization of the cultural text during capitalist cultural production'. Admittedly, a proper analysis of the commodification of race would need a fuller historical account than I can offer here. However, I argue that within the context of my sociological study of commodification, this formulation of the racialization of cultural commodity – in terms of the penetration of race-thinking into the cultural commodity as it is being produced – still holds.

tration with media power (his critique is of a functionalist reading of media power), Hesmondhalgh (2013: 194) highlights the direct and indirect ways that this might in fact occur when he argues that the first and second tiers of global and national media companies 'have an enormous impact on the cultural industry landscape in terms of policy lobbying and the standards they set for what constitutes standard practice in the cultural industries'. As I will demonstrate, such standard practices include rationalization (formatting, use of the star-system, market research, inflated publicity and marketing costs) and bureaucratization (see Ryan, 1992). The question of policy is something I address in the next chapter. But to conclude this chapter, I want to suggest that the impact of marketization, specifically on the dynamics of cultural production, is felt more acutely by racialized minorities – and not just in terms of how their artistic and political goals are undermined by the overwhelming commercialism of the cultural industries. In the remainder of the book, I want to demonstrate how the very forms of rationalization that constitute the production process in the cultural industries contain within them racializing dynamics.

Conclusion

In chapter 1, I referred to Herman Gray's account of US black television production in the 1980s and 1990s, where he describes how policies of deregulation – and the industry restructuring that ensued – both enabled and constrained its development. Gray literally speaks to the enabling/constraining dynamic of cultural production that I shall unpack in more detail in chapter 5. However, I want to conclude this chapter by stressing that cultural production under capitalism is mostly constraining. The ambivalence at the heart of both commodification and the cultural politics of race does not mean that anything goes, and anything is possible; that it is aleatory. Under neoliberalism, the scale is tipped very much towards oppression and domination. When it comes to the representation of the Other in the media, it is much more profitable to tap into the nation's postcolonial melancholia than to disturb its imperial fantasies, which includes exploiting the desire for and fear of the Other.

Nonetheless, stressing the dialectical nature of the production of representation, shaped by the intertwining legacies of empire and structural forces of capitalism (and their inherent ambivalences), highlights the limits and possibilities, the constraints and potentiality of representational strategies. I argue that reconceptualizing commodification as a technology of racialized governmentalities, and as a process that contains intrinsic racializing dynamics, is the most productive route to thinking through the cultural industries' role in the governance of race under racial capitalism. But this is only part of the story; a better understanding of how cultural commodities are racialized entails a microlevel analysis of the processes of cultural production, which I shall explore in chapters 5 and 6. But before that, in the following chapter I want to complete the macro picture by focusing on media and cultural policies that have played a significant role in the experience and representation of race in the media. The policies that I will cover have specifically been designed to address the marginalization and misrepresentation of minorities in the media. The question, though, is the extent to which they have intervened in or facilitated the reproduction of historical constructions of the Other.

4

'Diversity' in Media and Cultural Policy

Introduction

With high production costs/low reproduction costs, cultural industries are capable of generating vast profits. But they also wield great social power. It is because of this influence that the governments of the advanced Western capitalist nations, with which this book is concerned, even in the most commercial contexts, are compelled to apply regulation to curb excessive media power. Such regulation is conducted in the name of maintaining media 'diversity', a key tenet in a liberal pluralist model of communications that emphasizes how an open, independent and free media system is central to the sustenance of a well-functioning democracy. It is this notion of 'diversity' that features the most in media and communications scholarship. Yet this chapter's concern is with 'cultural diversity' as a particular policy approach engaged with the question of how to best manage a nation's diverse communities. In this sense, the goal of cultural diversity policy is to foster 'social cohesion, to enrich cultural resources in the cultural industries, and to facilitate cultural development' (Napoli, 2008: 320). For the purpose of this chapter, I draw from Gavan Titley's work and define diversity in the context of the cultural industries as the process of 'mediating, and being seen to mediate, lived multiculture' (Titley, 2014a: 248). As the chapter will demonstrate, the way in which cultural diversity is understood and applied in the cultural industries (in terms of the mediation of lived multiculture) has specific race-making effects. My argument is that media and cultural policy in the Western nations that are the subject of this book, against the backdrop of the shift towards neoliberalization, acts as a technology of racialized governmentalities, much like the way I described commodification in the previous chapter, which shapes representations of race in particular ways. In other words, this form of racialized governance is not just unique to the commercial sector. Once again, my stress is on ambivalence, and how such policies have both constrained and enabled (though mostly constrained) the practices of racialized minorities.

As Napoli (2008) highlights, the cultural industries are formed through both media and cultural policies. He argues that cultural policy is mostly associated with the subsidized arts sector, based on a distinction between commercial and noncommercial endeavours, and the belief that the arts, which have historically been supported through patronage, should be protected from the market.[1] Media and communications policy has tended to be analysed in terms of economics and politics – in terms of competition, efficiency and monopoly, and as a result has a more commercial orientation. Very broadly – in the context of the advanced capitalist liberal democracies in the West – both types of policies have been shaped by a shift towards neoliberalization and the principle that the market (and a profit-making imperative) is the most efficient way of producing and distributing cultural goods. This has seen the opening up of cultural industries to market forces – even in the supposedly noncommercialized sectors of the arts and public service broadcasting – in the name of facilitating competition and greater diversity. As Hesmondhalgh (2013: 125) states, 'in general, policy bodies in modern capitalism work towards combining the accumulation of capital on the part of businesses with a certain degree of popular legitimation'. And for Hesmondhalgh, this has led to the victory (although not total) of marketization.

Noting the shift towards neoliberalism and marketization is important to our understanding of how particular media and cultural policies have attempted to tackle the 'problem' of multiculturalism and cultural diversity. I describe this as a problem, as policy approaches towards addressing the increasingly heterogeneous nature of the nation have become a fraught business. Globalization has intensified flows of migration, which for Western nation-states poses immense challenges (though by no means has the West borne the biggest brunt of the vast displacement of people in the twenty-first century) and has led to some highly troubling reactions. A supposed 'crisis in multiculturalism' (Lentin and Titley, 2011) has been the consequence of a populist feeling in many nations that there is 'too much diversity' (Jakubowicz, 2014: 227). As we shall see, a key aim of media and cultural policy is not just to ensure efficiency but also to foster a universal national culture and identity. Thus, changing demographics and the political pressures that these developments bring makes the question of diversity an increasingly critical and challenging area for those involved in media and cultural policy.

---

[1] This follows deep-rooted ideas, especially shaped by the romantic movement of the nineteenth century, regarding art and aesthetics as autonomous from, and potentially devalued by, commerce.

The aim of this chapter is to unpack the particular effects of policy upon the experience, representation and race-making practices within the context of the cultural industries. To reiterate: policy approaches frame these issues in terms of multiculturalism and/or cultural diversity, rather than race (and certainly not antiracism). I am going to focus on three areas where policy has most explicitly addressed minority issues: (1) diversity initiatives (by which I mean efforts to increase the numbers of minorities working in the media), (2) arts funding policy and (3) public service media (PSM). Two threads run through each of these areas. First, diversity management (including recruitment), PSM and the arts have all been affected by a broad shift in policy, from multicultural policy focused on meeting the needs of specific racial and ethnic groups, to cultural/creative diversity policy where race is one of many diversities to be represented and 'catered' for in the mainstream. This, I argue, produces very particular (and ambivalent) ideological effects, which leads to the second thread: that diversity as a discourse has a structuring power upon race-making practices that I argue needs to be understood as a form of racialized governmentalities. That is, the manner in which 'diversity' is discursively constructed within cultural diversity policy (which in some contexts has developed into a new 'creative diversity paradigm') is a technique of power (Gray, 2013: 776) that has transformed the way that race is understood and made sense of, specifically in the way that it suppresses and obscures the experience of racism. Once again, I will underline how the shift towards new conceptions of diversity is nonetheless an ambivalent process. Before I begin, I need to stress that the aim of the chapter is not to offer detailed accounts of specific media and cultural policies in particular national contexts (which could be a book in itself); nor is the aim to evaluate whether certain policies have 'worked' or not. Following the approach that I have laid out in this book, the chapter looks for broad historical trends to see how 'diversity' policy as applied in the cultural industries makes race.

Diversity initiatives in the cultural industries

To start with, I take a slight detour from the subject of cultural production and focus on a nonetheless very relevant issue relating to race and the cultural industries: policies designed to address the lack of diversity in the creative workforce. Across both privately and publicly owned cultural industries, it is recognized (to varying degrees) that minorities are being failed. This is in terms of media content, but also the lack of diversity in the media itself. Such an acknowledgement reaffirms how even the most commercial of operations recognize the social responsibility of the media. The aim of this opening section is to critically examine policy attempts (both public and corporate) to increase the numbers of minorities working in the cultural industries. It will demonstrate how the emphasis on a more diverse media workforce is increasingly rationalized in neoliberal terms that stress the benefits of diversity for competition and economic growth, rather than for political, let alone ethical or moral, reasons. While this rationale, with its clear appeal to corporate (and public) interests, has seen the issue of diversity placed high on the policy agendas across the media, diversity initiatives have arguably failed, in that film studios, broadcasters, major record labels and publishing houses remain overwhelmingly white. The reasons for this are multiple, complex and varied, but in this section the attention is specifically on how policymakers and industry figures attempt to address the institutional whiteness of media industries. I do not have the space to detail specific diversity initiatives across all national contexts. Instead, my aim is to explore these developments from a macro vantage point to discover broad trends and how these impact upon race-making in the cultural industries. Drawing from critical whiteness studies, critical race theory and feminist scholarship, my argument is that diversity initiatives rather than failing actually serve an ideological function that sustains the institutional whiteness of the cultural industries even while they claim (often genuinely so) to do something more inclusive.

Numerous industry reports and academic studies have demonstrated how there is a lack of diversity in the cultural industries workforce across all sectors (Gray, 2016; Hunt and Ramon, 2015; O'Brien et al., 2016; Smith et al., 2016). This is usually discussed in two ways: (1) the low employment of minorities in the media as a whole (Wilson and Gutierrez, 1995; Hunt and Ramon, 2015) and (2) the lack of minorities in senior roles (Wilson and Gutierrez, 1995). What are the implications of a lack of diversity? As I have explored in previous chapters, there is an assumption – again in both industry and academic scholarship – that the reason that racial minorities are portrayed so poorly in the media is because of the institutional whiteness of the cultural industries, and that, consequently, increasing the number of minorities working in cultural production will automatically improve the quality (and quantity) of representations of racial minorities. This rationale is shared throughout the cultural industries, but is particularly strong in public service media and subsidized sectors like theatre. In commercial sectors, however, there is a more explicit economic rationale for increasing diversity. In the US newspaper industry, for instance, there is a strong sense that the need to increase diversity is of economic urgency, a response to diminishing circulations and shrinking profits (Johnston and Flamiano, 2007). The fear, as expressed most strongly by the American Society for Newspaper Editors (ASNE), is that newspapers are potentially missing out on a huge section of future markets, in a society going through profound demographic change where, by the mid-twenty-first century, non-Hispanic whites will become a minority (Coffey, 2013; Adams and Cleary, 2006). It follows that hiring more journalists from racial and ethnic backgrounds in the newsroom will allow newspapers to reach out to those journalists' respective racial and ethnic communities.

There are two assumptions that underpin diversity policies in the cultural industries. As just described, and touched on in previous chapters, the first is the assumption that diversifying the workforce will automatically improve the quality/range/amount of diversity in media content. The second is an assumption, based on what Gray (2016) describes as the 'representation and demography' approach, that 'fixing' the problem of diversity is based on reducing the 'racial parity gap' (McGill, 2000). In other words, the goal is to match the percentage of particular racial and ethnic groups working in the media with the percentage of that racial and ethnic group in society at large. The representation and demography narrative is exemplified in the following quote from Coffey (2013: 156): 'If news media outlets are to be true representatives of their local constituencies, then the on-air personnel should physically resemble, and editorial content of the community should reflect, the diverse constituencies that a local news outlet serves.' Indeed, in Western liberal democracies, the calls for greater diversity in the media – in both policy and academic accounts – are shaped by the normative principles of a liberal pluralist model of media (a topic I shall unpack further in the section on public service media) that it should mirror exactly the make-up of a nation.

Yet, as stated, this ideal is rationalized in increasingly economic terms in neoliberal contexts. The politics of recognition – that is, the demand of minorities to be recognized – has been reframed as a commercial imperative (rather than as an ethical/moral one), where particular demographic groups become 'recognized' as market niches. As Gray (2013: 777) states, in this current conjuncture, 'at both the level of the individual and population, differences are foundational in constituting markets, distinguishing and circulating brands, designing and caring for the self'. In essence, the celebration of difference and cultural diversity goes hand-in-hand with neoliberal principles of 'privatizing public resources, reinventing government and marketizing public policy, and consolidating entitlement and property among the wealthy' (Gray, 2013: 777). In this context as described by Gray, racial neoliberalism 'willingly concedes, even celebrates differ-ence' (Gray, 2013: 780).

Against this backdrop, various scholars and researchers have problema-tized diversity initiatives. For instance, researchers examining workplace dynamics in the media reveal how minorities are expected to simply blend in (Thomas and Ely, 1996) or are given special assignments that are spe-cific to their identity groups – what Pritchard and Stonbely (2007) describe as a form of 'racial profiling'. In addition, workplace studies show how diversity initiatives, when they appear to work, can produce resentment, especially when minorities get promoted (Johnston and Flamiano, 2007; Thomas and Ely, 1996); but when they fail, they feel tokenistic, reflecting a lack of investment by senior management (Johnston and Flamiano, 2007). Journalism studies scholars (who have conducted the most research into diversity in the media) expose how news media in the US and throughout the West are institutionally and structurally white and privilege white-ness (Johnston and Flamiano, 2007; Fleras, 2016), with senior roles still dominated by whites who maintain white news agendas (Jenkins, 2013; Johnston and Flamiano, 2007) that are difficult to budge (Byerly and Wilson, 2009). It is in light of this that Mellinger (2003: 146) describes diversity initiatives and the practitioners involved in implementing them as 'unwitting defenders of the privileges of whiteness'.

Building on Mellinger, I develop a more critical angle and argue that diversity initiatives serve an ideological function of racial capitalism. Reflecting the shift from the soft antiracism of multicultural policies to a broader, raceless version of cultural diversity that I mentioned in the introduction (and shall be detailing further in the following section), how diversity initiatives are narrated within policy discourse tends to eradicate more contentious issues such as equality, equal opportunities and social justice (Ahmed, 2012). Rather than bringing people of colour to the core, schemes focused on increasing minority participation produce what Hall (1996b: 471) calls 'segregated visibility' – a method of including minorities but simultaneously distancing them. With the demand for greater visibility and recognition on the part of minorities, diversity initiatives subsequently act as a form of governance. Gray (2013: 792) goes as far as describing them as an instrument of biopolitics, where 'claims for increased visibility and greater representation will likely intensify normativities, managing through difference in the name of diversity, market choice, and consumer sovereignty'. Again, Gray is articulating how in this neoliberal conjunc-ture, race, diversity and difference have become 'qualities', as Callon et al. (2002) put it, incorporated into a process of production differentiation though strategically emphasizing certain qualities that a particular good offers. Thus, resonating with my argument in the previous chapter, the way that 'diversity' is deployed in the cultural industries acts as a form of racialized governmentalities, not least, as I shall describe shortly, because it involves a question of commodification.

In light of these arguments, I highlight two ideological functions in particular that underpin diversity management and governance in the cultural industries. First, diversity initiatives reproduce whiteness. Critical whiteness studies demonstrate how whiteness is part of the binary that structures race (Dyer, 1997). But while race is marked by its supposedly recognizable difference, whiteness is unmarked; its ability to stay in power precisely draws from its ability to remain invisible and beyond reproach. In other words, whiteness depends on race and being able to mark out race in order to sustain itself. In journalism studies of race in news content, whiteness is strongly evoked when discussing 'news frames'. Fleras (2016), for instance, discusses how the way that racialized minorities are framed in news stories does not just normalize 'natural' conceptions of race; it also reproduces whiteness (see also Pritchard and Stonbely, 2007). In other words, whiteness is the invisible frame through which stories on minorities are produced. But a critical approach to whiteness is also key to under-standing diversity initiatives in institutions. Again, Fleras (2016: 27) high-lights how such initiatives are a way of governing difference; as he states, whiteness 'endorses diversity as long as it doesn't cost or inconvenience and, in the process, confirms a mainstream right to define what counts as differences and what differences count'. Sara Ahmed argues that diversity policy is used to strengthen institutional whiteness. Drawing from Nirmal Puwar's (2004) work on racialized and gendered bodies in white spaces, Ahmed (2012: 33) states that 'the very idea that diversity is about those who "look different" shows us how it can keep whiteness in place'.

Mellinger (2003) develops this argument on whiteness through a critique of ASNE campaigning on diversity, which, she argues, has an ideological dimension in terms of managing the intake of nonwhite journalists while allowing 'white identity to continually, if silently, reconstruct itself over and against categories of colour even as the diversity initiative pursues an explicitly inclusive end' (2003: 134). One target in Mellinger's critique is the focus on recruitment and training as a way of fixing diversity, which puts the onus on the minorities to fix themselves in order to allow the media to be more diverse. Thus, diversity initiatives, and their intrinsic whiteness, 'maintain racial distinctions by constructing and policing boundaries, and the emphasis on entry-level hires and the failure to promote journalists of colour in significant numbers serves this purpose' (2003: 140). In other words, diversity schemes are paradoxically a way of keeping minorities in their place. For Mellinger, the promotion of a disproportionately small number of minority employees does not effectively challenge white hegemony but resecures its dominance; and, moreover, the lure of inclusion produces division among groups that are excluded from the privileges of whiteness. In other words, recruitment and retention discourses, which purport to promote inclusion, are in fact technologies of exclusion.

According to Mellinger, ASNE's ideal of inclusion advances the commodification of those who are Othered by whiteness, which brings me on to the second ideological function of diversity initiatives: that they transform race and racial identity into a commodity. This is an argument made by Leong (2012), who claims that the commodification of Otherness is a characteristic of racial capitalism – though this is not a reference to Robinson's (2000) notion of racial capitalism. Leong (2012: 2190) defines racial capital as 'the economic and social value derived from an individual's racial identity, whether by that individual, by other individuals, or by institutions'. Racial capitalism in this sense is 'the process of deriving social and economic value from the racial identity of another' (2012: 2190). Mostly it is whiteness that extracts this capital (Leong cites examples of businesses and education institutions using people of colour in promotional material as a recruiting tool). Leong's point is that this is not just disingenuous, but is part of the ideological process underlying racial capitalism that reinforces the white status quo. As she states, 'by showcasing nonwhite employees in prominent positions, employers signal that unsuccessful nonwhite employees are responsible for their own failures' (2012: 2190). And echoing Mellinger, such a process maintains a system in which white employees are in fact preferred and the whiteness of the institution remains intact.

Leong is a legal theorist and is talking about diversity in workplaces generally, but she raises a point that is particularly pertinent for the cultural industries and this book's interest in how the material shapes the symbolic. I am referring to when she describes how diversity policies pressure nonwhite people to do identity work. Part of the value of nonwhite people in a particular setting is tied to their nonwhiteness, which they are subtly – or not so subtly – encouraged to perform in a way that meets with the approval of the dominant culture. I am reminded here of my own research on British South Asian theatre practitioners (Saha, 2013a), who described how the money that the Arts Council ring-fenced specifically for 'black, Asian and minority ethnic' (BAME) theatre companies put pressure on them to present or perform their Asianness in a way that the Arts Council understood. (I shall return to the issue of the funding of minority arts in the following section.) Framing the question of inequality in terms of representation reveals how it is not in spite of but *because of* diversity initiatives that representations of racialized minorities continue to be reduced to a handful of recognizable tropes, with little variation. Thus, diversity initiatives do not just reproduce whiteness; they also make race.

This is the argument of Gray, who regards diversity itself as 'race-making' (2013: 249) and a technology of racialized governmentalities. As he states (2013: 776), 'the cultural acknowledgment of racial difference operates as techniques of power that move from social and historical critiques of racism to celebrations of racial diversity'. Rather than an object that can be measured objectively, Gray instead suggests that 'diversity' is a practice – or a discourse that structures the understandings around, and the experience of, race in the media industries. As he (2016: 250) states, this reconceptualization 'shifts the industry and analytic assumption of equating diversity and social equality with access and representational parity to one where the calculus of cultural, economic, and political difference as a basis of the production of inequality *is central* to media industry practices' (my emphasis). To stress the point again, according to this perspective racial misrepresentation does not happen despite diversity initiatives, but because of them. For Fleras (2016), the misrepresentation of minorities is the fundamental logic of a news media that is intrinsically ethnically white and Eurocentric. As he puts it, it is systemic (that is, intrinsic) rather than systematic (deliberately distorting or omitting). It is in a similar fashion that Gray (2016: 249) argues that diversity initiatives in the cultural industries are 'race-making practices', a form of 'power/knowledge that operates as a logic of production'. It is this notion of racial governance as an intrinsic logic of production that I underline next, and will explore in more detail in the following two chapters.

While I am persuaded by the arguments that I have cited that expose the ideological function of diversity initiatives, I am less convinced by some of the solutions offered. For instance, Mellinger (2003), drawing from Nancy Fraser's concept of subaltern counter publics, argues that we need to support the alternative media of subordinated social groups that allow them to mount their own counter discourses and formulate oppositional interpretations of their identities, interests and needs. I am going to explore this in much more detail in the following chapters, but for now I will argue that while such alternative or ethnic media can certainly act as enabling spaces for minorities, I think there is danger in over-romanticizing media on the margins. One obvious reason is that it can lead to ghettoization, but more than that it fails to recognize how alternative media, often unwittingly, emulate the practices and behaviours of the core. This is an argument made by cultural industries theorists, who highlight that the real power of the types of oligopolies that characterize media markets is not (just) their ideological influence over society, but how they set the standards – specifically, forms of rationalization and bureaucratization – that other media organizations subsequently adopt and mimic (Hesmondhalgh, 2013: 209–215).[2] While smaller media companies can certainly resist these processes, and, indeed, actively do so, they can only do this up to a limit. As I shall argue in the next chapter, the processes of rationalization that shape cultural production under capitalism are embedded with racializing dynamics, and it is my contention that the subaltern media that Mellinger invests in are not immune to these processes.

Returning to the specific issue of diversity initiatives in the cultural industries, as much as they are a form of governance, we should still recognize how, as Ahmed (2012: 36) puts it, 'numbers can be affective . . . it can be surprising and energising not to feel so singular'. As we have already seen, Gray is critical of diversity initiatives and the 'representation and demography' approach that underpin them, but he still recognizes how 'increased visibility might in turn effect some measure of cultural justice, including empathy and sensitivity on the part of the powerful and the dominant groups to lives of poor, marginal, and dominated people' (2013: 791). Indeed, if we take fully on board Leong's Marxist critique of diversity initiatives as a form of commodification of the Other, then, according to a properly Marxist conception of the ambivalence of markets, commodification in this instance must have enabling qualities as well. I argue that Hall's conception of popular culture as the site 'where this struggle for and against a culture of the powerful is engaged' (1981: 239), is important here. Hall (1996b: 471) describes the struggle over cultural hegemony as 'never about pure victory or pure domination'; rather it entails 'shifting the balance of power in the relations of culture; it is always about changing the dispositions and the configurations of cultural power, not getting out of it'. In terms of a struggle over hegemony, the inclusion of minorities through diversity schemes, even though they serve to reinforce whiteness,

---

[2] Negus (1997), for instance, reconceptualizes 'major' and 'independent' record labels as 'major' and 'minor' labels, as he thinks that the term 'independent' over-romanticizes the extent to which indies are an alternative to the majors. Hesmondhalgh (2013: 209) similarly prefers to talk of 'smaller companies' rather than independents, not least since many companies that are considered independent have formal relationships with corporate companies. This will be unpacked further in chapter 6.

can still be read as a form of progress of sorts. While Hall admits that the gains made by marginality in popular culture amount to nothing more than segregated visibility, his point in fact is that, in a war of position,[3] segregated visibility represents a gain nonetheless. Although I argue that the reason minority access to the cultural industries is impeded is not in spite of diversity initiatives, but because of them, I would also go as far as saying that, when successful cultural transruptions do occur, it is *because* of these policies, however much it may feel as if they happened in spite of them.

Missing in the critiques of diversity schemes, however, is a discussion of the politics of representation. While the arguments I have presented go to great length to describe how the insertion of minorities into white spaces is governed in a way that sustains the very whiteness of media organizations, there is less discussion of what these minorities who have gained entry are able to achieve (or, rather, not achieve) in terms of their symbolic practices. Put another way, in diversity literature – whether academic or policy-orientated – there is less attention paid to the experience of cultural production itself. Earlier in this section I referred to journalism studies of newsrooms that have shown how the practice of minority journalists are constrained, and this is what needs further unpacking (and, as I have argued, such analysis needs to be underpinned by a fuller theory of race and cultural production). Crucially, what is lacking in the critiques and advocations of diversity policies is the question of the extent to which minorities are given the autonomy that would enable their creativity. The issue of diversity, representation, autonomy and creativity is at the core of discussions of public service media. But before I focus on PSM, I briefly turn to the issue of the funding of minority arts, as a way of opening up the discussion on diversity more specifically in relation to cultural production.

Arts funding governmentalities and politics of diversity

This book is mostly concerned with the core cultural industries – including film, music, television – where marketization, commercialism and commodification predominantly characterize the production of symbolic goods. Yet parts of these sectors, and peripheral cultural industries such as

---

[3] Hall is drawing from Gramsci's notion of a 'war of position', which refers to how, in a struggle over cultural hegemony, different classes compete to gain social influence. The war of position is more strategic, protracted and tactical (in contrast to a 'war of manoeuvre', which suggests a full frontal battle).

theatre, have been subsidized by arts funding bodies. This makes cultural policy and the arts a relevant topic for this chapter on policy approaches to race and the cultural industries. Cultural policy designed to financially support the arts often occurs in those industries where production is based on 'traditional' methods, such as writing music or books or plays.[4] The intention is to support cultural production especially in sectors with high production costs, where these sectors cannot be sustained by market demand alone. So, for instance, 'high art' like opera or classical music tends to receive funding, and so too do the artistic and cultural practices of minority groups. In fact, many arts bodies have specific diversity policies designed to give voice to and enable the production of minorities based on similar rationales found in PSM. As in that case, my aim is to consider how arts funding policy acts as a form of governance that makes race in particular ways. Since these policies only impact upon a relatively small portion of the cultural industries that I am interested in, this section will be relatively brief. Once again, my intention is not to provide a detailed treatment of specific policies in specific contexts, but rather to look for broader trends in arts funding in the West and unravel their race-making dynamics.

In many Western nations, the arts – and in particular 'culturally diverse arts'[5] – are subsidized by the state through independent funding bodies. As shall be made evident, cultural policy in this sphere faces very similar challenges to PSM, with Western nations feeling the effects of globalization and a struggle with the unsettling questions around multiculture that arise. The funding of the arts in most Western nations, no matter how meagre, demonstrates a fundamental belief in the key role that the arts can play in providing cultural cohesion. The Danish context (Skot-Hansen, 2002) is typical of European contexts in this regard in that its cultural policy has been characterized by two principles: (1) a democratization of culture approach, based on disseminating the national culture, that is, the 'good' culture, to the entire population, and (2) a cultural democracy approach involving a recognition that there are multiple cultures in Denmark and that growth possibilities should be created for these different cultures so that they could develop from below (Skot-Hansen, 2002: 199). While these two animating themes in cultural policy are often in tension with each

---

[4] Theodore Adorno (1991) distinguishes between two types of production in the culture industry: where production is based on traditional methods but the reproduction of the goods is industrial, and where the production process itself is entirely industrial (e.g., broadcasting).

[5] This is the term used by the Arts Council England, and reflects the shift from multicultural arts to a broader cultural diversity policy; see Moss (2005: 190–191).

other, they are both capable of being folded into the liberal pluralist principles that are at the core of cultural policy in Western democracies, albeit in distinctive ways.

The funding of 'culturally diverse arts' varies of course in different contexts, which I cannot go into fully here. But in certain contexts, cultural policy has taken the form of ring-fencing money specifically for minority practitioners. In the UK for instance, the Arts Council scheme 'Decibel: Raising the Voice of Culturally Diverse Arts in Britain' was based on having separate funds for 'cultural diverse' work 'aimed to make cultural diversity part of the mainstream in terms of showing of work, employment, governance and numbers of grant applications' (Moss, 2005: 191). (As I will demonstrate, the stress on mainstreaming both diversity and quantitative measures is typical of creative industries policies.) The ambiguity around what 'culturally diverse' consists of can be problematic; as Joop de Jong (1998) asks, in order to qualify for ring-fenced money, is it enough that the artist comes from a 'culturally diverse' background, or is it more important that her art be valuable from a multicultural or intercultural angle? In other contexts, there is no such special treatment. For instance, in the case of Denmark, even though both the State Art Foundation and other councils and committees have supported artists with non-Danish ethnic backgrounds as well as projects that include immigrants and refugees, it has not been their main purpose or part of a genuinely formulated policy (Skot-Hansen, 2002: 201).

Whatever the approach, cultural policy that attempts to address racial inequalities is fraught with challenges, not least the fundamental lack of financing in the arts, made worse by austerity measures introduced following the 2007 financial crash. One issue that is a problem for people of colour in the cultural industries as a whole, but is particularly felt in the arts, is negotiating Western conceptions of taste and quality, and the tension in applying Western universal aesthetic criteria to ethnic and cross-cultural art (Skot-Hansen, 2002; Moss, 2005). In the Netherlands (Jong, 1998), regional policy is based on fostering local culture, while national policy tends to be broader, based on the principles of quality or distinction; the government funds all artistic expression, including everything that is considered part of the national cultural heritage. But for Jong, while the meritocratic ideologies that underpin the European liberal state supposedly favour quality, when it comes to 'ethnic' arts what they appear to be looking for is cultural authenticity.

This begins to unravel the way in which cultural policy shapes discourses of race through what I call arts funding governmentalities (Saha, 2013a). As Jong (1998) suggests, the emphasis on authenticity often produces essentialism. For Moss (2005) a reified, essentialist form of minority culture tends to suit national policy much more than messier, hybrid versions. For instance, for Moss the particular policy of the biculturalism model adopted in New Zealand produces an essentialist version of Maori culture and arts 'that fit a folkloric stereotype'[6] (Moss, 2005). In the Danish context Dorte Skot-Hansen (2002: 206) cites an example of a 'hybrid' theatre company that has struggled to get funding because of its 'intermediary status', operating 'in the no-man's land between amateurs and professionals, the purely artistic and the socially engaged, and the local/global nexus'. Paul Gilroy (1993b: 110–111) observes how the structure of arts funding coerces a reductive type of representation in the context of black British arts when he asserts that 'the most unwholesome ideas of ethnic absolutism hold sway and . . . have been incorporated into the structures of the political economy of funding black arts. The tokenism, patronage and nepotism that have become intrinsic to the commodification of black culture rely absolutely on an absolute sense of ethnic difference.' Cornell West (1990: 20) echoes this point, referring to a 'double bind' in which black cultural critics and artists, 'while linking their activities to the fundamental, structural overhaul of these institutions, often remain financially dependent on them' (see also Saha, 2015). Garnham (1987: 34), in his critique of the cultural policy approach that is focused on funding the artist (and that he argues should be replaced with an audience-centred approach), describes this in terms of a 'Stockholm Syndrome' where creative artists unwittingly (or not) end up producing work 'for the only audience they know, namely the cultural bureaucrats who pay the bill and upon whom they become psychologically dependent even while reviling them'.

The way in which arts funding governmentalities manifest during cultural production is explored further in the following chapter. But to conclude this section I want to return to a discussion of policy itself. Specifically, I want to flag how cultural policy approaches to difference and, indeed, 'diversity' mirror PSM cultural diversity policy – that is the subject of the next section. As will be described, a powerful post-racial discourse has produced a race-less version of diversity. As Clive Nwonka (2015: 10) states, 'diversity policy is both political and depolitical; political in the sense that it is influenced by discourses of social inclusion and multiculturalism, but depolitical in the sense that it manoeuvres away from credible interrogations of discrimination into concepts of underrep-

---

[6] Moss (2005) finds an exception in UK arts funding, which in fact encourages more intercultural artistic practices.

resentation'. Approaches to cultural diversity take the same form – albeit, to varying extents, in different contexts across PSM, the arts and creative industries policies, shaped as they are by a racial neoliberalism and a post-racial turn that depoliticizes and neutralizes race issues that are, in fact, very much political and shaped by processes of racialization.

Yet once again it needs to be stressed that the cultural politics of cultural diversity policy are inherently ambivalent. In the context of cultural policy, Rimi Khan (2010), who explores the Australian arts organization Multicultural Arts Victoria (MAV), illustrates this effectively. Khan mounts a critical defence of – or, at least, wants to complicate the picture regarding – MAV's particular approach to representing multiculturalism, which is criticized for its marketized 'mainstreaming diversity' approach. Khan is offering an alternative to Ghassan Hage's (1998) argument that in cases like these multiculturalism is instrumentalized for dominant white culture, which, for Khan, problematically produces a binary based on the active and potentially cosmopolitan subject on one side and a passive ethnic object on the other.[7] Ultimately, Khan is arguing against 'a tendency – both within academic writing on the arts and amongst commentators from within the arts sector – to regard any instrumental use of culture as a compromise to the liberatory promise of the arts' (2010: 196). Instead, echoing Hall, Khan alludes to a war of position, where the efforts of MAV, despite its strong economic rationales that some find objectionable, nonetheless stand up to a right-wing government's vision of Australian national identity that is hostile towards multiculturalism.

What Khan is in effect describing is the ambivalence at the core of both the politics of multiculture and cultural production under capitalism, albeit in an arts funding context. Yet, as stressed in the previous chapter, such an observation should not be taken as an argument that anything goes with the production of cultural commodities. Industrial cultural production fundamentally has enabling/constraining tendencies. But the historical analysis that the cultural industries approach applies highlights how at specific conjunctural moments powerful political economic/postcolonial currents affect the balance of this dynamic. The aim of this chapter thus far has been to demonstrate how in the current conjuncture, media and cultural policies – specifically those that shape arts funding – are shaped by neoliberal ideologies even while they are operationalized in nonmarket contexts. This becomes particularly evident in the case of public service media.

---

[7] Keith (2005) makes a similar point defending ethnic entrepreneurs who actively self-commodify for their own economic gain.

Public service media and mainstreaming diversity

One of the key spaces for minorities in the cultural industries is PSM.[8] In many national contexts, it is the main, or indeed the only, arena where the dominant culture consciously and in a concerted way attempts to engage, accommodate and understand difference. PSM content varies across different national contexts, but what unites it is an emphasis on the social value of broadcasting. Of specific relevance for this chapter, PSM is primarily engaged with the task of fostering national identity and conversation – what Kyle Conway (2014) frames as producing and maintaining hegemonic ideas around national identity. This involves recognizing and catering for the full diversity of a nation, particularly its minority populations who tend to be underserved by commercial channels that pursue audience maximization strategies in order to generate revenues from advertising (Horsti, 2014; Gray, 1993). But crucially, PSM's aim is to create a universal national identity that (somehow) subsumes the full diversity of the nation into one. For Hall (1993: 25), 'access to broadcasting has thus become a condition, a sine qua non, of modern citizenship'. As such, PSM remains critical to the construction of a coherent and convincing imagined community that people are invested in across their difference. In an ever intensifying commercialized markeplace, PSM has come under immense commercial and political pressure, yet it still forms a significant part of the broadcasting market in many nations, constituting between 30 and 50 per cent of audience share in Western Europe (Titley, 2014b).

All national PSM systems are distinct, yet they share fundamental common features, including accountability to the public, an element of public finance, regulation of content (such as space reserved for news or children's programming), universal service across the nation and audiences addressed primarily as citizens. Differences between national systems lie in types of funding, different levels of commercial broadcasting, the extent of state control, different forms of governance, different programming styles and mixes between education and entertainment (Hesmondhalgh, 2013: 137–138). This makes talking about PSM in any kind of generalizable form difficult, but there are two broad trends that have affected PSM systems across Europe, Canada and Australia, which are of the main concern here.

First, PSM has seen a shift towards marketization. This has been dis-

---

[8] I work with Iosifidis's (2010) notion of 'public service media' rather than 'public service broadcasting', since public service organizations increasingly use a variety of platforms to deliver their content, beyond traditional forms of broadcasting.

cussed at length in the previous chapter, but to reiterate, under neoliberalism in general the dominant ideology is that the market is the best way to allocate resources and to manage organizations – even in nonprofit contexts. The neoliberal policies behind various forms of media regulation (for instance, the 1990 Broadcasting Act in the UK, the 1993 Broadcasting Services Act in Australia) have invariably affected PSM – the privatization of the public channel TFI in France being perhaps the most extreme version of the impact of neoliberalism (Hesmondhalgh, 2013: 143–144). Of course, it should be noted that the extent of marketization varies between media systems with a significant PSM presence. But generally speaking, this trend has been felt in two ways. First, it has resulted in a more competitive marketplace, which national public service broadcasters have had to contend with in different ways. (For instance, in Britain there is pressure on the BBC to commercially perform in order to demonstrate its national and cultural relevance.) Second, as we shall see in more detail in the following chapter, it has resulted in new forms of managerialism, emulating the rationalizing practices and forms of bureaucratization found in the commercial sector (Born, 2004), which can be interpreted as the corporate takeover, to use Jonathan Hardy's (2014) term, of PSM and its values of universal access, social participation and citizenship.

The second broad trend that has had an impact upon European PSM in particular, but has also been felt in other Western nations, is the aforementioned crisis in multiculturalism. As stated, a universal element of PSM is fostering a sense of commonality and national community, though the particular approach adopted by a national public service broadcaster is determined by that nation's distinct relationship to its own multiculture. This might be shaped by histories of empire and colonialism, and/or more recent patterns of migration following broader geopolitical developments. Multicultural policies across Western nations vary along the spectrum between pluralism and assimilation (Siapera, 2010; Murphy, 2012). For instance, the UK and France have two opposing models of integration: pluralistic and republican, respectively. Sweden and Canada have similar pluralist models based on the principle that integration should take place without the need for cultural assimilation (Hultén, 2014). Germany adopts a particular 'ethnic' multicultural model (Siapera, 2010). But in Europe overall, we have seen a wholesale crisis in multiculturalism. With the impact of digital technologies, and satellite and cable television in particular, PSM was already struggling with the challenge of catering to increasingly fragmenting audiences that are no longer as reliant on PSM as they once were (Titley, 2014a; Skot-Hansen, 2002). This has been compounded by the so-called failure of multiculturalism – a reaction to the transformative effects of globalization, and the racial and religious tensions at home brought about by foreign excursions abroad – that produced an increasing suspicion of policies seen to be accommodating minorities, for the reason that they promote a 'problematic excess of difference' (Titley: 2014a: 249). As suggested in the previous chapter, it is not always clear what multicultural policies these critics are specifically referring to. Indeed, for Lentin and Titley (2011), what these crises actually reveal is the general anxieties of the dominant culture about the presence of racialized minorities, reflecting an increasingly culturalist conception of minorities whose cultures are considered deviations from European norms (see also Titley 2014a; Gilroy, 2004). Consequently, even within the nations that have had a strong history of pluralism, there has been a pull towards integrationism. But such an integrationist approach is not designed to address the issues of inequality and exclusion that impede the actual ability of different groups to integrate into society. Rather, it is based on 'merging an instrumental demand for economic utility with political concerns regarding cultural compatibility and socio-economic costs' (Titley, 2014a: 251). As Andrew Jakubowicz (2014: 233) puts it, such 'sociocultural conflicts are framed by political and economic concerns with crisis and free markets, and the reduction in state expenditures'. I interpret this as a particular dynamic of racial neoliberalism, a governance of difference according to market logics. The shifts towards marketization and integrationist policies are not, then, two distinct phenomena that just happen to run in parallel; they are in fact ideologically intertwined.

PSM is under great commercial and political pressure. It faces two challenges in particular: first, to underline its own relevance in an increasingly commercialized, globalized and fragmented marketplace and, second, to recognize the diversity of the nation while trying to produce a coherent and concrete sense of national identity. These challenges have been met in a similar way across different national contexts, through an approach that is known as mainstreaming diversity. This refers to how PSM no longer tends to produce niche programming for minority groups, but instead strives to include minorities in mainstream programming, or, put another way, to produce 'minority programming' that has mainstream appeal. Sarita Malik (2013a) unpacks this in detail in her mapping of a policy shift that she has identified in the case of UK public service broadcasting, from multicultural policy, to cultural diversity policy, to a new paradigm: 'creative diversity' policy. While Malik's case study relates specifically to the UK, this trend towards 'mainstreaming diversity' and the retreat from multiculturalist polices mirrors what has happened in other PSM contexts; as Titley (2014a) acknowledges, British PSM is held up in Europe as particularly influential in how it has managed cultural diversity. Through an exploration of policy developments in UK PSM, I argue that the shift to cultural and then to creative diversity is part of a broader, powerful neoliberal current working through the cultural industries, which constrains the expression of marginality in PSM, though it invariably contains enabling features too.

Following the first significant waves of immigration from the former colonies in the postwar period, PSM in the UK adopted multicultural policies to address its new audiences. Ben O'Loughlin (2006: 3) describes this as bringing minorities into the national conversation and 'moving towards the objective of a multicultural representation of an apparently multicultural society'. In the case of the BBC, its approach towards multicultural audiences was shaped by a Reithian version of public service that was paternalistic but accommodating (quite literally, a programme for the newly arrived Hindi-speaking immigrants was called 'Apna Hi Ghar Samajhiye', or 'Make Yourself at Home').[9] In the case of Channel 4 – the public service broadcaster launched in 1982 as a commercially funded but publicly owned entity – multicultural programming was embedded as part of its core practice and infrastructure. In other words, ethnic minorities, along with women and youth audiences, represented the channel's principal target groups in its remit to cater for distinct and neglected audiences. Indeed, its younger, fresher approach was a contrast to the establishment tone of the BBC (Hall, 1993; Malik, 2008). But both broadcasters adopted broadly similar multicultural policies, consisting of recruitment measures, targets and specialist slots and multicultural departments, all designed to explicitly position visible minorities such as Blacks and Asians on the media agenda. The inevitable downside was ghettoization (Cottle, 2000) and an essentialist approach to race, defined by a 'race-relations problematic' (Ross, 1995: 91), but Malik nonetheless has a fairly positive view of the multicultural moment:

> Multiculturalist principles employed an overt group-based approach in which certain ethnic communities were targeted for inclusion and access. Although not without its own politics of limitation and ghettoisation, this version of state multiculturalism should be noted for being written

[9] Lord Reith was the first Director General of the BBC. He saw the role of broadcasting as chiefly educational, which still shapes the BBC's approach (to varying degrees) and other PSM organizations like it.

into media policy and commissioning structures and for being grounded in a particular (albeit soft) version of anti-racism. (2013a: 230)

It is interesting that Malik describes these policies as softly antiracist in character. Indeed, she goes as far as saying that PSM during this period acted as a truly 'multicultural public sphere' (2008: 344).

Yet the increasing intensification of globalization raised a number of new challenges for PSM that forced it to revaluate its approach. As stated, the rise of satellite and digital technologies in particular meant that diasporic groups became less reliant on PSM. In the face of this 'delocalisation' (Malik, 2013a: 232), the need for PSM to act as the social glue for the nation became less important. Moreover, fragmenting audiences led to new forms of identity politics where it became more difficult to treat racial and ethnic minorities as clearly delineated, bounded groups (Cottle, 1997). The 'crisis of multiculturalism' has seen increasing calls for assimilation and social cohesion (and a rejection of accommodative policies), bound up in a discourse of 'post-race', which rather than striving for a society where racial equality has been achieved, can be better described as 'racelessness' – a way of removing race (and racism) – from the picture (Malik, 2013a). So, paradoxically, multicultural policies were seen as, on the one hand, failing to integrate minorities, but on the other as not reflecting the more inclusive, and post-race British society that had emerged.

The response of PSM in the 1990s was to shift from the multiculturalist language of race and ethnicity to a broader notion of 'cultural diversity' – race was just one of many diversities characterizing the nation that needed to be incorporated into the mainstream. Nwonka (2015: 4–5) points out that cultural diversity policy in this instance was constituted by the language of New Labour Third Way politics, which 'coupled social democracy's commitment to social justice with the requirements of the capitalist system'. The emphasis here shifted from tackling racism or marginalization to the broadening of access. Channel 4's CEO, Michael Jackson, went as far as saying that equality had been achieved since minorities were now part of the mainstream,[10] though, as Malik (2013a) points out, this was mostly driven by a fear of losing the core mainstream audience in an increasingly competitive sector with falling advertising revenue. Indeed, as Cottle (1997: 4) points out, this period is also marked by a 'shift away from public service ideals to the marketplace'. The 1990 Broadcasting Act created a

[10] Michael Jackson stated: 'In 2001 the "minorities" of those times [1982, when Channel 4 began] have been assimilated into the mainstream of society'; quoted in Malik (2013a: 232).

much more competitive environment where lighter regulation and technological change (specifically, the explosion of digital channels) put PSM under immense commercial pressure. In other words, the turn to cultural diversity belied the fact that channels, quite simply, could no longer afford to target niches anymore (Saha, 2012).

It was in the name of 'mainstreaming diversity' that we see the closure of the Afro-Caribbean Unit and Asian Programming Unit at the BBC, and the Multicultural Programmes Department at Channel 4. While multicultural policies were originally at the core of the Channel 4 remit, the channel 'now repositioned multicultural representations as part of a broader diversity agenda in which ethnic diversity was just one component' (Malik, 2008: 346). This admittedly did result in the increasing visibility of minorities onscreen, particularly in the reality TV and lifestyle shows that came to dominate prime-time viewing. But we see new challenges emerge for minorities in this new environment. First, with regulation stipulating that a certain portion of PSM programming has to come from the independent sector, rather than producing a competitive marketplace, this led to monopolization and the dominance of 'super-indies', at the expense of black-led companies that would most typically cover issues of race (Ross, 1995; Cottle, 1997). Second, as alluded to above, we see the emergence of 'new mangerialism' (Born, 2004), which Cottle (1997) argues constrains rather than enables minority programming. In this context, programmers, particularly those from minority backgrounds, suffer from insufficient finance, problems dealing with institutional gatekeepers and commissioners, and tension between political goals and audience demands. In a nutshell, cultural diversity policies have led to more black and brown people onscreen, but fewer stories about actual black or brown experiences.

In more recent times, we have seen a further shift towards a new paradigm, what Malik (2013a) defines as 'creative diversity' policy. The emergence of creative diversity policy is not necessarily a reaction to any major or sudden changes in broadcasting or in politics, but, as alluded to above, is constituted by the neoliberal current in advanced capitalist countries. This next stage in diversity policy mirrors the shift from cultural industries policy to 'creative industries' that emphasizes the role of creative industries in economic growth through innovation and competition, but with a social inclusion aspect: to enable access for everyone 'to the widest possible range of cultural experiences' (Garnham, 2005: 27). For Khan (2010: 185) creative industries policy is better understood as 'a move away from cultural development agendas towards a focus on the development of individual human capital, where new forms of value are attributed to the individual artisan or entrepreneur'. In other words, diversity is reframed in terms of innovation and creativity, with less emphasis on addressing actual inequalities (Nwonka, 2015: 7). In the context of PSM, the application of creative diversity policy is an attempt to solve the dilemma of multiculturalism and engage diverse audiences. Yet what emerges is a marketized version of diversity where 'cultural life is reconfigured as a post-racialized modality of public service' (Malik, 2013a: 235) that obscures the forms of inequality that continue to structure the lives of racialized minorities in particular. What creative diversity policy in effect works to do is remove the unsettling presence of 'race' and 'racism' – or 'culture' for that matter – reconceptualizing diversity in terms of supposedly universalistic, and much less contentious, notions of 'choice, innovation, efficiency' (Malik, 2013a: 235). Resonating with Khan's argument above, this shift towards what O'Loughlin (2006: 14) calls a 'flowing' version of cultural diversity (as opposed to the essentialist version that underpinned multiculturalist policies) is based upon increasing the social capital of individuals (rather than raising the standards of living of marginalized groups), which is seen as the route to 'democratic renewal, social cohesion, and economic productivity' (see also Titley, 2014a, 2014b; Horsti, 2014). Creative diversity, in other words, allows PSM to reconcile marketization, on the one hand, and diversity agendas, on the other. It can be read as the logical end point in the move towards mainstreaming diversity, from the softly antiracist politics of multiculturalist policies, to a non-antiracist policy of cultural diversity, to a race-less notion of creative diversity.

Although this case study is taken from the UK, the broad policy of mainstreaming diversity has also been adopted by several other national public service broadcasters, not least because they all have to contend with the same challenges: an increasingly competitive sector, technological change and a supposed crisis in multiculturalism (Titley, 2014b; Horsti, 2014; Jakubowicz, 2014; Leurdijk, 2006). So how does the mainstreaming diversity approach make race? In the neoliberal conjuncture, diversity neutralizes race, and is now more likely to act as a marker of consumer brands, lifestyle choices and post-racial cultural appreciation (Gray, 2016) rather than reflect the lived experience of multiculture. While again there has undoubtedly been an increase in the visibility of people of colour, this is often put down to the proliferation of reality TV and lifestyle shows that rely on having a variety of social types to add colour to a production (Malik, 2008: Titley, 2014a; Horsti, 2014). According to Leurdijk (2006: 41), in this move, 'popular appeal and innovation have become more important motivations than social realism or compensating misrepresentation or under-representation in mainstream programmes'. While Titley (2014b: 139) agrees that there is something potentially progressive about the mainstreaming of diversity whereby migrants and ethnic minorities are no longer 'ciphers burdened by messages they have to convey', he nonetheless argues that 'the unobtrusive inclusion of diversity [. . .] can be as depoliticising as it can be normalising'. Titley is wary of a post-racial valorisation of diversity as the basis for a turn away from the 'contested ideological terrain of cultural representation' (2014a: 253). To repeat, PSM programming has become less concerned with exploring black or brown experience, or even just social issues, and more concerned with finding a diverse range of 'characters' (Leurdijk, 2006). Thus, the shift to main-streaming diversity produces predominantly negative ideological effects for minorities. It reinforces post-race discourses where race and racism are removed from the picture, where any articulation of either is dismissed as anachronistic or as a reductive form of identity politics. Under the new creative diversity paradigm, racial and ethnic identities and experience are only recognized when they are collapsed into a generic and politically neutral notion of diversity, preferably conceived in terms of market goals contributing to the continued upward redistribution of resources. In this way, cultural/creativity diversity policy, including the rationales, logics, mechanisms and tools embedded within them, are a technology of racial-ized governmentalities; a form of power/knowledge that performs the ideological work of managing difference through operating as a logic of production.

Yet once again I want to stress the ambivalence intrinsic to the move to mainstreaming diversity. Creative diversity policies are depoliticizing as much as they are normalizing, but the fact remains that PSM, with its remit to cater for a nation's diverse communities, has nonetheless enabled the cultural production of minorities – perhaps more than any other cul-tural sector. This is the reason why I yet again underscore the complex-ity, contradiction and contestedness of PSM. As I stressed in the previous chapter, all advanced Western capitalist nations are fully embedded in globalization, which brings tensions as well as unique forms of syncretism and cultural exchange. As Jakubowicz (2014: 238) puts it, 'where the media are charged with recognizing and engaging creatively with these changes as part of the contemporary modernity of these complex societies, what had been bizarre or deviant instead becomes reprocessed and integrated into current narratives'. Rather than normalization, we can read the poten-tiality of PSM in terms of Stuart Hall's notion of multicultural drift – as an irreversible, albeit slow and incremental, transformation of national culture, where difference becomes ordinary. This has been evoked by several writers when speaking about the dynamics of multiculturalism in broadcasting. For instance, Ang et al. (2002: 34–37) refer to 'everyday cosmopolitanism', which Khan (2010: 193) interprets as 'an openness to difference based on everyday encounters and interaction'. Similarly, Gilroy's notion of convivial culture describes an ability to 'live with alterity without becoming anxious, fearful or violent' (2004: xi). Drawing from Gilroy in her own work, Malik (2013b: 515) stresses that convivial culture, in the context of PSM, rather than being a naive form of utopianism, becomes a potential 'manoeuvre for managing the potential challenges of living with multiculture (and the interactions it offers)'. I will develop these arguments further in chapter 6.

For now I want to return to Stuart Hall, who stresses the politics of representation as a war of position, neither wholly liberating nor wholly dominating. Again, while mainstreaming diversity policies can be interpreted as part of a post-racial discourse that attempts to de-race rather than address racial inequalities, PSM nonetheless remains a particularly enabling space for minorities to intervene. As Hall (1993: 36) puts it, PSM is the 'theatre' where cultural diversity is produced, displayed and represented and the 'forum' in which the terms of its associative life together are negotiated. However, while I conclude this section by stressing the ambivalence at the core of PSM cultural/creative diversity policies, which perhaps overstresses the potentiality of their development, adopting a more micro perspective, as I will do in the next chapter, highlights how the 'corporate takeover' of PSM has damaging effects upon the practices of cultural producers wanting to tell stories from the margins. It is when we combine this macro view of the cultural industries with an empirical approach to cultural production – the central theme of this book – that we attain a clearer view of mainstreaming policy as a form of racial governance.

Conclusion

The media and cultural policies of Western liberal democracies understand that cultural industries play a crucial role in fostering an inclusive national community. Policies specifically addressing diversity similarly see one purpose of national media as the integration of minorities into society. While the nations of the West have their distinct policy approaches to cultural diversity based on their own histories of migration and/or empire, there has been a broad trend towards neoliberalism across the advanced capitalist nations that applies a market logic to dealing with the 'problem' of race and diversity. Thus, in those nations once characterized by multiculturalist approaches based on a pluralist, accommodative model, we have seen a shift towards integrationism and an emphasis on fostering social cohesion based on increasing the social capital of individuals and enabling them to lift themselves out of poverty or existence on the margins so they can integrate fully into society (or indeed, the market). In other words, policy approaches to diversity have become less concerned with addressing racial inequalities (let alone racism) and more focused on how diversity can contribute to innovation, efficiency and competition in the new knowledge economy.

Yet one thing that has not been made apparent in this chapter is how the recognition given to racialized minorities – in public service broadcasting, in arts funding, in the calls for greater diversity in the cultural industries – is a consequence of the campaigning and activism of people of colour, from political interventions (in the UK well-known black celebrities such as Idris Elba and Lenny Henry have both addressed parliamentary commissions on the lack of diversity in the cultural industries) to hashtag activism (e.g., #oscarssowhite). As I have argued, in response to these actions neoliberal media and cultural policies act as a technology of racialized governmentalities, appearing to address the demands of minorities but doing so in a way that produces a form of segregated visibility; a simultaneous inclusion and distancing. Yet my stress here, as it has been throughout this book thus far, is on complexity, contestation and contradiction. So rather than a case where minorities continue to be marginalized by the dominant culture, I see the field of popular culture and news media, and cultural production itself, as a 'war of position', which has been enabled and constrained by diversity policies in particular ways in specific contexts. Yet, as I have argued, under the current neoliberal conjuncture both commercial forces and media/cultural policies have shaped the cultural industries in such a way that cultural production has become a mostly constraining process for those wanting to explore the experience of racial marginalization.

In the remainder of this book, I want to explore the dynamics of cultural production in relation to race. This involves gathering those empirical studies (including my own) that have analysed various practices of race-making in the cultural industries. Building upon Part II, I want to consider how marketization and policy developments have shaped production and race-making in different contexts. With a stress on ambivalence, the next two chapters will focus, respectively, on the enabling and the constraining dynamics of cultural production under capitalism. In chapter 6 I will examine those moments where practitioners have been enabled by, for instance, a public service remit, or an arts policy, or indeed, a particular negotiation of commercial forces in order to produce a version of race that is disruptive, transcendent, unsettling and convivial. First, in chapter 5 I want to examine more closely how cultural commodities are racialized in reductive ways. That is, I want to examine those points in production where Orientalist and neocolonial ideologies manifest. Chapters 4 and 5, with their macro focus on capitalism, nation and empire, have suggested that racial governance is inextricably intertwined with the logic of production. In what follows, I am going to demonstrate how exactly this is the case.

Part III

The Cultural Politics of Cultural Production

5

The Racialization of the Cultural Commodity

Introduction

Having fleshed out the macro factors that shape the production of discourses of race in the cultural industries, the purpose of the following two chapters is to look more closely at the production of representation at the micro level. This entails getting to grips with the particular nature of cultural production under capitalist conditions – what Bill Ryan (1992) calls the corporate form of production[1] – bearing in mind that representations of race are consumed in the form of cultural commodities. Cultural production in contemporary times is shaped by the market, but also by forms of policy that attempt to regulate the market, though under neoliberalism regulation involves facilitating the spread of market logics into previously noncommercial spheres and work cultures. Legacies of empire and colonial ideologies impact also upon the production of representations, and of course help explain – though not entirely – the resolute persistence of historical constructions of Otherness. Pulling these strands together, I argue, first, that the production of representations in contemporary times is a process of commodification, and takes on an increasingly industrial form; and, second, that commodification acts as a technology of racialized governmentalities. I have stressed throughout that this is an ambivalent process, but within the neoliberal conjuncture commodification is mostly constraining and reductive in terms of labour and ideology. The aim of this chapter is to demonstrate, through a greater focus on cultural production, how the cultural commodity is racialized. It unpacks the ways in which cultural industries continue to make race in a remarkably consistent and

---

[1] Ryan's notion of 'corporate production' is indeed referring to commodity production within media corporations. However, he also makes clear how this corporate form of production has spread into noncorporate spheres of the cultural industries. As such, like Ryan, when I talk about 'corporate production', I am essentially referring to the industrial practices that characterize the core cultural industries, employed by both corporate and independent entities.

homogenous fashion, despite the attempts of cultural producers – not least those from minority racial and ethnic backgrounds – to subvert and destabilize the reproduction of racist and Orientalist tropes. To illustrate this, I draw from empirical research into cultural production, often based on participant observation and interviews with those involved in the making of what Karim Hammou (2016: 70) calls 'Othered cultural goods'.[2] I will also include case studies from my own ethnographic research into British South Asian cultural production.

As explained in chapter 2, there is a relatively small number of studies of production in relation to race in the fields of production studies / media industry research and of critical race studies, but there is growing interest in these areas. One body of work I did not cover in that chapter were studies of cultural production in the context of race critical studies. The few examples that exist in this field mostly approach this issue in terms of authorship, shaped by cultural studies roots in literary studies, where an analysis of the author's practice is seen to deliver a deeper understanding of the aesthetics and meaning of the text (Gray and Johnson, 2013; Chow-White et al., 2015). When thought through more explicitly in terms of production, the study of authorship involves an interest in 'how meanings are produced and negotiated' (Acosta-Alzuru, 2003: 1) and how a text is encoded – or 'transcoded', as Martin (2015) puts it – with meaning. Georgina Born is one of the most important writers on authorship, describing how 'by eliciting producers' exegeses about their creative work, and by elucidating the wider critical discourses that attach to the cultural object' (through ethnographic work in particular), we get a deeper understanding of the aesthetic discourses that surround said cultural object and the practices that go into their making (2010: 191). According to contributors to a weighty volume on authorship (Gray and Johnson, 2013), contrary to Roland Barthes's famous pronouncement, 'the death of the author' has been greatly exaggerated. But the essays within this collection do stress a need to broaden the way that we understand authorship. Particularly rel-

---

[2] Hammou (2016: 70) defines the 'Othered cultural good' as a commodity whose value is determined by its conceived distance from the 'reference group' or dominant culture. This is a useful definition as it distinguishes between the practices of those minority (and nonminority) cultural producers who foreground, articulate and / or explore a particular racial or ethnic experience in their work in an assertive way, and those minorities who do not do so (of which there are many). Like Hammou, my interest is in the ways that cultural goods become 'Othered' during production. One of the key questions is whether or not this Othering is in line with the producer's intentions.

evant to this book is the idea that, as Busse (2013), for instance, shows, it is still important to recognize the role of the author – albeit in terms of the Foucauldian notion of 'authorial function' – since this helps us to understand how particular discourses work and gain power. Gray and Johnson (2013: 10) argue that authorship under capitalism is increasingly shaped by industry practices, where it exists in a 'direct relation to the commodification of culture and the reification of social identities'. In other words, industry practice takes on an authorial authority in itself, which in turn shapes dominant discourses of race. What this literature on authorship underlines is the importance of production contexts to our understanding of the text, and of particular discourses of race. But what remains under-researched is how cultural industries construct racial discourse. As I have stressed throughout, addressing this lack is critical to the development and formulation of counter strategies that can transform the standardized and reductive representation of race into something more unsettling and productive.

I use this brief discussion of authorship[3] to open up the notion that industrial production has an authorial function, within which the actual author of the text is just one component.[4] The task of this chapter is to unpack the industrial processes, including the behaviours and actions of the individuals who operate within them, that determine the production of representations. As I argued in chapter 2, the cultural industries tradition is best equipped for exploring the different dimensions of cultural production; in this chapter I take cues from this approach, paying particular attention to the dynamics between structure and agency, and macro and micro forces, while being sensitive to complexity, contestation and contradictions. As stated, the aim of this chapter is to unpack in more detail the notion of the racialization of the cultural commodity that I outlined in chapter 3, which argues for a more discursive take on the making of race in the cultural industries in contrast to the functionalist and determinist tones of a certain argument regarding the 'commodification of race'. The chapter asks: how do the cultural industries make race during the production process? How are cultural texts racialized at specific stages in the production process? To answer these questions, I will initially examine

---

[3] For a fuller discussion of authorship in relation to race and production, see Havens (2013: 11–14).

[4] Indeed, this point has been made by the 'production of culture' perspective (see Becker, 1984; Peterson and Anand, 2004), though my formulation of cultural production will stress issues of conflict and struggle to a much greater extent.

some of the general ways in which the impact of media production on representation has been understood, including the burden of representation, questions of risk and the concept of segregated visibility. I then focus on a particular cultural studies approach to race and production. This approach draws attention to the knowledge that creative managers work with – what Havens (2013) calls 'industry lore' – that goes into the production of representations. Cultural studies scholars who explore this issue stress how such 'lore' is not just economically derived, but is constituted by broader social, cultural and political values, and indeed common-sense societal-held ideas around race. This provides a very persuasive argument about the unconscious biases and behaviours that feed into cultural production that can help explain why historical constructions of Otherness persist. Yet, as I will demonstrate, there is a gap in this argument in that it neglects how racial ideologies become entrenched within industrial logics and processes themselves. The final part of the chapter will detail my notion of the 'racializing/rationalizing logic of capital' that draws attention to how the very forms of rationalization that constitute cultural production in its corporate form are, far from being race-neutral, instead deeply racial in their effects. This, I argue, offers a more satisfying and fuller explanation for the reproduction of Orientalist discourses of race, and the one-dimensional, reductive and devastating manner in which race continues to be made in the cultural industries.

Media production as racial governance

The topic of race and cultural production is relatively underresearched, but that is not to say that scholars interested in media representation have not considered these issues. As stated, authorship is the frequent starting point for scholars of race and media intrigued by the question of production. One common line of discussion is in terms of the burden of representation. As Gilroy (1993b: 98) states, 'in the ironic milieu of racial politics, where the most brutally disposed people have often also proved to be the most intensely creative, the idea that artists are representative public figures has become an extra burden for them to carry'. This 'burden of representation' once figured widely in discussions of racial cultural politics (Hall, 1996b; Mercer, 1994; Gilroy, 1993b). As an example, Rupa Huq (1996) deals with this issue in relation to British South Asian popular culture, using the case study of the post-Bhangra music scene. In this example, she interviews British Asian musicians, who demonstrate how they at times resent the burden of having to speak on behalf of – or to – what is in fact a diverse and heterogeneous community, especially when their music doesn't sound particularly 'Asian'.

As Huq states, 'the burden of representation is intrinsically bound up with media representation because of the mass media's role in legitimation of cultural production' (1996: 67). What Huq is referring to here is how the media, through the burden of representation, limit the possibilities and scope of representation for Asian cultural producers in particular. However, there is little discussion in her account of how the media actually enforces this burden. While the notion of the burden of representation is useful in helping to understand those moments when people of colour working in the media feel a tension between wanting to represent their community narratively but not wanting to be contained within their ethnic or racial identity,[5] the predominantly cultural studies accounts that explore this issue are limited in that they do not really have an explanation of how this burden manifests itself during production, and nor are they able to identify its source (that is, whether it is commercial or sociocultural). Put another way, absent in these accounts is the question of the structural determinants that constrain the creativity of minority cultural producers, where the burden of representation is just one expression of the multiple ways that their practice is impeded, as this chapter will demonstrate.

The obvious place to begin to unravel how the structure of the media constrains symbol production for minorities is by stressing how cultural production is inherently risky and creative managers in response often act conservatively. The risk-averse nature of the cultural industries invariably has a negative impact upon black and brown cultural producers in particular, who are seen as a dangerous[6] investment (Greene, 1994; Ross, 1995; Gandy, 1998; Fitts, 2008; Fuller, 2010; Molina-Guzmán, 2016). Cultural industries scholars (Garnham, 1990; Ryan, 1992; Hesmondhalgh, 2013) explain risk in terms of the intrinsically unpredictable nature of the cultural commodity form, whereas political economists, particularly in the Schiller –McChesney tradition (Hesmondhalgh, 2013), tend to focus on how the conservative nature of cultural production is an outcome of commercialization and media concentration. As outlined in chapter 3, according to this perspective media concentration has led to an oligopoly where media conglomerates, wanting to protect their market share, finance only products

---

[5] This is a common theme in journalism studies and research into the experience of journalists from minority backgrounds; see Cottle (2000) and Johnston and Flamiano (2007).

[6] In this instance, I mean 'dangerous' in commercial terms.

seen to have commercial value. This disadvantages minority cultural production, which is perceived as lacking mass appeal. As an example of this political economy approach, Blevins and Martinez (2010) analyse the fallout following the repeal of the Minority Tax Certificate Programme in the USA – a programme that, following civil rights campaigning, was a way to incentivize black media ownership. Its abolition in 1995 unsurprisingly led to a drop in the number of black-owned media. But in response, Blevins and Martinez argue that rather than campaign for the reinstatement of tax-incentive policies specifically designed to address racial inequalities in media ownership, the focus should instead be on regulation that breaks up monopolies. They argue that it is the intensification of media concentration that has had a bigger impact on the fall of minority ownership rather than the repeal of the tax incentive. This argument is typical of a particular political economy approach to media diversity that engages at the level of redistribution rather than recognition or representation.

As should be clear by now, I have serious misgivings about such an argument for underplaying the ideological nature of media production. Put another way, media concentration is not enough to fully explain why historical constructions of Otherness persist. A more productive way of understanding the particular governance of race by the cultural industries comes when we look at Stuart Hall's (1996b: 471) concept of 'segregated visibility', as discussed in chapter 4. Hall uses this concept to describe the limited nature of the gains made by black cultural production within the mass media – a form of inclusion at arm's length.[7] Hall is talking about this at the level of ideology (in terms of visibility and the politics of recognition), but we can apply it to the structural governance of race in the cultural industries.

Segregated visibility is apparent in Keith Negus's account of the way that rap music is governed within the music industry, amounting to what he describes as 'regimes of containment' (1999: 93). In his empirical study of corporate music production, based primarily upon interviews with executives and cultural intermediaries, Negus[8] describes how rap is some-

---

[7] While Hall (1996b) admits that the gains made by black cultural production amount only to a form of segregated visibility, he argues that we should understand them as gains nonetheless.

[8] Negus (1999) is interested in the nature of corporate production in the music industry rather than in race-making per se. However, his study of the production of both rap and salsa music provides rare in-depth case studies related to the topic of race and cultural production and is the reason why his research receives significant attention in this chapter.

what disparagingly regarded as a 'wild cat' operation by executives who are 'uncertain about its future aesthetic changes and nervous when trying to predict "potential market growth", and by business personnel who are uncomfortable with the politics of black representation foregrounded by the genre and anxious about confronting political pressure from the moral opponents of rap' (1999: 87). Negus refers to two logics that define the production of rap – one that is economic (rap as perceived as not having the same longevity as other genres, nor having the same catalogue value), and one that is cultural (the feeling that rap music is controversial, and too culturally specific, lacking international appeal). The play between these logics will be unpacked further in the next section. But the point here is that particular economic and cultural understandings of rap have led to its formal separation from the core music industry, through (1) the creation of rap divisions within corporate record labels and (2) independent labels, where the major label acts as a financier and distributor. In terms of the first pathway and the formation of separate rap divisions within the major labels, Negus highlights how this industry move was in part a product of the civil rights movement, where campaigners were fighting for the recognition of blacks in the cultural industries. But it additionally follows a logic of bureaucratization (Ryan, 1992) following a 1971 report by the Harvard Business School, which, since black music exists in its own separate sphere – with separate radio stations, promoters, touring circuits, record stores and so on, all relying on specialist knowledge – recommended the formation of black music divisions. The benefit of this move was the creation of a space where black personnel could be employed in an industry otherwise structured by racial hierarchies, and where black artists could be supported by staff who understand the music, its production and its audiences. Yet these divisions are vulnerable to cuts and corporate restructuring. Black divisions are historically the biggest victims of such cutbacks. Negus cites an instance where Capitol Records closed its urban division in 1996 – sacking 18 members of staff, most of whom were black. As one insider speaking to Negus (1999: 89) said, '"this happens so much whenever there is a budget cut to be made; it's always the black department that suffers"'. Having to contend with boom–bust cycles once the cultural industries were fully embedded within structures of financialization (Winseck, 2011), black divisions became the most exposed. This is further compounded by under-investment in rap, which as a genre does not receive the same resources as, for instance, rock (Negus, 1999; Fitts, 2008). In terms of the second pathway that Negus identifies, in which major labels manage rap acts via an independent label, he finds that sharp boundaries are created between the label and the act/genre/scene, amounting to another regime of containment. In these relationships, the major labels effectively only deal with those cultural entrepreneurs who bring in and manage acts. Thus the way that major labels place the responsibility of producing rap acts on independent labels, for both economic reasons (it is the indie that bears most of the financial risk) and cultural reasons (since rap acts are seen as unpredictable), is a form of spatial management that can in turn be read as a form of racial governance.

Culture makes industry and the racialization of production

In contrast to political economy accounts that simplistically place all the blame for the poor representation of minorities on an inherently conservative media, Keith Negus's notion of 'regimes of containment' opens up a more productive route towards unravelling the governance of race in the cultural industries. An important component of his argument is the attention he draws to the ethnocentric understandings of black music held by creative managers, which become another obstacle for black cultural producers to surmount in addition to the general commercial challenges intrinsic to industrial cultural production. A particularly interesting part of Negus's analysis of rap is his discussion of the discourse of 'the street' that is the language through which the production of rap is organized and made sense of. I shall unpack this specific example in more detail shortly, but first I want to highlight the connections between Negus's conceptualization of 'the street' in the context of rap music to Timothy Havens's (2013) notion of 'industry lore', originally discussed in chapter 2, as they both describe a specific dimension to how creative workers manage production. With this chapter's interest in the micro practices that shape the production of representations, 'lore', as I will show, has particular value.

Havens formulates the concept of 'industry lore' specifically in relation to the making and global circulation of African American television. But we can extend its use and define 'industry lore' more broadly as a form of power/knowledge that shapes the production and distribution of cultural commodities in general. As discussed in chapter 2, industry lore is produced through a complex web of knowledges: commercial, regulatory and technological, which coalesce to form the 'lore' that informs decisions about what type of cultural commodities get produced and how. Lore then is the executive's understanding of how an audience is going to react to a particular cultural good, gleaned from a combination of market research, experience and gut feeling. Lore is additionally shaped by trade magazines and industry reports (such as the Harvard Business School report cited above). While Havens dwells slightly less on this point, the individual actor's own cultural and social values inform industry lore, as I shall explore shortly. Consequently, when it comes to the making of Othered cultural goods, industry lore has a racialized dimension, which of course is Havens's precise point.

Havens is particularly interested in international syndication, since television shows are, increasingly, very rarely made with just domestic audiences in mind. As such, the industry lore that shapes black programming forms around the specific question of how particular shows will be received by international audiences. One dominant lore, particularly prevalent in US cultural industries, is that black actors/films/TV shows do not perform well internationally (Quinn, 2013b). Former singer turned law professor Dennis Greene (1994: 29) alludes to lore in relation to cinema when he refers to the 'self-serving and self-fulfilling myths based on the unspoken assumption that African-American films can never be vehicles of prestige, glamour, or celebrity'. He continues:

> The relationship players have convinced themselves that black films can do only a limited domestic business under any circumstance and have virtually no foreign box office potential. They assume that the only dependable African-American audience is teenagers. They also assume that films that exploit black urban violence are all the black teenage audience and the limited crossover audience want to see about black life. Any significant increases in production and marketing costs are projected as a wasted expense that cannot greatly increase the audience for African-American films. (1994: 29)

This demonstrates not just how black representations of black experience are sidelined in the name of common business sense, but how particular types of representations of black experience are privileged – in this case, a spectacularized version of black urban life that appeals to the fantasies of black youth and the 'crossover audience'. Lore is strongly evoked when Greene describes how the 'relationship players have *convinced* themselves' (my emphasis) that this is the way that black films are received. The important thing to note here, I argue, is not necessarily the question of whether this conviction is grounded in reality or not, but rather how it becomes the dominant lore that ultimately determines how much money black cultural production receives for production and marketing.

Returning to Havens (2013), his interest is in US television, exploring the industry lore that formed following the huge and unexpected success of black-cast sitcom *The Cosby Show*. Havens argues that executives downplayed the racial and class elements of the show and instead chose to explain the sitcom's success in terms of its universal family themes, which supposedly transcend race. In other words, television executives produced a lore that suggested that *The Cosby Show* was a success in spite of its blackness. Cultural industries rely on formula, but, as Havens demonstrates, rather than resulting in a proliferation of 'non-stereotypical' representations of black life, the industry lore that formed around *The Cosby Show* instead produced a spurt of more conservative (nonblack) family sitcoms. Yet, stressing the mutability of industry lore, Havens describes how the unexpected international success of other black-cast sitcoms *Fresh Prince of Bel Air* and *Moesha*, both of which contained a more unabashed representation of blackness, led to the questioning of this lore, whereby executives began to consider how the particularities of African Americanness, rather than alienating foreign audiences, can actually resonate with them in a number of ways (albeit both progressive and conservative). What I want to underline in Havens's analysis is how the concept of 'industry lore' provides an account of the way in which production determines representation, but in a way that challenges the determinist and functionalist tendencies of weaker forms of political economy analysis. Note as well that the lore can have enabling potentialities, as in the case of the success of *Fresh Prince of Bel Air* and *Moesha*, something that I shall explore in much more detail in the following chapter[9].

Industry lore is a relatively new concept, but it is evoked in other studies of race and cultural production, particularly when explaining how executives anticipate and make sense of audience reaction to Othered cultural goods.[10] For instance, Wolock and Punathambekar (2014) explore the failure of two US-based desi productions – a brand new MTV network called MTV Desi, and NBC sitcom *Outsourced*. The authors argue that both were impeded by an understanding of – or, indeed, the lore around – the US desi audience, constituted by essentialist ideas of Indian American culture: 'a pleasant, reductive image of a highly educated and pliant "Indian" demographic' (2014: 674). That is, the US desi audience is primarily constructed in terms of its Indian rather than its North American identity. Wolock and Punathambekar demonstrate 'how the American

---

[9] Both programmes were the product of the industry strategy of 'narrowcasting' that, as stated, will be covered in more detail in chapter 6.

[10] As Negus (1996) states, the production of cultural commodities is not based on what will sell well, but on what is perceived to sell well – or what is *seen to be* commercial.

television industry's imagination and cultivation of minority audiences remains mired in a nation-centric understanding of race and ethnicity' (2014: 665), where lore based around national characteristics is seen by executives as being less controversial (in contrast to its being based upon supposedly racial traits). On the contrary, Wolock and Punathambekar find that the creation of the desi promotional subject and audience in these two cases was in fact reductive, essentializing and, indeed, racist. In another example, taken from his research into the corporate production of music, Keith Negus (1999) describes how US-made salsa music suffers from a lore based on a lack of knowledge and expertise. Negus argues that creative managers struggle with the production of salsa, and one reason for this is that they are working without accurate data, since so much of the sales of salsa music comes through independent, local Latino stores not covered by Soundscan – the technology used to track sales – which is installed only in major record stores and the bigger independents.[11] The absence of data produces uncertainty in an already unpredictable market, so labels defer to the distribution divisions that are perceived to have a better understanding of the salsa audience. But these have no more market knowledge than the label managers themselves and salsa music therefore falls down their list of sales priorities in contrast to other genres like rock, which can be more confidently dealt with. The lack of specialist knowledge means that, quite often, Latin division personnel, when asking for more resources, encounter ignorant responses from the executive board – for example, that they should not expect any extra investment until their acts sing in English. The point is that the knowledge around salsa – and the lack thereof – means that it is treated as a niche market at best, and a cultural ghetto at worst. As the president of marketing at WEA Latina states, in Negus's account: "'the Anglos don't want to know that Latin music will cross over. That's the bottom line. The bottom line is that they want to keep us in the ghetto, ghettoised"' (1999: 145).

The types of lore referred to in these examples explain the ways that minority cultural producers get sidelined and silenced. In addition – and this is particularly relevant to my argument in this book – it is not hard to find case studies that draw attention to how a form of industry lore comes to shape representations of difference. For instance, Isabel Molina-Guzmán (2006) explains that the pressure to appeal to global (rather than local) Latina/o and non-Latina/o audiences led to the particular Orientalized

---

[11] Of course, the new forms of digital production and circulation would now give record companies much more data not just on sales, but also on listening habits.

aestheticization of the film *Frida* – the biopic about Frida Kahlo starring Salma Hayek. According to Molina-Guzmán (2006: 241), the 'use of accented-English, tropical colours, indigenous cultural artefacts, folkloric Mexican music, and Hayek's eroticised Latina body evoked dominant panethnic constructions of Latina/o identity'. Thus, the production of *Frida* was based on a lore that states that selling Latina/o culture to global audiences depends on delivering a strong sense of the 'authentic' – but, as Molina-Guzmán states, such an authenticity is constructed around what are in fact essentialist tropes of Latina/o identities. Returning to the case of music, Fitts (2008) discusses the formulaic nature of hip-hop videos – specifically, the production of the 'booty-video' genre – in spite of directors' attempts at innovation and originality. Fitts explains this in terms of the labels' unwillingness to take risks, but also in terms of a type of lore, where the booty-video 'fits a packaged image or a stereotypical urban sensibility that consumers unconsciously desire and that producers attempt to mimic in order to sell albums' (2008: 223). So the continuous reproduction of hypersexualized representations of black women in rap videos is formed through a lore that is fearful of rejection from what Fitts describes as the 'Top 40 demographic', who (are perceived to) have a clear expectation about what rap is and should be.

The key point I want to underline, and what is most troubling about these different takes on what Havens calls industry lore, is how the racialist logic is disguised as common business sense. To illustrate this point we can return to Negus's (1999) discussion of rap, and the unique challenges rap music faces, which, it should be stressed, remain in place despite the genre's huge commercial success. Negus finds that although record labels say that the decisions behind the underinvestment in rap, or cutbacks in personnel – or indeed the closing of divisions – are purely economic, they are in fact 'informed by a number of value judgements and cultural beliefs' (1999: 88). These judgements and beliefs can be unpacked via a deconstruction of the discourse of 'the street' through which the production of rap is made sense of. 'The street' clearly has racial undertones but, surprisingly, Negus sidesteps this issue,[12] focusing instead on how 'the street' is merely the language used to describe rap music's promotional practices – for instance, embodied in the industry lingo 'taking it to the streets' (i.e., marketing) and

---

[12] Hammou (2016), on the other hand, refers explicitly to the racial dimensions of 'the street' in the production of rap, describing how this discourse falsely equates originality and innovation with cultural singularity and supposed authenticity, which leads to 'discriminatory management based on exoticist assumptions'.

'bringing it from the streets' (i.e., market research). The point here is that what appears as common business sense belies its racialist effects in terms of the containment of rap. Negus (1999: 91) suggests that 'racial identity, racism and the history of racial antagonism inform relationships that are often blandly referred to as "business decisions" within the corporate suite'. He additionally describes how 'broader cultural political tensions *are structured into* what are often taken to be straightforward economic organizational practices' (my emphasis) (1999: 146). Thus, disguising racist logic as common business sense is not merely disingenuous or a discursive trick, but something that is structured into, or embedded within the very industry logics of cultural production. This is a crucial point, but one that Negus does not unpack further (perhaps because his interest is more on corporate music production rather than the making of race). However, it will strongly inform my main argument, which I unpack in the following section.

In a nutshell, while Negus is specifically interested in the dynamics of cultural production, what we can take from his case studies on rap and salsa is an understanding of how assumptions about race from the outside inform the production of race inside the cultural industries. In this sense, the lore or rationales that shape the production of Othered cultural goods can be interpreted as a form of unconscious bias that reproduces social values and understandings of race during the production process. 'Unconscious bias' is a term currently in vogue with industry and policy-makers, with many media workers undertaking 'unconscious bias' training as part of an organization's diversity initiatives, focusing on exposing how hidden assumptions about racial difference inform work practices and treatment of minorities in particular. In scholarship on race and cultural production, unconscious bias features less explicitly as an explanation for the marginalization of race. However, it is alluded to in many of the cases cited in this section. For instance, Molina-Guzmán (2016: 441) describes how 'mainstream media's tendency toward homogeneity, structural stability, and binary representations of Otherness is a result of implicit and explicit racial and gender biases by those in control of the production of popular images and narratives'.

Drawing on Hall's particular reading of Althusser and the mass media as ideological state apparatus, Molina-Guzmán is trying to make sense of the persistent whiteness and maleness of Hollywood. According to this argument, Hollywood acts as a cultural institution constituted by and constituting broader social inequalities in society. Consequently, the reproduction of historical constructions of Otherness are a result of colonial ideologies that are still strong in society and also the biases of those who are responsible for the production of representations. This has strong resonances with Negus's argument, although he, like other sociologists of media industries, argues strongly against the more functionalist tendencies of a Althusserian approach to the media, contending that production is a much more contested and contradictory process than a notion of media as ideological state apparatus would allow. This is articulated strongly in Negus's (1997) call for a shift in emphasis from the notion that *industry produces culture* to the idea that *culture produces industry*. In this formulation, he is challenging political economy approaches that focus solely on the production of culture in terms of ownership, concentration and commercialism, arguing that such analysis tends to be functionalist, deterministic and instrumentalist. He is dismissive of the predictable conclusions of political economy that insist that corporate control amounts to social control over the artist and the consumer, and how this has a detrimental effect on the music. Fundamentally, he criticizes political economy for ignoring human mediations, 'which come in between the corporate structures and the practices and sounds of musicians, most notably the work of intermediaries of the music and media industries' (1999: 16). Utilizing the work of Bourdieu and focusing on these 'cultural intermediaries', Negus (1999) describes how artistic work is not just contained within an organization, but is influenced by broader, social, economic and political contexts where aesthetic judgements are made and cultural hierarchies established. As such, his aim is to see how class divisions, lifestyles and habitus intersect with corporate practices; how knowledge is collected about consumers, how this influences strategies and how this knowledge becomes the 'reality' – or, as Havens would put it, the industry lore – that guides the industry personnel. In relation to this chapter, the way in which aesthetic judgements are made and cultural hierarchies established has a clear racial component and will inform how race is understood and made within the cultural industries. What, in effect, the studies cited in this section argue is that industrial cultural production is inscribed by understandings of race that circulate in wider society, which, when they encounter industrial cultural production, take the form of (unconscious) racial bias wrapped up as common business sense that shapes the production of representations of race. Since common-sense understandings of race are formed through the lingering, though no less powerful, effects of empire, this then provides a persuasive explanation for why historical constructions of Otherness persist in the media.

However, I have reservations about this argument. One concern is that if we follow the logic of this argument to its conclusion, it suggests that inserting more minorities into the cultural industries will inherently challenge, or provide an alternative to, the unconscious biases of the media's predominantly white workforce. Greene (1994) tries to explain the persistence of certain industry lore around black cinema and puts it down to two main reasons: first, industry executives grew up in a time where there was a limited range of black representation in the cinema, and, second, these executives fundamentally do not want their status challenged (which is what black cinema inherently does). Thus, one would surmise that the increased presence of people of colour in the production process should have an inherently destabilizing – and productive – effect. This returns us once more to the question of whether increasing diversity will lead to more diverse representations, something that I have questioned throughout this book. The fact remains that racial minorities can often be the very authors of representations of race that reproduce Orientalist, racist tropes. Greene (1994: 29), for instance, attacks those 'desperate and Machiavellian African-American film producers, directors, and writers who would transform *The Birth of a Nation* into a black musical if that would provide them with gainful studio employment'. This statement is typical of a particular account of racial betrayal (Kennedy, 2009) that slips into polemics. Karen Ross (1995: 82) produces a more nuanced account when she describes how 'the ambiguous relationship between black filmmakers and their sponsors raises issues about the politics of representation and the intentions of black filmmakers to either integrate themselves into the existing codes of film production or to forge a new cinematic language which embraces the diversity of the African American experience'. What Ross is alluding to here is how black filmmakers are coerced into accepting the status quo and common-sense ideas about what types of blackness sells. As I discussed in chapter 2, journalism scholars, in my view, produce a more sensitive account of how people of colour, or rather their management, come to reproduce whiteness. For instance, Peter Parisi (1998) demonstrates how black reporters internalize white mainstream understandings of race. Similarly, Drew (2011: 363) quotes a black journalist who discusses the totalizing effects of whiteness: "'If you get writing for a white newspaper for long enough, you start to write and even think in a white voice".'

I argue that there is a further point to be made. It is not just that the production of cultural commodities is inscribed with the social and cultural values and understandings of race that creative labourers bring with them to work each day. Instead, there is something about the processes and logics of industrial cultural production that steer the production of representation in reductive ways. Most troublingly, this can happen despite the cultural producer's explicit intention to challenge Orientalist or racist representations of race. This is not a slip into economic determinism, as I still insist that contradictions do occur. But in the final section of this chapter I want to argue that the very processes of standardization and rationalization that characterize cultural production in the corporate age are ingrained with racial logics, or, rather, paraphrasing Negus, have racial logics structured into them that ensure that race is made in a consistent, reductive and homogenous fashion. This argument will become evident when we directly address how cultural commodities come to be racialized in the cultural industries.

The rationalizing/racializing logic of capital

In chapter 4, I referred to an argument by Gwyneth Mellinger which suggested that more minority-owned media would provide a space that would allow those groups to mount their own counter discourses and formulate oppositional interpretations of their identities, interests and needs – an argument shared by media scholars and activists alike.[13] I challenged this assumption based on a cultural industries argument that independently owned media do not necessarily act as an alternative to corporate media, not least since they often work according to the same market logics and adopt the same processes and industrial standards (Ryan, 1992: 180; Negus, 1992: 18; 1996: 42–45; Hesmondhalgh, 2013: 235).

For instance, Chávez and Stroo, in their study of the production of the black-owned US television network ASPiRE, conclude that 'despite having greater control over the means of cultural production, African-American television owners remain beholden to industry practices that indelibly shape their social mission' (2015: 67). ASPiRE was a new television network founded by basketball superstar Earvin 'Magic' Johnson[14] that set out to provide an alternative, positive and, indeed, aspirational vision of

---

[13] Indeed, in the USA the question of media ownership was a civil rights issue in the 1960s. Campaigning led to the creation of the Minority Tax Certificate Program, a policy intended to support the sale of broadcast properties to minority owners on the basis that '[f]ull minority participation in the ownership and management of broadcast facilities results in a more diverse selection of programming' (FCC, quoted in Blevins and Martinez, 2010: 222).

[14] ASPiRE was one of several minority-owned channels that Comcast were required to carry in order to acquire a stake in NBC Universal (following pressure from pro-diversity campaigners).

African American life; as Johnson states, 'I wanted a vehicle to show positive images and to have stories written, produced and directed by African Americans for our community' (quoted in Braxton and James, 2012). However, Chávez and Stroo argue that the emphasis on this upwardly mobile black community (at the expense of the working-class black community) did not reflect a social mission, but was born out of economic necessity, as a middle-class construction of blackness was seen as holding greater appeal to advertisers. They state:

> As a commercial television network whose primary goal is to remain profitable, ASPiRE must actively find ways to solidify their subscriber base, minimise production costs while seeking greater advertising revenue. Thus, it is limited in its capacity to act as a transformative agent within the field of television production. Industry practices such as brand positioning, audience segmentation, and programming strategies are designed to enable television networks to efficiently channel resources. The employment of these practices, however, locks owners into a logic that indelibly shapes the network's mission. (2015: 78–79)

In this example, Chávez and Stroo demonstrate how industry practices shape the supposed social and cultural goals of black cultural production. Put another way, they show how commercial pressures determine the particular representation of black experience shown on ASPiRE, which they claim is not as progressive or radical as the network thinks it is, and in fact produces something rather more conservative. What I want to highlight in this quote is the reference to industry practices (brand positioning, audience segmentation, programming strategies), as it is these rationalizing techniques, which are employed in the cultural industries to bridle the unpredictability of the market, that effectively shape ASPiRE's mission (both commercial and representational). In this final section, I develop this line further and argue that technologies of rationalization become the means through which cultural commodities get racialized – commodification as a technology of racialized governmentalities. This adds a different dimension to narratives on industry lore, or culture produces industry perspectives regarding how race is governed in the cultural industries. Before making this argument, I will unpack what rationalization in the cultural industries actually entails, focusing primarily on the work of Bill Ryan (1992) and his comprehensive account of the specific nature of corporate production.

In his historical political-economic account of the development of cultural production in capitalist systems – and following Nicholas Garnham (1990) – Ryan sees rationalization as the defining logic of the corporate form of cultural production. Alongside Hesmondhalgh's (2013) notion of the 'complex professional era' (which is his own modification of Raymond Williams's (1981: 38–56) description of the 'corporate professional' age of production), cultural industries theorists are essentially describing the moment that cultural production takes on an industrial form, mostly along capitalist lines, marking a separate stage from when the making of culture took a more artisanal, craft form.[15] Ryan himself highlights a shift from an era when the relations of artistic production governed the process of creation (that is, the patronage stage – see Williams, 1981), to the corporate era, characterized by the industrialization and marketization of cultural production, where relations of capitalistic / economic production – including forms of rationalization – now govern creative practices. The employment of rationalizing techniques – encompassing bureaucratization, formatting, packaging and marketing – is the method through which creative managers deal with the inherent unpredictability of the cultural market, but also the unpredictability of cultural workers and symbol makers. Bureaucratization, for instance, entailing the management and standardization of workplace practices, was the corporate response to shop-floor conflict and growing unionization, and is a method to make worker behaviour more predictable. For Ryan, bureaucratization consequently has an ideological dimension (controlling workers through habitual day-to-day practices rather than direct hierarchical intervention) as well as a profitable one. Bureaucratization is based on both written forms of policy (rules, codes, best practices, memos, manuals, trade magazines) and discursive forms within the cultural organization that construct 'the everyday understandings and values of workers and management' (Ryan, 1992: 149). Negus (1999: 102) effectively describes a form of bureaucratization in his discussion of the role of portfolio management in rap music, 'as a way of allocating staff, artists and investment, [which] directly intersect with the deployment of a particular type of knowledge used to understand the world and to produce a "reality" that informs the perceptions and activities of staff'.

If bureaucratization represents the corporate response to the unpredictability of the worker, then formatting is a form of creative control that is the corporate response to the uncertainties of the cultural marketplace.

---

[15] Hesmondhalgh (2013) highlights how the complex professional era, which, as he states, began roughly in the 1950s, consists mostly of the corporate form of production, but also other types from earlier periods, including public service, and patronage and 'market professional' models.

Formatting – that is, creating a cultural text according to a production format or formula – is also the way in which creative managers deal with the fundamental tension within corporate cultural production between an urge to homogenize and standardize cultural production (in order to keep costs low), and the need to produce something original and different in order to keep audiences satisfied. Formatting involves market research – defining audiences, their demands, their size and propensities – and producing goods according to a format, which (1) meet these demands, and (2) can be reproduced. The most common form of formatting is through genre (e.g., romantic comedy films, or country music), but there are other forms of formatting, such as serials (e.g., James Bond or Tyler Perry films or Tom Clancy novels) or stars (Tom Hanks or Will Smith) (see Hesmondhalgh, 2013: 31–32). Formatting in essence is producing an original to type – or, as Ryan (1992: 163) puts it, 'stylistic variations on known themes' – where the creative imperative shifts from the artist to the creative manager. Ryan (1992: 168) continues: 'The right to imagine, once the preserve of the artist, is structurally relocated and authorised as the (cultural) task of the general management (including the producer), and transformed into the bureaucratic power to determine what will be produced.' But, as he stresses, even in the most commercial settings, artists can never be wholly dominated by formatting, not least since managers understand that, while their job is to encourage authors to understand how formats work, they cannot impose it wholly as this will impede their ability to come up with an original (albeit according to type). Therefore, in a nutshell: 'By transforming the production of originality into a process governed by company-advocated rules, formatting serves to rationalise the otherwise arbitrary and idiosyncratic play of imaginative creativity and routinely steers artists towards repetition of the particular cultural forms in which companies have invested' (Ryan, 1992: 178). There is an inherent flaw within formatting though, as reputation and formula can be rejected by audiences. Therefore, large sums of money need to be spent on marketing in order to differentiate products that follow the same type. Thus, formatting depends on effective marketing – another way to discipline the marketplace – in order to differentiate products that are essentially the same. Indeed, for Ryan, marketing has 'displaced prices as the primary form of competition' (1992: 187).

Marketing in the cultural industries consists of two components: research and promotion. It entails turning cultural commodities/producers into brands, constructing their identity and promoting them as such. They are brands in the sense that extra values and qualities are associated with them – a guarantee of worth, which deems a brand to be superior or at least equal to other brands (often based around fantasies of upward mobility and increased status). In this regard, packaging is a key component of marketing the cultural commodity – a way of making the product stand out from the field of indistinguishable and similar products. Ryan describes packaging as the 'textualization of identity'. He states:

> symbols are made to surround its physical form, playing upon and becoming, in effect, its external surfaces . . . designers select signs from various discourses and collect them and their conventional meanings around the object. As a text, the packaging becomes a polysemic but powerful voice apparently emanating from the commodity itself. (1992: 190–191)

For Ryan, then, marketing and packaging involve positioning the commodity in a market and segmented niche, and then branding it in a way that places upon it a higher status. Moreover, through its aestheticization the cultural commodity becomes a powerful carrier of particular discourses. This speaks to the intrinsic symbolic nature of the cultural commodity, which becomes particularly apposite to the discussion of racialization that is to follow.

The relatively detailed analysis of rationalization that I have provided underpins the next stage of my argument regarding how cultural commodities come to be racialized. I argue that the processes of bureaucratization, formatting, and marketing/packaging, as presented by Ryan, contain strong racializing tendencies or logics – such that even minority producers cannot at times escape them. This challenges theories of unconscious bias, or weaker takes of the culture produces industry perspective (i.e., where the racialized nature of cultural production is simply put down to the media as an extension of a wider, racist society), suggesting that the rationalized nature of cultural production itself steers the production of representation in very specific ways. It is through what I call the rationalizing/ racializing logic of capital that this happens.

Murali Balaji (2009) offers an excellent entry into a discussion of how cultural industrial production is racializing, at the same time demonstrating the value of a cultural industries approach to race and cultural production. The case study that I want to focus on is his account of the formatting of former child actress Keke Palmer as she moved into a pop music career. Balaji describes the tension between Keke and her label Atlantic Records, which wanted to present her as a more raunchy, urban star, despite her middle-class, non-urban African American identity (for a closer examination of how the format of rap genders and sexualizes black women, see Fitts, 2008). Keke, wanting to present or, indeed, commodify herself as a more wholesome, teen singer (in the early part of her career she worked with Disney), resisted Atlantic's attempts to format her as an urban singer. As a consequence, she fell out with Atlantic and eventually left the label. Working within Ryan's framework, Balaji initially explains the logics behind formatting: that it helps guide creative intermediaries during the production process and is a safe way for corporations to (re)produce commodities that minimize risk and increase the potential for high profit. But Balaji also argues that formatting is inextricably bound up in processes of racialization and sexualization. Indeed, his aim is identical to mine: to demonstrate how the rationalized nature of cultural production leads to the reproduction of historical constructions of the Other. As he states (2009: 229): 'Attempting to make Keke into the Other, in much the same way as other black female artists, involved little innovation and few resources, but it has the potential to reap significant rewards for the corporations.'

There are three things that I take from Balaji's argument. First, rather than being an example of the commodification of race, the production of race where minorities are involved is a process of self-commodification. Balaji stresses how Keke is not resisting commodification itself, just the particular way that Atlantic Records was attempting to commodify her; she wanted to commodify herself in an alternative way. This simple point needs to be foregrounded in any analysis of the nature of symbol production in the complex professional era. Moreover, it underlines how a notion of the racialization of cultural commodity better captures the dynamics of race and cultural production, more so than the concept of the commodification of race that, to repeat once again, too often slips into an economist and functionalist interpretation of the media. As a further point, Balaji's research, following the cultural industries tradition, highlights how this process should be understood as contested and a site of struggle, occurring through a fraught dynamic between structure and agency. Indeed, as shall be explored in much more detail in the following chapter, self-commodification is an ambivalent process and contains intrinsically enabling properties as well as reductive ones.

Second, formatting has a strong ideological dimension, and involves a complex interplay between economics and culture. As Balaji says in relation to Keke, 'representations of black women might be grounded in historical constructions of Otherness, but the way in which their identities are produced, distributed, and marketed is inherently linked with the economics of culture' (2009: 227). His account of how formats become racialized and gendered complicates weaker versions of the 'culture makes industry' perspective discussed earlier in this chapter; or rather (like Negus to be fair[16]), he stresses how cultural production has both the 'culture produces industry' and 'industry produces culture' dynamics working simultaneously. The point here though is that formatting contains an ideological function where production formats set black artists as the Other, 'restricting their ability to move too far outside of an ideologically constructed zone that caters to dominant culture's perceptions of blackness' (Balaji, 2009: 229). Formats effectively get tied to particular types of authentic experience – producing very powerful understandings of how black artists are supposed to sound and appear,[17] which is particularly constraining for women of colour.

The third factor that I take from Balaji's account of Keke is a challenge to the simplistic pariahization of white men in suits. While the media remains 'hideously white', as former BBC Director-General Greg Dyke once famously put it (Hill, 2001), blaming poor representation on white executives alone is a rather lethargic explanation for the marginalization of race in the cultural industries. Balaji, on the other hand, produces a more nuanced take in his analysis. So, for instance, he recognizes the 'Anglocentric' nature of cultural production (see also Ross, 1995) that attempts to commodify Keke in a racialized and sexualized way. But he also wants to challenge the argument that Negus slips into, and others like him (see Basu, 2006), that the struggles of black production mostly result from the cultural values of predominantly white music executives who run the cultural industries. As Balaji (2009: 228) states: 'Negus's argument overlooks the fact that the creative intermediaries tasked with producing the artists often have intimate knowledge of how to connect the artist to a market of consumption.' The point he is making here is that, whether white or black, cultural intermediaries are following the logic of the market, where formatting appears commonsensical (as Balaji argues, it

[16] My reference to weaker versions of the 'culture versus industry' perspective is in contrast to Negus's own conceptualization, which is a more nuanced take on the interplay between culture and industry. However, Negus's determination to critique crude Marxian accounts of the production of culture means that he can occasionally sway too much towards a culturalist perspective of production – overemphasizing the 'messiness' of human agency in cultural production, while downplaying the structural constraints placed on the individual actor's labour.

[17] While she does not refer explicitly to formatting, we can find an example of the ideological dimensions to formatting in Ross's (1995: 82) analysis of African American film production when she describes the challenges facing those black filmmakers who 'don't fit neatly into Hollywood's perception of what African American film should look like, that is, they should portray African American communities as a permanent underclass without a sustaining culture or heritage'.

is the way for the corporation to maintain control without appearing to do so), disguising its ideological, racializing underpinnings. So while he is claiming that pinning the blame on white men in suits is far too easy, Balaji is also challenging the idea that people of colour working in the cultural industries have no agency or should know/act better. Put another way, struggles in cultural production occur over the question of how to format, rather than should we format in the first place.

This returns us to the rationalizing/racializing logic of capital. The purpose of this concept is to understand, first, how rationalization produces racializing effects and, second, how this is the particular logic of capital in the corporate era of production. This, I argue, is more satisfying than the 'culture produces industry' perspectives, as it highlights the specificities of cultural production that steer the production of representation in a way that reproduces historical constructions of Otherness. As I am going to illustrate further, when it comes to the cultural production of people of colour, the logic of rationalization – and by extension, capital – bound up in processes of bureaucratization, formatting, marketing and packaging, racializes their cultural goods in very specific ways. There are two aspects to this that need stressing. First, drawing from Negus, rationalizing processes appear during production as bland or neutral common business sense, obscuring their ideological function such that these processes go unchallenged. Second, we can see how people of colour working in the cultural industries are also steered into producing reductive tropes of race and gender despite their best intentions. As Balaji (2009: 228) puts it, 'these intermediaries are ultimately bound to profit-making imperatives of the corporations they work for'. Crucially, this also happens in the independent sector when minorities own the means of representation. Indeed, this is what my own research into British South Asian cultural production finds, and to end this section I want to refer briefly to three of my own case studies that illustrate how the racializing/rationalizing logic of capital works on racialized minorities, providing an empirical illustration of how commodification acts as a technology of racialized governmentalities.

My first example comes from a case study on British Asian independent record labels and the experience of self-formatting (Saha, 2011). The labels I worked with were involved in the 'new Asian dance music' (Sharma et al., 1996), which was a club scene that emerged in the mid-1990s that fused South Asian musical influences (classical Indian, Bollywood soundtracks, etc.) with Western dance genres like drum and bass and breakbeat. At first, the scene was lauded by scholars and cultural critics alike for its defiantly syncretic aesthetic, in both images and sound, which challenged normative understandings of Asian youth (as uncool, conformist, passive, victims of racism), while constructing a more inclusive notion of Britishness – it was no longer the case of being Asian or British, but *British Asian* (see Sharma et al., 1996). But eventually this aesthetic became co-opted, or, indeed, made into a production format that bracketed all Asian music together, transforming the formerly disruptive potential of the hybrid musical form into exoticized, reified difference (Sharma, 1996). My study examined the challenges facing one particular independent label which was struggling to cross over into the mainstream. On the one hand, the label complained about being seen as just an 'Asian label', and articulated a desire to transcend the 'Asian dance niche'. But in trying to find a brand identity and a unique selling point (USP) (specifically in order to attract the attentions of a major label that had shown an interest in developing a distribution deal), the label formatted itself according to its most visible characteristic: its *Asianness*. As a consequence, this self-branding employed a slightly exoticized, Orientalist depiction of Asian culture that the label was, in fact, critical of in other labels. My argument is that rather than internalizing white perceptions of Asianness, the label in fact internalized corporate promotional techniques that steered it in a direction that ultimately led to self-exoticization, compounding its status as different and Other in the process.

In an example based on theatre (Saha, 2013a), I demonstrate how arts funding governmentalities steer the work of a British South Asian theatre company called Rasa Productions into reproducing racialized tropes. Rasa, founded by a Malaysian woman of South Asian descent who was the main writer and performer behind all the company's productions, was the beneficiary of ring-fenced money from Arts Council England as part of the Decibel scene, mentioned in chapter 4. This money was ring-fenced for 'culturally diverse arts' and, as the only culturally diverse theatre company in the particular region that the money was set aside for, Rasa attained highly coveted regularly funded status. The nature of the funding suited Rasa, which was unashamedly *culturally diverse*, with a strong postcolonial feminist narrative running throughout its work. Like the label discussed above, Rasa adopted the rationalizing, formatting techniques that, along with forms of bureaucratization and managerialism, had spread into arts production from the corporate sector (Fraser, 2004). These techniques worked to great effect when Rasa marketed its play *Curry Tales*, which, from the title, to the hyper-eroticized/exoticized (albeit kitsch) promotional image, to the gimmick of real curry being made live on stage, gave Rasa, to quote the producer, '"treble USPs"' (Saha, 2013a: 827) – which helped the play become a relative hit. By Rasa's own admission, it purposefully played with Orientalist images to draw in a white, mainstream audience, based on the rationale that these Orientalist assumptions would then be challenged inside the theatre by the subaltern, feminist themes of the play. But with its next production, called *Too Close To Home*, about a Muslim family and a son involved in a terrorist plot, Rasa avoided an 'ethnic' production format, and tried to do something universal in order to downplay the racial/religious element of the storyline that it feared could be sensationalized. In other words, it went in the complete opposite direction from that of *Curry Tales*. Yet *Too Close to Home* was poorly reviewed and commercially not as successful as *Curry Tales*, which led the producers to question the way that they were originally lauded for *Curry Tales*; those press reviews, while glowing, had tended to reproduce an Orientalist reading of the play (featuring lots of curry-flavoured puns), which Rasa, in hindsight, became ambivalent about. In other words, breaking from the ethnic format that had been such a success for Rasa had serious repercussions on how the company felt that its future work was received and how it was allowed to represent itself.

In my third and final case study, I draw from an example in broadcasting, and a culture of 'noise'-making that leads a British Muslim commissioner into producing what many strongly argue are sensationalist representations of Islam (Saha, 2012). This case study involves the head of religion and multicultural programming at Channel 4 – a commercial channel with a public service remit that, at the time of the research, had adopted a mainstreaming diversity policy. The commissioner in question was a British-born Pakistani with working-class roots, who, in our interview, spoke of the challenge of developing religious programming for prime time viewing. Knowing that religious programmes do not generally attract high ratings, the commissioner described to me his strategy of making 'noise' instead – that is, by generating press coverage and winning awards, and ensuring that a programme gets talked about. He explained this strategy of 'noise-making' as something he learnt on the job, a process of getting to know the culture and feel and '"flavour"' (Saha, 2012: 433) of the channel – very much echoing Ryan's description of the discursive forms of bureaucratization. But Channel 4 has received a lot of criticism for its sensationalist representation of Islam (Campion, 2005; Malik, 2008; 2014) and looking at the titles of the shows he commissioned – *Inside the Mind of a Suicide Bomber, The Cult of the Suicide Bomber, Women Only Jihad, The Fundamentalist, The Road to Guantanamo, Putting the 'Fun' in Fundamental* – one can see why. These titles appear sensationalist, though I stress that the shows themselves for the most part delivered a sensitive and nuanced take on controversial topics. Yet the way that they were presented nonetheless played on very powerful discourses. While the programmes themselves might have tried to challenge a particular take on Muslim experience, their titles and the way that they were packaged contribute to a discursive formation (including other popular cultural texts, news stories, political speeches, anti-terror measures and so on) that reinforce the idea of Islam as absolutely and irreconcilably different from Western culture.

The aim of presenting these brief case studies is to show how the rationalizing/racializing logic of capital takes hold during cultural production – through (self-)formatting, marketing and packaging. This I argue is the way that race is governed in the cultural industries. To reiterate: what the concept of the rationalizing/racializing logic of capital refers to is how the very forms of rationalization that characterize industrial cultural production in the complex professional era are the means through which historical constructions of Otherness are reproduced in an unchecked form (during production at least). The assemblage of processes, apparatus, rationales and logics that are embodied in each stage of production is what I refer to when I describe commodification as a technology of racialized governmentalities. And it is through these means that commodities come to be racialized in a reductive way that reflects the interests of the dominant culture. To answer the question that has run throughout this book about whether increasing the number of minorities working in the cultural industries will 'improve' the quality and diversity of representation, my response is they will not do so as long as minority cultural producers have to contend with the rationalizing/racializing logic of capital.

Conclusion

Although I assert that increasing the number of minorities in the cultural industries by itself will not lead to a more diverse and varied range of representations of race, let alone to the destruction of historical constructions of Otherness, to conclude this chapter I want to raise a question that is less certain: based on the case studies covered, is it ideology or economics that primarily defines the making of race in the cultural industries? Of course, the easy and no less correct answer is to say both. Yet I argue that the industry standard of making commodities according to (racial arche)type can in fact be commercially self-defeating. For instance, in Balaji's study of the commodification of musical act Keke, he questions the executives' choice to format her as a black, urban, sexualized female given that she could have sold a lot of records if they had instead targeted the much larger (and whiter) pre-teen and teen market. Balaji concludes that the label's decision to commodify Keke according to a black urban format was ideological, describing this tension between the economic and the cultural as the contradiction of cultural production. Negus similarly suggests that in the cultural production of Othered cultural goods such as rap or salsa music cultural values trump economic fact; as he states (1999: 146; my emphasis):

> Uncritically received cultural assumptions and common-sense ideas about a world of discrete markets and separate social worlds are inscribed into business practices. These are deployed systematically, ignoring all evidence of the contrary (*which would, I suspect, produce a type of cognitive dissonance that would undermine the logic of the system*), and this contributes to the separation of knowledge and experience.

Negus's comment – that challenging common-sense ideas about the 'world of discrete markets', or, put another way, whole groups of people, would lead to 'cognitive dissonance that would undermine the logic of the system' – is said off the cuff in parenthesis, and, frustratingly, he does not unpack this point any further. But what I take from the quote is how it highlights the very entrenched nature of cultural – or indeed racist – values in production that, if exposed and called out, would in effect undermine the entire logic of the system. The idea that cultural production is characterized by a 'separation of knowledge and experience' where all 'evidence of the contrary' is ignored again highlights the ideological dimension to cultural production in relation to race and ethnicity.

It is in this way that I argue that commodification is a technology of racialized governmentalities. The process of commodification in the context of the cultural industries is precisely the way that race is governed. As Balaji (2009: 235) put it, 'the production of culture is not purely an economic process, but one driven by ideological considerations as well'. The rationalized processes that constitute cultural commodification – bureaucratization of the workplace, formatting strategies, packaging and marketing – are the means through which commodities are racialized. In the production of Othered cultural goods, each of these processes is shaped by common-sense understandings of race, but conducted in the name of following standard business practice. There are three points that I have discussed that I want to reiterate. First, while rationalizing processes are not inherently racist, due to the institutional whiteness of the cultural industries, Eurocentric, ethnocentric understandings of race are structured into them (for instance, in the way Balaji argues that formats are racialized and gendered). Second, the logic of rationalization (embedded within these racializing logics) is so strong that it is internalized and adopted by workers throughout the cultural industries, which helps explains why minorities themselves are steered into reproducing historical constructions of Otherness. Sometimes this process occurs following the direct interventions of white gatekeepers, but this can also happen when there are no white gatekeepers in sight – which is why the concept of governmentality has value. Third, the ideological dimensions to the representation of race in the cultural industries are hidden within supposedly neutral commercial reasoning. What appear as purely commercially rationalized and race-neutral processes are in fact deeply racial in their effects. To reiterate, I am not arguing that rationalization is inherently racializing, rather that it is the vehicle through which racialization occurs undetected. Thus, once again, commodification in the context of the cultural industries acts as a form of governance that reproduces racist discourses. The fact that it is hidden by common-sense business speak is how this reductive process persists.

Yet, as I have stressed throughout, commodification nonetheless has intrinsically enabling capacities (as well as a constraining one), and the cultural worker does have agency in the face of the rationalizing/racializing logic of capital. As such, there are still spaces within the cultural industries for resistance and contestation and the enactment of a politics of production that can open up representational practices. This is the topic of the final chapter.

6

Enabling Race-Making in the Cultural Industries

Introduction

In this book I have argued that commodification acts as a technology of racialized governmentalities. It is the vehicle through which racialization of the cultural commodity occurs, where race-thinking is structured into the production process – most evident in how certain standard formats are racialized and gendered. Moreover, the logic of rationalization under the corporate age of production is powerful enough to be adopted and internalized by workers, white and nonwhite, explaining the constant churn of historical constructions of Otherness in terms of race, gender, class, sexuality and so on. Yet I have also stressed throughout that commodification is an inherently ambivalent process, that is, it contains both enabling and constraining tendencies. This being the case, what are the enabling features of commodification for racial and ethnic minorities working in the cultural industries?

In this chapter, I shed light on and unpack those spaces and moments where cultural practitioners invested in the production of cultural goods that deal with 'political, thematic, or cultural concerns' (Havens, 2013: 7) relating to race have been facilitated, whether purposely or unwittingly, by the cultural industries. The chapter rests on two foundational ideas. The first is to do with a characteristic of the cultural industries that I have covered already: while cultural industries, for the sake of cost, gravitate towards formula and standardization, audiences crave originality and difference as much as familiarity, and, as a result, cultural industries are almost obliged to invest in new and innovative products even though it is inherently risky and at times counterintuitive. Thus, in the production of cultural commodities, even in the most commercialized, marketized settings, there is always an opportunity for different, alternative, experimental, thought-provoking, counter-discursive narratives to emerge (though in the neoliberal conjuncture such opportunities are shrinking). The second underlying principle of this chapter, which I introduce now but which will be unpacked further shortly, is that, while I have referred to racialization in negative terms, in terms of how, as a process, it inscribes people, cultures and objects with meaning derived from historical modes of racial thinking – 'race-making', as Gray puts it (2016: 248) – it can at times be productive, subversive and radical. It is for this reason that I have avoided the normative ways that representations of race are usually evaluated in research into race and media – in terms of authentic/stereotypical, positive/negative, truthful/biased – not least because, at times, what appear as inauthentic, stereotypical, spectacularized depictions of race can in fact be radical and unsettling. The implications of a more discursive take on racial representation, in terms of race-making, is that it prevents a slip into an assumption that the best way of countering racialization is to remove race entirely from the picture (which can end up reinforcing a post-race discourse in the process – namely, that we have somehow left race and racism behind), or that any articulation of race is immediately reifying. Instead I am thinking of ways to articulate race that contribute to its undoing – a form of race-making that exposes the spuriousness of biological notions of race, that deconstructs the ethnic absolutism that underpins cultural racism, while creating solidarity among racial communities in the struggle against inequality. This is something that I shall develop further in the next section of the chapter.

This chapter's main purpose is to explore those moments when minority cultural producers have encountered or prised open spaces within the cultural industries to represent race in ways that unsettle and disrupt hegemonic ideas around racism. As in the previous chapter, my arguments are based on case studies from scholars who explore what I label the politics of production either directly or indirectly, to shed light on the ways that cultural commodification can have enabling effects. After unpacking the politics of race-making, the remainder of the chapter will consider the different modes of production within the cultural industries where the representational practices of minority cultural producers have been opened (albeit, always constrained). First, I will consider forms of ethnic/community media and independent/DIY modes of production, which, whether they are not-for-profit or commercial enterprises, to various degrees reject or work outside the standards and logics imposed and practised by media corporations. I then examine those spaces within the core cultural industries that have provided a fertile environment for cultural producers wanting to explore and articulate the politics of race. This necessitates a discussion of public service media; despite my critiques in chapter 4, PSM is still one of the most important spaces for minority practitioners in terms of access and the potential for broadcasting stories from the margins to the mainstream. But I end this chapter with a discussion of moments within highly corporate and commercialized spaces where people of colour have managed to produce something disruptive and unsettling. Indeed, one of the key arguments in this chapter is that even as cultural industries shift evermore towards marketization and corporate forms of production, this inevitably leaves cracks, tears and contradictions where cultural political interventions, in the form of Othered symbolic goods, amount to, in Hesse's (2000) terms, multicultural transruptions. This becomes particularly evident in the final section of the chapter when we consider that representations of race as embodied in cultural commodities are no longer confined to the nation-state, and instead are absorbed into global flows, landing in new locales, where they are taken up, rearticulated and redeployed in ways that produce new types of industry lore, understanding or awareness that, in turn, shape the production of representations in domestic cultural industries. It is following a discussion of these different case studies that explore the dynamics of the multiple modes of production within the cultural industries that we can then begin to formulate a politics of production designed to harness the enabling properties of commodification for the benefit of the cultural politics of difference.

Making race productive

Gray (2016: 249) refers to 'race-making' in terms of a form of 'power/knowledge that operates as a logic of production'. While I demonstrated in the previous chapter that race-making under the corporate form of production has overwhelmingly reductive tendencies, I argue that it can nonetheless be productive. If such a statement is difficult to swallow, I would contend that it is the exact reason why Stuart Hall says that popular culture matters. Before I return to the question of cultural commodification and its generative potentialities, the first point I want to make about the value of race-making is that it does not have to be essentializing or reifying. Inversely, a purely pluralist position on race and culture has little political merit; as Gilroy (1993a: 32) states, pluralists, who see 'black' as an open signifier and celebrate the polyphony of black culture, are 'insufficiently alive to the lingering power of specifically racialized forms of power and subordination'. Thus, following Gilroy, I am thinking of race-making within an anti-anti-essentialist frame, which can produce commonality, community, solidarity, self-affirmation and self-love; a way of highlighting the diversity and the ongoing, unfolding of cultural identity, in the process undermining the spuriousness of exceptionalist logics of race, while underlining how all identities are embedded in structures of dominance (Hall, 2000). Productive race-making involves uncovering a location from which minorities can speak, against modernity's hidden racialized epistemologies. It is in these terms that Gilroy (1993a) conceptualizes the expressive cultures of the Black Atlantic as a counterculture to modernity.

One common way that the value of race-making has been articulated is in terms of strategic essentialism, widely accredited to Gayatri Spivak (despite her own ambivalence around the term). Strategic essentialism refers to the adoption of temporary positions in order to resist and challenge dominant ideologies. It explores how the mobilization of particular racial or ethnic identities can have value in specific circumstances. Spivak herself refers to the 'strategic use of essentialism' (Spivak and Harasym, 1990: 109; she notes that it is impossible to be non-essentialist, as the subject is always centred; instead there are 'good' or 'bad' strategies of essentialism) as the articulation of an irreducible otherness – when groups of people who are internally differentiated present themselves publicly, advancing their group identity in a simplified, collectivized way to achieve certain objectives (see also Eide, 2010). A well-known example comes from Britain, where antiracist activists reclaimed and politicized the term 'Black' as a way of uniting and mobilizing the Afro-Caribbean and Asian communities against the severe racial provocation faced in 1960s and 1970s Britain (Gilroy, 1987; Hall, 1996a; Brah, 1996). In a discussion of British South Asian popular culture, Sanjay Sharma, while deconstructing normative understandings of the term (South) 'Asian', simultaneously seeks to 'reclaim it against prevailing culturalist notions and regressive shifts towards ethnic particularisms that close down political opportunities over the contestation of this signifier' (1996: 33). For Sharma, the signifier 'Asian' can be one of 'many temporary positionalities that offer us strategic places from which to speak in this racist Britain' (1996: 33).

There is not the space to enter a discussion of identity politics in full, but in the context of this book I argue that a more productive route towards understanding the value of race-making comes from the recognition that commodification, as it occurs in the cultural industries, is not always reductive. In chapter 2, I stated that while we should avoid celebrating all minority cultural productions as evidence of their resilience, we shouldn't dismiss interactions with commerce as immediately undermining the political or aesthetic value of cultural production. Indeed, I critiqued weaker accounts of the 'commodification of race' that foreclose the political potential of cultural expression once it has apparently been commodified. One interesting alternative to the commodification of race narrative which I did not cover comes from social geographers Dwyer and Crang (2002), who argue that ethnic identities do not exist in a pure state prior to commodification, but are rather reproduced through the social and material processes of cultural production itself. While I believe the authors dangerously underplay the fundamentally reductive and exploitative character of commodification in terms of ideology and labour respectively (see Saha, 2013a: 820–821), the argument that racial and ethnic identities are made during commodification deserves recognition. It echoes Balaji's case study on the musical artist Keke Palmer, which he understands as a process of self-commodification. Rather than resisting commodification, Keke's struggle in the music industry was centred on how she was to be commodified. In her account of the commodification of black/Latinadad, Molina-Guzmán (2013) describes how slow transformations in the media industry have allowed some Black Latina/o actors to accrue 'racial capital' (in the Bourdieusian sense rather than in Nancy Leong's (2012) Marxist conception) in their commodification. On the one hand, the racial capital of the black Latina/o actor is constrained by hierarchies of race, sex and gender and the multiple forms of oppression that emerge through production, casting and narrative practices, as well as by audience demand and expectations. But on the other hand, racial capital can be harnessed by the individual in productive ways during the process of commodification and, in doing so, offers black Latina/o actors in particular the scope to 'negotiate their symbolic status, and participate in the transformation of the institutional status quo' (Molina-Guzmán, 2013: 216), including the decentring of whiteness.

In his fascinating analysis of the struggles of French rap music, Karim Hammou (2016) describes how the producers of rap (labels, promoters, entrepreneurs, the acts themselves) attempted several disconnected 'paths' of commodification – through adopting particular aesthetic and promotional strategies – as a way to gain artistic/cultural legitimation. One path of commodification sought to construct rap as a serious aesthetic form based on its innovations in 'composition, poetry and delivery' (Hammou, 2016: 72). This was refused by the gatekeepers of music and media industries and subsequently rap commodified in this way remained underground. Another path saw rap commodified as an oppositional voice, less about the music and more about articulating the experiences of racial and class exclusion. But this form of commodification relegated French rappers to the status of spokespersons for their deprived communities, rather than credible artists. A third path of commodification attempted to present rap as a mainstream music – which followed the regulation stating that 40 per cent of broadcasting has to come from French-language music – but in doing so rap music had to shed its reputation for being the voice for deprived suburban youth, with labels forcing acts to sanitize their lyrics and sound. The problem with this path was that rap was seen as a fad and not supported for the long term. Eventually, rap music in France gained legitimation when it commodified itself in terms of the 'oppositional avant-garde' – a fusion of the aesthetic path and oppositional path that stressed how French rap was being produced by disenfranchized suburban (racialized) youth, and how it was explosive and credible 'rather than promoting consensual thematic and non-threatening public images like its predecessors' (Hammou, 2016: 74).

Detailed and nuanced production studies like Hammou's contradict reductive deterministic takes on cultural commodification, providing empirical evidence of its inherent constraining/enabling properties particularly in relation to race-making. Thus, rather than seeing commodification as something negative that happens to the authentic expressive culture of racial and ethnic minorities, it is just one of multiple social forces or processes that, to quote Gray (2005: 3–4) again, structures 'the conditions of possibility within which black cultural politics are enacted, constrained and mediated'. Gray alludes to a conjunctural approach to understanding black cultural politics, based on unpacking the spatial and temporal contexts of black cultural production, and the struggles over meanings of blackness that unfold. For the purposes of this chapter, I want to underline how race-making can be destabilizing as well as conforming. While Gilroy (2000) is correct in saying that the logical solution to the 'crisis of raciology' is to denounce and end all types of race-thinking and race-doing, that does not mean we can afford to ignore or disavow race and racism in the immediate present, as post-race discourse implores that we do. Rather, productive race-making entails crafting narratives that destabilize the very ontology of race. For instance, Gray (2005: 16) refers to black musicians who produce 'musical styles which unsettle and destabilise, if only momentarily, the music industry's racialized approach to musical production, marketing and classification'; in other words, cultural productions that attempt to defy the rationalizing/racializing logic of capital. As such, commodification needs to be understood as a process of articulating 'competing claims on blackness' (2005: 20). Gray (2005: 21) continues: 'specifying blackness as the subject of different social positions, competing cultural claims, conflicting political interests, and shifting market imperatives highlights the strategic necessity (in matters of cultural politics anyway) of thinking about the processes and relations of black cultural production in institutional, structural and cultural terms.' To reiterate, race-making is generative when it produces destabilizations around the categories of race. This can include messy, hybrid cultural productions (Moss, 2005; Gilroy, 2004) or overtly essentialist forms (Zook, 1999; Saha, 2013b). We must be careful not to burden a song, film, TV documentary, book or, even, a collection of these things with the task of liberating humankind from raciology. But we can judge them on the extent to which they contribute to hegemonic struggle. That being the case, what production contexts lead to enabling forms of race-making?

Minority ethnic media and independent cultural production

Many scholars of race and media, whether they are interested in production or not, believe that one way of addressing the misrepresentation of minorities entails more minority-owned media. Often this is based on an assumption that such media will have a strong social mission element, or at least will be more sensitive to minority concerns, whether these are not-for-profit or commercial. I challenged this assumption in the previous chapter, arguing that minority-owned media – including independent, or community / ethnic media – can in fact emulate core cultural industries in terms of adopting corporate forms of bureaucracy and rationalization that have modes of race-thinking structured into them, which steer cultural producers into, often unwittingly, reproducing historical constructions of Otherness through the rationalizing/racializing logic of capital. But that is not to downplay the role of alternative forms of media in enabling representational practices, particularly when they reject and resist corporate modes of production. The fact remains that independent production – whether commercial or noncommercial – intervenes in hegemonic commercial media representations of blackness, not least since it allows for greater self-representation and self-definition (Florini, 2015b). In what follows, I explore this cultural political potential, beginning with a discussion of minority/community media, followed by an analysis of independent production, including the new forms of digital cultural production.

Minority ethnic media

Minority-owned media that is specifically made by and for particular communities goes by lots of different labels: diasporic media (Georgiou, 2005), community media (Lewis, 2008), ethnic media (Cottle, 2000), and minority ethnic media (Husband, 2005). Charles Husband is one of the key research-ers of such media, so I work with his notion of minority ethnic media, which includes newspapers and broadcasting (particularly radio). Analysis of minority ethnic media organizations and their minority ethnic person-nel is a neglected area as far as Husband is concerned, which is especially confounding since minority ethnic media is often the dominant media for minority communities. It is also surprising that there is a relative lack of attention paid to production within this small body of literature, as the structural challenges facing minority ethnic media strongly define their impact. This issue is missing in many accounts.

Minority ethnic media can be described in terms of grassroots, bottom-up initiatives that seek to empower marginalized communities – whether migrants or indigenous groups – allowing them to self-represent (Lewis and Booth, 1989; Riggins, 1992). They are often not-for-profit organiza-tions and sometimes receive grants from local, national or European funds (Lewis, 2008). Another common trait is the use of minority languages (Georgiou, 2005). Minority ethnic media is seen to have multiple values, based on its commitment to supporting specific migrant communities. It provides an important resource for newly arrived migrants in terms of producing information about services and benefits (Hartley, 2000), mediating mainstream news (Georgiou, 2005), providing training and education (Lewis, 2008), and facilitating dialogue amongst listeners, that is, members of the community (Georgiou, 2005). Furthermore, as Lewis (2008) points out, in the radio context the broadcasting of 'local' music is an underestimated aspect of minority media radio, acting as an impor-tant cultural resource that enables forms of community. Minority ethnic media is criticized in some quarters for encouraging self-segregation and ghettoization, but evidence suggests that it has a strong social inclusion element. According to the UK's 2004 Community Radio Order, minor-ity ethnic media produces 'social gain' for its listeners (Lewis, 2008). For Deuze (2006), minority ethnic media is inherently participatory. Using the example of London Greek Radio and its impact upon the Greek com-munity, Georgiou (2005: 493) states that the station provides 'a source of information they trust and which speaks their own language'.

Community radio then is generally seen as offering alternative spaces for the articulation of minority experience which run counter to the domi-nant framings of race found in mainstream media. In this regard, with its stress on collaboration that privileges community need over profit, it is easy to read minority ethnic media as oppositional, or at least as contrary to corporate media (Deuze, 2006), where a community rejects mainstream media and forms its own media. As Ross (1995: 175) states (albeit, rather dramatically), minority ethnic media represents 'a bottom-up project of recuperation rather than a top-down doctrine of subordination'.

However, while it is easy to valorize minority ethnic media in terms of providing an oppositional new source and resource, scholars researching this field are more focused on countering the fears that such media leads to the fragmentation of the public sphere. For instance, Deuze (2006) argues that community media does not oppose, but contributes to the media sphere as a whole. Community radio as an alternative media sphere that supplements the core public sphere is evoked when Hartley (2000: 158) describes the National Indigenous Radio Service in Australia, which acts as a network of dozens of local stations 'necklaced together into an alternative "national broadcaster" for the Indigenous "nation"'. Lewis describes community media as a Third Sector sphere – that is, not public or commercial – acting as a 'local form of public service' (2008: 12), based on its core characteristics, which set it apart from other local (and commercial) forms of media: not-for-profit and accountable to the community it serves, which involves participation from the community in its production. One of the most nuanced writers on the subject, Myria Georgiou (2005), in her discussion of diasporic media, reiterates that even though it is tempting to think of these media as excessively particularistic, or as symbolizing a rejection of the universal European values that the mainstream media seemingly embody, diaspora media in fact exist along what she calls 'the universalism particularism continuum'. She states (2005: 483): 'Even when their content promotes insularity and closure, diasporic media depends on universalistic values ingrained in the modern nation-state (that supports them with money and infrastructure), on universal human rights and the freedom of communication (that protects their rights to exist).' What I take from Georgiou's argument is that diasporic media, rather than being in opposition to mainstream media, in fact relies on it (as much as the latter relies on the former), and embodies – as well as depends upon – many of the same universal values that underpin and sustain the media sphere in modern Western nation-states.

These arguments on the social significance of minority ethnic media are very persuasive but, as stated, there is a surprising lack of attention paid to the political economic challenges facing community media. If minority ethnic media holds such important value in Western societies then the question of their preservation and sustenance must be an urgent one. But, as stated, there is much less written on this topic. An exception comes from Husband (2005) who provides an overview of the structural challenges facing minority ethnic media, highlighting three issues in particular. First is the lack of finance; advertising is harder to attract 'because of the perceived limited disposable income of the target audiences' (2005: 467). Second are demographic challenges. In the USA, the size of African American and Hispanic audiences is large enough to sustain minority ethnic media, but this is not the case in Europe where minority communities are smaller in scale, much more internally heterogeneous and more dispersed. Third are staffing resource issues. According to Husband, members of particular minority communities who aspire to work in the media can often be discouraged. Moreover, individuals' class and educational background may hinder their entry into media professions, and they may also be put off by the poor – or indeed, in many cases, complete lack of – pay. And the fact remains that the best minority media professionals have ambitions to enter more commercial, mainstream organizations, which pay better, provide more resources, and are more professional operations.

Important in Husband's analysis is the attention he draws to commerce–creativity tensions, or rather commerce–ethical tensions in the production of minority ethnic media. Husband identifies how there can be a conflict between a minority ethnic media outlet's social mission and commercial imperatives/pressures. As he states: 'The moral concerns of identity politics with cultural viability and survival do not sit comfortably with the economic logic of media production and distribution' (2005: 468). What he is referring to here is the tension between journalistic codes and the organization's social mission, where, potentially, 'resources are likely to be squeezed in order to maximise the socio-political impact of the enterprise' (2005: 470). How this works will depend on a worker's self-definition, and whether workers see themselves more as, say, community activists or as media professionals. What Husband is referring to is the particular challenges of working in minority ethnic media that are more likely to define its output in terms of identity politics – which can in fact throw up different challenges for minority professionals.

One of the critical issues for Husband is how a combination of structural and professional challenges steers minority ethnic media into self-essentialist forms of representation. Facing the challenge of having to deal with a diverse and heterogeneous community that is spread beyond specific locales and is not very well off, minority ethnic media find themselves forced to define their audience in the widest sense. As Husband (2005: 463) states, 'where topography, audience demography and relative economic privation intervene, minority ethnic media may de facto find themselves required to service generic audiences defined in broad ethnic terms'. A similar argument about the self-essentializing nature of minority ethnic media is made by Florini (2015b) in her account of the popular US podcast *This Week in Blackness* (*TWiB*), which is caught between wanting to assert a common blackness but which also recognizes and caters to the diversity of black experience. For Florini, *TWiB* does not always pull this off – slipping into an essentialist form of blackness that can justify 'the racism colour-blindness seeks to obscure' (2016: 342).

While this paints a rather negative picture of the supposedly enabling properties of minority ethnic media, I want to reiterate the clear benefits for minorities that such media provides in the way that Georgiou (2005) and Deuze (2006) argue, in promoting an active glocalization and contributing productively to the mediascape of the city and its migrant populations. This remains the case despite the challenges posed by a marketized media, where minority ethnic medias find their operations increasingly constrained, whether by financial, cultural or technological factors. Nonetheless, independent media entities and community media have much more autonomy to self-define and self-represent. In the following section I examine how independence in relation to the cultural politics of race has been explored more generally.

Independent production

Seen as commercially unfeasible by major media corporations, cultural producers from racialized backgrounds have historically relied upon independent media companies for (limited) financial and creative support. The main difference between independent and community/ethnic media is that the former is often commercial (Lewis, 2008). But independent media companies similarly define themselves according to broader social, artistic or political goals. In light of the longstanding concern with the severe concentration of the mass media, many theorists have seen independent organizations as a way of challenging the major corporations' dominant economic and aesthetic order. Independent record labels in particular have been seen as 'innovative and creative oases for new or unconventional musicians in the midst of a capital-driven and profit-orientated record business' (Lee, 1995: 13). In theory, independents do not have the same commercial agenda as the majors, are not under pressure from shareholders to make a profit and therefore have more space to produce aesthetically innovative music that challenges the mainstream (Lee, 1995). They are able to react faster to changing cultural tastes and can pick up on new trends and bring them into the market, as Marcus (1991) and Gillett (1996) demonstrate in their accounts of the emergence of rock 'n' roll. Additionally, through affiliation with nonmajor manufacturers and distributors, they can create alternative industrial channels and can subsequently contest the control of large corporations (Lee, 1995).

Returning to the subject of race, one of the key enabling elements offered by independent media organizations is how they, in theory at least, provide minority cultural producers with the autonomy and freedom to tell the stories they want to tell. Quite simply, more autonomy and creative freedom allows for more authentic self-representation. Two case studies that provide an account of independent black production in a relatively pure sense are found in cinema: the Black Film Workshop (see Ross, 1995) that ran in the UK in the 1980s and the 'LA Rebellion' film scene (see Field et al., 2015) based around the Media Crisis Unit programme at UCLA during the 1960s, 1970s and 1980s. Both scenes were based on collectives of predominantly black filmmakers (though involved members of other racial and ethnic groups). While each scene included a diverse range of filmmaking styles on a diverse range of topics, they all in some way explored past and present black lives in the USA and UK and across the African diaspora. The autonomy of the scenes was established in different ways. While the Black Film Workshop was publicly funded – a result of the 1981 Workshop Declaration that was an attempt to create a separate, autonomous grant-assisted financial structure for independent filmmaking practices (which included funding from the recently established Channel 4 Television and the Greater London Council) (Ross, 1995) – the LA Rebellion was enabled by higher education and the civil rights gains that provided entry for racial and ethnic minorities to UCLA's film school (Field et al., 2015).[1] The scenes were radical in three ways: (1) in their depiction of black experience that challenged the mainstream cinema's denigration and dehumanization of black folk; (2) in their commitment to developing new aesthetic forms that again challenged Hollywood/mainstream norms and conventions; (3) in their defiant independence, rejecting any relationship with mainstream cinema in order to build a more community-oriented film scene (particularly pronounced in the case of the LA Rebellion). Both the Black Film Workshop and LA Rebellion were committed to the project of producing

[1] Led by activists/educators such as Elyseo Taylor, who obtained funds from the Ford Foundation, the nonwhite film students had their own programme called Media Urban Crisis, which provided both practical training (and equipment) as well as formal film studies education, particularly in the new film movements – French New Wave, the New German Cinema and New American Cinema – that were helping to decentre Hollywood's dominance (Field et al., 2015).

an alternative cinema – in narrative, style and practice. While the films produced by these scenes struggled to reach a wider audience, they still left behind a significant archive of material that has influenced future filmmakers in terms of their aesthetics, their narrative-scope and their exploration of the cultural politics of race.

These cases represent independent production in its most autonomous form. But there is a danger in assuming that independent media companies represent an alternative to mainstream media. For instance, independent media companies can be just as commercially oriented and profit-driven as major media companies, and can be just as exploitative of their acts (Negus, 1996). Under immense financial pressure, independents are more likely to work with media corporations rather than against them, through a variety of different types of deals including stakeholder, international licensing or distribution deals (Negus, 1996; Hesmondhalgh, 1996). It is for this reason that Hesmondhalgh (2013) works with the term 'smaller companies' rather than 'independents'. But while I broadly agree with these arguments, the significance of independent media companies has to be a key part of a discussion on the enabling properties of commodification, for, as is the case with the Black Film Workshop and LA Rebellion, independent modes of production have at the very least allowed minority cultural producers to enter the cultural industries on their own terms without having to go through the channels of the mainstream media that have traditionally blocked their entry or demanded conformity.

Appreciating that the relationships between independent media companies and corporations is increasingly symbiotic, I argue that Hammou's (2016) study of French rap referred to earlier offers a more nuanced approach to independent production, which both recognizes the significance of independent cultural production for minorities in particular, and also does not overvalorize independent companies as an alternative to, or as somehow existing outside, capitalism. Hammou focuses upon the success of an influential compilation record called *Hostile Hip Hop* as illustrative of the 'oppositional avant-garde' path of commodification featuring the scene's most credible rappers, endorsed by the indie label scene, hip-hop entrepreneurs and parts of the mainstream. In his analysis of how this compilation helped to legitimate rap music, Hammou stresses the promotional (and highly commercial) strategies employed in the making of this particular cultural commodity, including 'a marketing strategy that showcases marginality and a high regard for aesthetic innovations' (2016: 74). The success of the *Hostile Hip Hop* compilation spawned an alternative cultural industry that centred around the oppositional avant-garde path

154 The Cultural Politics of Cultural Production

of commodification, adopting its aesthetic, including the establishment of a national radio station, new record labels and rap-specific magazines. As stated, Hammou's interest is in how French rap gained artistic and cultural legitimation. But what I take from this argument is how it draws attention to the way that indies, like majors, are still involved in a process of commodification, and how commodification can in fact facilitate the cultural politics of difference. According to Hammou's narrative, the producers behind the *Hostile Hip Hop* compilation, through an effective politics of production, created a new path of commodification that foregrounded multiracial, working-class (sub)urban experience, while ensuring that the artistic innovation of the rappers involved was recognized and taken seriously.

My argument is that effective independent cultural production, in terms of its propensity for the opening up of representational practices, is not a case of resisting commodification, but rather of harnessing its enabling properties, for the sake of creative innovation and social impact. To reiterate, independent production does not mean that it is not also commodified. As an extreme version of this, we can turn to Eithne Quinn's (2013a) critical defence of African American entertainer, writer and producer Tyler Perry, one of the wealthiest men in entertainment, who has forged a successful career by working completely independently of the major Hollywood studios. Although working autonomously, Perry applies the same rationalizing techniques of corporations (such as formatting techniques – much of his output is prefixed with 'Tyler Perry's . . .') that targets a very specific black audience, literally churning out films that give them what they want. Perry's unprecedented success can be put down to two factors. First, he has stayed independent. Working with independent distributor Lionsgate has allowed him to retain a majority of the profits as well as keep full creative control. Second, audience engagement work is at the core of his promotional strategy, employing community outreach marketing strategies including garnering audience feedback after every performance, and the collation of a massive mailing list that allows him to engage his audiences directly. In essence, Perry has kept publicity targeted and cheap, which, with film production costs kept low, has allowed him to make huge profits. Perry has effectively taken advantage of a high production costs/low reproduction costs dynamic of the cultural industries; by keeping production costs lower, the scale of profits rise.

Quinn does not discuss the politics of representation in Perry's films in too much detail, but nonetheless argues that, while Perry has been criticized for his stereotypical, heteronormative and conservative depiction of black life, a common narrative in all his films and television shows involves working-class victories over rich powerful elites, which advocates a politics of redistribution. Anticipating a critique from the likes of Gilroy regarding the commodification of blackness and the rise of a hyperconservative/consumerist version of the black subject, Quinn defends Tyler by placing him within the pragmatist tradition of African American cultural politics, which has transformed play into labour, and sees entertainment as a path to social mobility. According to Quinn, Tyler Perry has effectively created his own cultural industry with its own infrastructure and studio, all owned by himself. What I take from Quinn's and Hammou's case studies in terms of the value of independence for race and cultural production is that it is not about how independent production resists capitalism, but how effective independent practices harness commodification for the sake of aesthetic, sociocultural, or political-economic goals.

Digital media

While independent production has provided an enabling space for producers, it can be severely impeded by commercial pressures. Ross (1995) argues that a deregulated market can provide more opportunities for smaller, independent media (with lower barriers to entry), but she is less optimistic about its chances in the face of competition from powerful media corporations. But Ross is writing at a time before new digital technologies have impacted upon the cultural industries, particularly in terms of delivery and distribution. While we should remain guarded about the true democratizing and decentralizing capacities of new media, digital technologies have undoubtedly provided new opportunities for minority cultural producers.

There has been much written about the Internet and the emergence of new online racial identities (Murthy, 2010; Nakamura and Chow-White, 2012; Daniels, 2013; Nakamura, 2013; Sharma, 2013), but less about the experience of digital production in relation to the new online audio video content. I am referring here to the online platforms (both corporate and independent) that allow minorities to self-publish and distribute their films, web series, books or music. An immediate consideration is that the Internet and new media technologies have lowered barriers to entry for minority producers, who can theoretically make and distribute their own independent productions, again with benefits for the scope of self-definition and self-representation. One exploration of the opportunities afforded by online streaming services comes from Molina-Guzmán (2016), who presents a case study on Hulu show *East Los High*, a young adult drama based around the trials and tribulations of a group of final year high school students, featuring a predominantly Latina/o cast and crew. For Molina-Guzmán, *East Los High* offers a counter-hegemonic take on Latina/o experience, while remaining relevant to urban Latina/os (in other words, this is not just a positive corrective to negative 'stereotyping'). Molina-Guzmán sees the more radical depiction of Latina/o identity, especially in relation to gender and sexuality, as enabled by two qualities of streaming services. First, she argues that the production is enabled by virtue of working outside the context of white patriarchal Hollywood (even though on streaming platforms the decision-makers and the majority of original programming production are dominated by white men). While I complicated the white man in suits narrative in the previous chapter, there is certainly something that appears more radical about the approaches of streaming services such as Netflix and Hulu for minorities.[2] Second, for Molina-Guzmán, streaming services such as Hulu do not have the same content regulation as network television and therefore they can challenge narrative norms and representational boundaries.

A lot of these issues are not new, and relate to the experiences of minorities working on cable TV, which I shall unravel shortly. But I do want to temper a utopian view of the impact of digital technologies that exists in both media studies and public discourse. Critical political economists (McChesney, 2013; Curran et al., 2016) have argued that the new media is better understood as an extension of corporate cultural industries rather than as a challenge to it. In relation to race, two newer production studies provide a critical take on the potentiality of new digital cultural production. For instance, Sarah Florini (2015a; 2015b) in her exploration of the politics of urban podcasting – that is, US podcasts from a particular African American perspective, including the *This Week in Blackness* (*TWiB*) podcast referenced earlier – begins with the observation that the very architecture of social media produces a 'networked individualism' (2015b: 3) rather than emancipatory forms of community that utopian takes on the Internet suggest. But in her critical analysis of *TWiB*, Florini finds that it manages to resist 'the individualism at the centre of both contemporary racial logics and digitally networked sociality' and instead produces a strong black collectivity. And for Florini, this stems from the nature of *TWiB*'s function as both a broadcast and digital social network and the immersive sonorous

---

[2] For instance, the television series *The Get-Down* was Netflix's most expensive series to date – costing $120 million – and perhaps, more staggeringly, featured an almost entirely black and Hispanic cast, most of whom were unknown. See http://www.vanityfair.com/hollywood/2016/07/the-get-down-budget-netflix.

experience offered by radio that leads to enhanced feelings of community, blending 'together multiple traditions for the production of Black counter-publics' (2015b: 4). In other words, the success of *TWiB* in facilitating forms of community and solidarity is, in a particular sense, in spite of the Internet rather than because of it.

In his analysis of *A Real Girl's Guide to Everything Else* – previously tackled in chapter 2 – Christian (2011) produces a similar account of the radical potential of the web series. As he describes, the producers and writers of *A Real Girl's Guide to Everything Else* wanted to emulate *Sex and the City* of which they were big fans, while also aiming to put right the mainstream's misrepresentation of queer women of colour in particular, taking advantage of the low barriers to entry offered by the new online platforms. Like Molina-Guzmán, Christian stresses how the potentialities of the web series lie in having the freedom to challenge existing norms around diversity in mainstream programming. But in line with the cultural industries scholars, Christian avoids a narrative on heroic independents. Crucially, he stresses how, while the fan practices behind this particular production were an attempt to address the poor representation of race and sexuality in *Sex and the City*, they did not necessarily comprise a challenge to its explicit commercialism; the producers self-consciously poached certain narrative formulas and marketing/publicity strategies. In fact, the production is just as much about commercial ambitions as about cultural political ones. Christian (2011: 5.5) argues that the producers behind *A Real Girl's Guide to Everything Else*,

> saw a television industry consistently refusing to cast marginalised people as leads. So they seized the opportunity to try to correct imbalances through industrial practices, not outside of them. They would craft a marketable narrative, produce it well, and sell it to distributors – the growing number of independent networks – who packaged stories for advertisers and made it easier for viewers to find them.

Christian (2011; 2012) paints a complex picture throughout his research into the online video services, where new media, rather than existing outside, or challenging/subverting old media, has to work with it in order to survive. Because fundamentally, like minority ethnic media and minorities working in independent media more generally, the ultimate challenge for those working in new media is the lack of rewards that they receive for their labour. As Christian argues, 'independent participants in the new media market make valiant attempts to harness their creativity and package it to advertisers; yet those products can be undervalued, necessitating more corporate-friendly responses to their labour' (2012: 84).

In conclusion, independent production – whether commercial or not-for-profit – reflects the ambivalence of commodification. It has both revolutionary and realist tendencies. It faces huge political economic challenges in terms of trying to survive in a highly competitive market. But while we should be careful about over-romanticizing independent cultural production, we should be aware that it undoubtedly does offer greater autonomy to minority cultural producers. Speaking in the context of television, Ross (1995: 176) defines the potential of independently made black-originated content in terms of representing a 'response to the poverty and paucity of black and other minority images which are available across mainstream programming'. But, as I have argued, independent production should not be conceptualized in terms of resisting or working outside commodification, but of harnessing its enabling qualities for primarily aesthetic and/or sociocultural gain.

Mainstream cultural industries

Public service media

Minority ethnic media and independent media certainly offer greater scope for self-representation; but in a highly competitive market, minority cultural producers working in these sectors of the cultural industries can find themselves stranded on the periphery. While minorities have been responsible for great art and forms of cultural expression, as well as for bringing alternative experiences and perspectives to a pathologically white media, their biggest challenge remains making an impact in the core of the cultural industries. As I demonstrated in chapter 5, the more intensely commercial cultures of production in these sectors are particularly stifling for minority producers. Nonetheless, the core can produce enabling spaces for minorities, with public service media representing a particularly important sphere. In chapter 4 I critiqued a trend within PSM across European systems in particular, from multicultural programming to a new cultural/ creative diversity paradigm that I read as part of a shift towards neoliberal approaches to multiculture, where minority experience is de-raced and collapsed into a post-race discourse of diversity. As I said in that chapter, while we are more likely to see more black and Asian faces, we are less likely to learn about black or Asian lives. Nonetheless, PSM still has value for minority producers in particular. PSM is often seen as an alternative to a commercialized globalized media where profit comes first. Despite its difficulties with issues of diversity, PSM is one area of the core cultural industries where minority broadcasters have managed to gain access, not least because of PSM's core remit to cater for the nation in its diversity. In other words, PSM provides a potentially enabling space for minority producers to intervene in the hegemonic construction of national identity.

While creative diversity policy is neoliberal in character, encouraging individualization over community, the turn to mainstreaming diversity following increasing commercial pressures on PSM has had some enabling effects for minorities. The end of the weekly multicultural magazine-style format (Horsti, 2014) has coincided with the ascendency of populist and generic programming (Born and Prosser, 2001) and lifestyle programming and reality television in particular, which, needing a diverse range of characters, embrace racial and ethnic diversity. For Malik (2014: 34) these programmes, somewhat perversely, result in a 'hyper-visibility of multicultural societies'. This can be critiqued as a form of 'corporate multiculturalism' that seeks to '"manage" minority cultural differences in the interests of the centre' (Hall, 2000: 210), but it nonetheless has some productive effects.

For instance, Malik (2014) suggests that, because they are unscripted, the reality TV and documentary series that characterize contemporary PSM programming tend to avoid criticisms of misrepresentation. Horsti (2014) concedes that the tone of these programmes is less paternalistic and overly educational than the older versions of multicultural programming, and more likely to stress universality and commonality (Horsti, 2014). While stories about race and racism are less covered, representations of cultural difference, which stress the universal, are in fact sought after. Leurdijk (2006) notes a rise in PSM programming that takes universally shared experiences – birth, marriage, death – but tells these stories from minority perspectives. As she states, 'looking for universal emotions and experiences, or focusing on remarkable individuals, are seen as the best ways to keep viewers attracted' (2006: 35). The victory of British Bangladeshi (and hijab-wearing) Nadiya Hussain in the hugely popular BBC series *The Great British Bake-Off* encapsulates this new emphasis. Indeed, for Jakubowicz (2014: 238), reality television can be unexpectedly enabling for people of colour: 'where people of colour, of odd shapes and sizes, and of new eclectic creativities, can emerge as cultural heroes'. Of course, we should be careful not to put too much value on these moments. As Malik (2014: 34) recognizes, the new PSM reality formats fulfil a post-race discourse that 'neutralizes' racial difference, simulating a world where meritocracy rules – in sharp contrast to actual lived realities. But the point I want to stress here is that commercialism does not necessarily result in less visibility for minorities. As Malik (2014: 35) adds: 'To this degree, reality television has become the most ubiquitous and racially varied form of programming today.'

These largely textual accounts point to the enabling features of the turn towards creative diversity policy. But I argue that, in each different PSM system, to varying degrees, public service's key principle remains firm: to produce programming that commercial television cannot or will not make. A public service remit can still produce radical output. This insight has come from more production-oriented studies. Cottle (1997: 3–4) for instance, in his ethnographic study of news and current affairs production in the BBC, considers the factors that lead to the moments when something inclusive and progressive is produced in relation to race. He sees this as due to several factors, including 'a developing newsroom awareness of multiculturalism; the pursuit of minority ethnic audiences as a means of increasing the programme rating; and the programme's populist "visualisation", enacted daily by producers, which informs the mix of selected news stories as well as their subject treatment'. Cottle here draws attention to the way that various motivations, whether moral (an awareness of multiculturalism), or commercial (increasing ratings), combine to facilitate minority representation. He also refers to the daily enactments of producers, who, according to Born and Prosser (2001: 669) – speaking in the context of the BBC – can come to embody public services principles: 'Among some creative and production staff there thus remains a vital commitment, lived out in everyday practice, to certain core values in a direct line of descent from Reith's values of serving and stimulating the audience, justifying the licence fee, and quality and integrity of output.' The fact remains that PSM is remarkably resilient (Horsti, 2014), and is at its most progressive when it realizes that difference and diversity are irreversible facts of modern life; as Hall (1993: 34) argues, 'the public service idea can only survive in this changed climate if it can adapt to it, pluralising and diversifying its own interior world, its buried assumptions'. And, arguably, it continues to achieve this, to varying degrees. In this regard, more production-oriented case studies best illustrate the enabling qualities of PSM, as I shall now demonstrate using two examples.

Little Mosque on the Prairie (2007–12) is a Canadian sitcom that lasted six seasons, produced and broadcast by Canadian PSM broadcaster CBC. It is a gentle and somewhat traditional sitcom, albeit set in a mosque in a prairie town in Saskatchewan, which stresses the ordinariness of Canadian Muslim lives. In his study of the green-lighting process behind the series, Kyle Conway (2014: 655) describes how *Little Mosque on the Prairie* had 'more diversity among Muslim characters than on other shows: plot structure and setting made it possible not only to present a range of perspectives but also to explore how characters grew more complex over time'.[3] Indeed, the main motivation of the writer Zarqa Nawaz was to challenge hegemonic representations of Islam in the media. Broadcast on CBC, one would assume that *Little Mosque on the Prairie* was commissioned via CBC's public service mandate. But while Conway acknowledges how CBC's multicultural and regional mandates of course provided an impetus for the network to green-light the show, he argues that the main reason was because it would fit with CBC's promotional strategy where it uses its public service credentials – which *Little Mosque on the Prairie* encapsulates – as a form of market differentiation from its competitors. Thus, Conway is suggesting that the counter-hegemonic representation of Muslims in *Little Mosque on the Prairie* was enabled in fact by a commercial imperative. In addition, he recounts the difficulty that the show faced in gaining syndication in the USA, due to campaigning from conservative groups and a more risk-averse commercial sector, which for Conway reads as an illustration of how PSM is still able to make programming that the commercial sector will not touch. Therefore, while 'the potential of policy to encourage alternative discourses about Islam was real but indirect . . . one important thing mandates can do is provide a reason for public broadcasters to take a risk' (Conway, 2014: 661).

In my own research (Saha, 2013c), I explored the case in the UK of Channel 4's *Bradford Riots* (2006), which was a two-part docudrama based on the real events that took place in Bradford in 2001. The story follows the lead-up to and aftermath of a riot between the police and Bradford's predominantly working-class Pakistani youth, who were given disproportionately large sentences for rioting. *Bradford Riots*, like *Little Mosque on the Prairie*, should not be seen as a totally radical depiction of Muslims, since it reinforces strong discourses around what Alexander (2000) calls the 'Asian Gang' – but nonetheless it was a damning indictment of the British state and legal system. The drama was a critical and commercial success, enabled by a big promotional campaign that included a significant marketing push consisting of trailers, a billboard campaign and a two-page advert in all the daily newspapers. Indeed, the film was commissioned around the time that Channel 4 was applying its new strategy of mainstreaming diversity. Neil Biswas, the writer and director behind *Bradford Riots*, explained

---

[3] Conway stops short of calling it a truly radical representation as the characters and storylines were still tethered to particular tropes on Muslims.

to me in an interview that the production of the series was enabled by a risk-taking culture at Channel 4 – particularly striking, since he was a first-time director. Biswas recognizes that this in part was informed by how the story fitted in with Channel 4's brand, which targets a young, urban audience. But he also went to great lengths to acknowledge the political motivations of individual executive producers in supporting *Bradford Riots*. For instance, he recounted a story where, following the temporary shut-down of the production as it struggled to get permission from various local authorities to stage the riot scene, the producers offered £1 million to build a bespoke set:

> I think [Channel 4] did *Bradford Riots* because they felt politically it had to be addressed . . . you remember, part of their remit is to do ethnic programming . . . programming that is there for a minority interest, so it couldn't have been more up their street in terms of their remit. But I think in terms of their political positions they all felt this was a really important story to be told that hadn't been told. (Quoted in Saha, 2013c: 222)

According to this account, the production was enabled by Channel 4's remit to cater for minorities, but also the political motivations of the channel that was, in Biswas's words, 'radical' and 'gung-ho' (Saha, 2013c: 223). Thus, in contrast to the majority of cases I encountered in my research into British South Asian cultural production, where symbol creators would describe feeling alienated or pressured by senior executives to sanitize or tone down their narratives, Biswas expressed his amazement at how Channel 4 and its co-producers flouted all the standard commercial conventions, and took risks over a production that would probably have generated press interest based on subject-matter alone, but was not guaranteed to be a commercial hit.

Corporate production

There are two things that I take from these case studies. First, although the practices of PSM are constrained by political economic and policy shifts, it still embodies a set of principles that individual actors come to personify at particular moments; this is the reason why PSM remains a productive – and attractive – space for racial and ethnic minorities, despite the challenges. Second, these two case studies demonstrate how the writers and producers were aided, not by a public service remit alone, but by an inter-action between public service and commercial rationales. In the *Bradford Riots* example, I referred to a comment from Neil Biswas regarding how the drama was commissioned because it fulfilled Channel 4's branding criterion (which targets a younger, urban demographic) as well as its remit do to 'ethnic programming'. Branding such as this is adopted from the corporate sector – evoking Hardy's (2014) description of the 'corporate take-over' of PSM (see also Born, 2004). But while it is assumed that the imposition of promotional strategies is a negative force on minority cultural production (Davis, 2013: 193), several production scholars of race demonstrate how 'branded diversity' (Kohnen, 2015) or 'narrowcasting' (Zook, 1999) have in fact enabled minority cultural production in highly commercial settings. Indeed, in Kohnen's study of branded diversity in the case of American Broadcasting Company (ABC) drama *The Family*, about a lesbian couple and their adopted interracial family (a form of branded diversity that ABC used to break from conservative conceptions of the family in order to appeal to millennials), the main target is a political economy approach that dismisses the political potential of popular culture based on its corporate production.

Two of the most well-known studies of race and cultural production as a whole come from Herman Gray (1995) and Kristal Brent Zook (1999), both of whom take as their subject narrowcasting strategies in US network television and how, if only for a moment during the 1990s, they led to an explosion of black programming never seen before in this context. The Rupert Murdoch-owned Fox Network was the innovator in this regard following its launch in 1986, but other network channels, such as WB and UPN, have subsequently adopted similar narrowcasting strategies trying to emulate Fox's success. Narrowcasting can be considered a form of rationalization, something that the TV networks adopted in the 1990s against the backdrop of heightened competition (Fuller, 2010). Narrowcasting essentially means targeting 'niche' audiences or, rather, specific audiences, and meeting their particular needs, rather than producing programmes that appeal to the biggest audiences.[4] It is, in addition, a method of constructing viewers in a way that advertisers understand and can buy into. So, for instance, in this new environment the act of scheduling (Ellis, 2000) became less about trying to maximize audiences and more about creating a channel's brand in order to attract advertisers (Fuller, 2010).

By focusing on niches and working quickly and efficiently, these newer networks have found success, particularly Fox, which successfully broke

---

[4] Narrowcasting strategies have traditionally been used by cable networks; structural changes in network broadcasting have led to network channels emulating these practices (Gray, 2005; Zook, 1999).

the oligopoly of the Big Three television networks ABC, CBS and NBC (the gains made by WP and UPN have been more modest). As Zook (1999) stresses, when Fox was launched it was well aware that it could not compete with the Big Three, initially at least, so it adopted narrowcasting strategies of the kind previously used by cable channels. NBC had found some success with black-cast sitcoms (*The Cosby Show, A Different World* and *The Fresh Prince of Bel-Air*), so Fox focused on attracting black and urban audiences, referred to controversially by one Fox executive as the '"Nike and Doritos audience"' (quoted in Zook, 1999: 4). This came through green-lighting black-cast programmes, and counter-programming against other networks to suit that audience's taste. And it worked: Fox success-fully attracted black audiences, representing 25 per cent of its total audi-ence. During this period, Fox – which wanted to portray itself as the 'rebel network' (Zook, 1999: 5) – subsequently became an incredibly enabling space for black producers who were encouraged to hire black staff like them – other writers, performers and producers – who shared the same vision. Zook finds as well that the network was more open to risk-taking than film studios. She makes the point that, while the popular sketch show series, *The Wayan Bros.*, would not have aired in the 1980s because it would have been considered too ethnic, in the 1990s it allowed Fox to distinguish itself from others in the market.

Zook then considers what these structural contexts meant for the poli-tics of representation. What she finds in particular is that these liberating spaces enabled black showrunners to draw from autobiography and the black aesthetic of improvisation that ordinarily would have been con-strained or discouraged. At their best, shows such as *A Different World, The Fresh Prince of Bel-Air, Sinbad* and *Living Single* are characterized by Zook as embodying a combination of black nationalist desire (these programmes were defiantly black in contrast to colour-blind *Cosby Show*) and an open-ness to discussions of blackness and what it means to be black, specifically in relation to interracial identity, classism and colourism, sexuality, gender and romance (as embodied in the programmes *Martin* and *Living Single*).

However, while Fox no doubt facilitated some radical (relatively, at least) black programming, this was unintentional. It goes without saying that Fox was more interested in alternative programming and market differentiation than in exploring black cultural politics. Drawing on inter-views, Zook explains that even when the new breed of black-cast shows were at the height of their popularity, networks were not really invested in them, socially or culturally. And eventually this explosion of African American television receded: while initially targeting black audiences, networks began to switch their focus to the more affluent, and lucrative, elite white group (Fox did this through the purchase of NFL rights). While trying to 'seek white "legitimacy",' Fox cut black shows or limited them to a single night, demonstrating how black audiences were no longer a priority (Zook, 1999: 23). Gray (2005) notes that by the 2000s black-cast sitcoms had almost disappeared from network television.

Zook's important study is an older example, but we find a similar case of narrowcasting/branding strategy in contemporary cable television. In contrast to network TV, cable is not reliant on advertising, which enables/constrains black cultural production in different ways; As Fuller (2010: 291) states: 'For cable, with its reliance on a subscriber base, black viewership has a different meaning than it does for broadcasters.' Audiences for cable are smaller, but they have loyal audiences that allow them to adopt niche programming – in fact, it is financially beneficial to do so. It is for this reason that black take-up of cable is high and it is for *this* reason that cable channels boast of their appeal to racial minorities. Why might black programming be enabled by cable TV? First, cable is less risk-averse, since it is not reliant on advertising revenue that depends on attracting the biggest audiences (Molina-Guzmán, 2016; Fuller, 2010). Second, as we have seen, black show-runners have benefited from cable television's recognition of its black audience (Fuller, 2010). But, naturally, there is some ambivalence. Paradoxically, while boasting of their black audiences, many cable channels downplay the 'blackness' of their programmes even when they are in fact predominantly black-cast. Instead, they brand them in terms of universal notions of quality. This can be read as progressive (refusing to reduce by race) or reactive (not wanting to alienate white audiences). But what Fuller further finds is that black programming on cable television is framed not only in terms of quality, but also in a supposedly non-raced notion of 'edginess' (see also Banet-Weiser, 2007). Fuller is drawing from the case of Comedy Central's popular *Chapelle Show*, written by and starring African American comedian David Chapelle. In her analysis, Fuller describes how Comedy Central downplayed the show's strong race dimension and up-played the show's riskiness and edgy humour. By the third season, the promos more actively focus on Chapelle's relationship with white audiences, selling the *Chapelle Show* on the idea that white people become 'cool' by watching it. Chapelle famously quit the show during the third series, worried that his material was being misinterpreted by white audiences.

Thus, while cable television channel's use of blackness to promote its brand – through black culture's association with all that is edgy, urban and cool – is certainly successful (by which I mean profitable) and indeed enabling for black cultural production, this is only the case up to a certain point. (In Chapelle's case, his breakdown echoes the black alienation described by Frantz Fanon – see chapter 1.) Nonetheless, it still represents a cultural political gain in the Gramscian sense. Returning to her study of ABC's *The Fosters*, Kohnen (2015: 96) draws from Lisa Henderson (2013) in her description of how the 'longstanding denigration of commercial pop culture fails to recognize the struggles for a queer presence within mainstream media'. She argues that, in the case of *The Fosters*, branded diversity 'opens up a space for a critical interrogation of interracial and lesbian identity in contemporary culture' (2015: 100). My argument is that even in the most commercialized and profit-driven of spaces, minority cultural producers can find areas where their representational practices are opened. These are often fleeting, and limited in their gains. But if we relieve popular culture of the burden to emancipate us in full, then they represent transgressions nonetheless.

Conclusion

One of the fundamental arguments for the enabling properties of com-modification in relation to race is that cultural industries, if we are to crudely regard them as an extension of capitalism, can never control either how cultural commodities are consumed or the meanings that are made from their consumption. This is particularly evident when we consider the global nature of race-making, race-circulation and race-consumption. As Jakubowicz (2014) argues, all advanced Western capitalist nations are fully embedded in globalization and this can be generative in terms of intercul-tural exchange, as much as it can result in reactionary outcomes. And this, to paraphrase Stuart Hall, comes without guarantees, especially when cul-tural production is concerned. As Jakubowicz continues: 'Where the media are charged with recognizing and engaging creatively with these changes as part of the contemporary modernity of these complex societies, what had been bizarre or deviant instead becomes reprocessed and integrated into current narratives' (2014: 238).

The inherent unpredictability of cultural production in the context of globalization is articulated in Negus's (1999) account of the transnational production of salsa music and his concept of the 'salsa matrix'. The salsa matrix describes the ways in which salsa moves between different locales – beyond the New York–Miami–Puerto Rico network – extending to Venezuela, Colombia, Cuba, parts of Europe (including Spain and Canary Islands) and Africa. Negus argues that salsa can subsequently only be fully understood in terms of its transnational constituents – highlighting the inadequacy of thinking of music in terms of nation. The transnational character of the 'salsa matrix', according to Negus, underlines how

> musical recordings are not simply 'distributed' by the music industry but moved through complex cultural matrices of meanings, social practices and transformations on their way to meet new listeners, dancers and musicians. The idea of the cultural matrix is an attempt to suggest that a range of different dynamics are involved in the circulation of commodities, and that these cannot be reduced to any straightforward logic of the music business or capital, nor simply to the transformative creativity of musicians or active consumption of audiences. (1999: 149)

Negus is arguing that the production – or consumption – of salsa is not determined by its corporate production, but happens in a much more ad hoc fashion influenced by 'the actions of fans, friends, managers promoters, disc jockeys, collectors, journalists and general music enthusiasts' (1999: 150). This is a crucial point in understanding how discourses of race circulate, evoking the research of material culture scholars who track the social lives of things, including cultural commodities, and the different meanings they take through space and time.

Yet, this does not really engage with the question that is central to this book: namely, why it is that media discourses of race remain persistent and resolute and very rarely change form. This question remains regardless of whether those representations come to mean something different in another spatial or temporal context. In that sense, what is more valuable about understanding cultural production in its global dimensions is in how, as Havens (2013) demonstrates most acutely, domestic cultural industries are forced to think globally, in terms of international syndication, which then shapes race-making in the domestic context. That is, assumptions (whether evidenced or not) about how global audiences will react to certain representations of race subsequently influence the form those representations take. As Gray (2000: 125–126) puts it:

> Now (black) programme makers and buyers can ask, for perhaps the first time, how will black television programming play in the distant reaches of the vast corporate marketplace made possible by satellite, cable, the Internet and other forms of global delivery? Will the demands of distant markets rob locally based black programming of its specificity and historicity? Is the prerequisite for black television shows (and cinemas) that they travel well? That they speak in a universal language? And if so, what is that language and what is the embodied representation(s) through which it is expressed? Is it the naturalized (racialized) athletic and dancing

black body? Perhaps it is the body endowed with musical prowess? Is it the black corporeal body of liberal civil rights? Perhaps it is the neo-nationalist subject of hip-hop discourse?

What is underlined here is how race-making takes on an increasingly global character. This is a point I accept fully. Yet what I in turn add is that race-making in Western cultural industries remains based on Western understandings of race (whether the athletic black body, the rhythmical black body or the civil rights black body) and commodification and the rationalizing/racializing logic of capital is how racial tropes get repro-duced. In other words, very powerful discourses of race, shaped by empire and capitalism, still dominate and persist in Western media, and are diffi-cult to dislodge, subvert or transcend.

Yet there is always scope to do so. The purpose of this chapter has been to explore the different spaces within the cultural industries that enable the counter narratives of minority cultural producers. Clearly, minority-owned media – particularly independent and community media – offers the most autonomy and creative freedom for minorities and the ability to craft the stories that they want to tell. But in this chapter I have argued that we should not readily dismiss the enabling capacities of corporate cultural production. Eithne Quinn (2013a: 205) refers to Hollywood and blackness, but could be speaking of the cultural industries and race more generally:

> [While Hollywood] seems overwhelming, [it] is not all-absorbing or monolithically efficient – its racist assumptions present some opportuni-ties for minority cultural producers. Indeed, when such corporate fault-lines are combined with the rich performative and subcultural resources of black America in an increasingly synergistic, celebrity-fronted industry environment, the opportunities presented can be substantial.

Thus, as I have stressed, even in the most commercialized and profit-obsessed spaces, filled with white executives with the most racist attitudes, cultural commodification can still be enabling. This is why race and cul-tural production matters, and why we need to give a damn about it.

7

Conclusion

The fact is, we see more people of colour in the media than ever before. And while huge improvements remain to be made, there are probably more minorities working in the media than at any point in history. So why is the media's representation of racial and ethnic minorities so limited, rather than diverse? Why do these minorities continue to be represented according to particular tropes that appear to emanate from colonial times? Why do cultural industries make race the way that they do?

There has been much scholarly work that deconstructs popular culture and news, revealing the deeply damaging representation of minorities; the best examples situate the circulation of symbols of Otherness within the legacies of empire and colonialism. But answering the questions posed above demands greater attention to the production of representations. Developing a keener sense of the reproduction of racial archetypes (so as to intervene in it) necessitates understanding the mode of production through which racial representations are shaped and then distributed. Yet in media research, the study of race in the context of cultural production remains a relatively minor area of interest. It is this lacuna that this book has attempted to fill, with the hope that it will inspire further research on the subject. In this concluding chapter I provide a brief summary of my approach and where I see its practical, as well as theoretical, intervention.

Race and the cultural industries

In approaching the production of representations in the cultural industries – as the cultural industries are the site within which racial representations are primarily made – I focus on two broad areas. The first is the issue of commodification, specifically the commodification of culture. Production in the cultural industries is essentially a process of commodification, transforming expressive culture into a good with exchange value. The term commodification is nearly always used negatively, in terms of the exploitation of the labour that goes into the production of the commodity, and

169

in terms of how it turns culture into private property, the access to which is limited (and runs counter to the idea of the common good). A further negative dimension of commodification is the extent to which commodities in the West embody the ideologies of capitalism and empire. This is a much more contentious issue, but one that is particularly pertinent to the issue of the production of representations of race.

My second area of focus is in the dynamics of industrial cultural production. Industrialization generally speaking is an aspect of commodification. While not all commodification is based on industrialization, the latter has intensified the spread of the former; the emergence of the cultural industries has facilitated further the commodification of culture. Hesmondhalgh (2013: 68–69), drawing on Lacroix and Tremblay, defines industrialization as based upon significant 'capital investment, mechanised production and the division of labour'. In the specific context of the cultural industries in its current corporate form, industrial production also includes the adoption of bureaucratization and forms of rationalization. Gaining a deeper understanding of the production of representations necessitates getting to grips with the specificities of industrial cultural production (that cultural industries scholars recognize as distinct from other forms of production due to the particular nature of the cultural commodity) and seeing how race penetrates into specific points of the production process. In summary, understanding the production of representation necessitates a macro analysis of the particular nature of commodification under late capitalism / racial neoliberalism, and a micro examination of the dynamics of industrial cultural production.

Addressing the question of how cultural industries make race, I argue, entails thinking through how cultural commodities come to be racialized. This reframing emerges in response to a particular discussion on the commodification of race, which is one explanation given by cultural studies scholars for why race is so negatively represented in the media. In a nutshell, the commodification of race argument conceptualizes commodification as the process whereby what begins as a radical expression of minority vernacular culture loses its political agency once it is co-opted by capitalism and converted into a commodity. While correctly foregrounding the industrial context of the production of representation (in contrast to postcolonial criticism, which tends to treat texts as non-commodities), the commodification of race argument, however, is undermined by a slip into a determinist and functionalist account of the cultural industries (impeded by a lack of empirical detail) that allows no room for contestation or contradiction. Indeed, the notion of the commodification of race immediately forecloses the disruptive potential of the cultural commodity, as, following the argument through, since cultural commodities are produced by capitalism, they consequently cannot have any disruptive effects upon it – a position that is far too fatalistic. Ultimately, this account of commodification is simplistic, and becomes an all-too convenient shorthand for capitalism's supposed co-option of the counter narratives of racialized difference and the production of its own form of corporate multiculture – a process that is much more complex than such a narrative allows. Thus, the shift from the notion of the commodification of race to a notion of the racialization of the cultural commodity reconfigures the production of representations as a process of race-making. This immediately comes up against polemical accounts that dismiss anything made by the culture industry as a pawn of capital or embodied with capitalist ideologies, while avoiding also an overly celebratory account of any successful minority cultural production as evidence of their resilience. The purpose of conceptualizing industrial cultural production as a form of race-making is to address directly the issue of why historical constructions of Otherness persist in the media, and why contradictions occur.

To unpack the racialization of cultural commodity, a theory of race and cultural production is required that offers a fuller, more detailed interpretation of capitalism's attempts to manage and regulate the counter narratives of difference through commodification. It must be attuned to the questions of power and domination and how ideologies of empire and capitalism manifest in the cultural industries, but also be able to explain the contradictions, complexities and sites of contestation that characterize the experience of cultural production itself. I develop a theoretical framework that combines the cultural industries tradition of critical political economy (encompassing sociological approaches to creative labour)' with postcolonial/critical race theory. It is aimed at ascertaining the dynamic between macro and micro dimensions of cultural work that form the richly layered cultures of production through which race is represented in the form of cultural commodities. It is concerned with structure and agency and how creative workers constitute, and are constituted by, the structures of the media, and the extent to which they conform to or can challenge standardized industrial practices that restrict their creativity. It thinks through how the cultural industries and their role in society are shaped by capitalism and legacies of empire, while examining the specific dynamics of cultural production on the ground, and the relations between them. Overall, it foregrounds the way in which race-making activities occur via a complex interplay between different sedimentary layers: between the text, the symbol creator and other cultural intermediaries involved in the making of the text, the cultures of production of the media organization, the political economy of the cultural industries, and the wider global cultural economy. Such an approach does not just help us understand the reproduction of historical constructions of Otherness, but also offers an important insight into the complex, entangled relation between capitalism and race in general.

In adopting this approach, I make two theoretical arguments in particular. The first involves (re)conceptualizing commodification as a technology of racialized governmentalities. This concept exposes how racial governmentalities within the cultural industries – through the broad process of commodification – attempt to steer, direct and shape the production of racial meaning, and sustain the absolute difference between European and nonwhite. In describing commodification as a 'technology', I refer to the processes, apparatus and machinery, as well as to the production rationales and logics that constitute industrial cultural production and, in turn, the commodification of culture, which are the means through which the counter narratives of difference are regulated and transformed into reified, essentialist symbols of race in the form of cultural commodities. The concept has a macro and a micro element. In terms of the macro, it describes how race is managed through power/knowledge and techniques of power that are used to sustain and reproduce an absolute sense of ethnic and racial difference upon which Western national identity depends. In the context of cultural production, it refers to how racial knowledge becomes embedded in production – that is, how it becomes the very logic of industrial cultural production. In terms of the micro, the concept of commodification as a technology of racialized governmentalities offers a route to thinking through how the production of racial knowledge actually occurs, through what Rose (1999: 3) describes as 'rationalised schemes, programmes, techniques and devices which seek to shape conduct so as to achieve certain ends'. Again, when grounded specifically in the cultural industries, the concept explains how actors (both minorities and non-minorities) adopt the logics of production through their everyday practices, rituals and habits, which appear to be neutral but are in fact racialized, reproducing racialized representations (and other inequalities of gender, sexuality, class and so on) in the process.

The second main theoretical argument concerns what I call the rationalizing/racializing logic of capital. This concept refers specifically to how the increasingly rationalized processes that characterize production in its corporate form are what steer minority producers into reproducing historical constructions of Otherness. That is not to say that rationalization is inherently racializing. Instead, rationalizing processes such as formatting, packaging, marketing and promotion have common-sense understandings of race structured into them (a consequence of the intrinsic whiteness of the cultural industries). To reiterate: they become the very logic of production. Crucial to the rationalizing/racializing logic of capital is the manner in which the racialization of the cultural commodity manifests as common-sense, race-neutral business practice that obscures its ideological dimensions. So, for instance, it explains the process that leads to the racialization and sexualization of standard production formats – for instance, hyper-sexualized urban R&B or hyper-masculine gangsta rap. Indeed, if formatting is the production of culture to type, as Bill Ryan (1992) puts it, then, in the context of race-making, formatting becomes the making of race according to racial archetype. Minority cultural producers, following these rationalizing techniques, reduce their own work to racial tropes. As argued in the previous chapter, sometimes this is following the direct interventions of white gatekeepers, but also this can happen when there are no white gatekeepers present. This is why the concept of governmentality has a function, as nonwhite managers, intermediaries and creatives have internalized the rationalizing/racializing logic of capital. This then explains the constant churn of racialized, Orientalist representations of racial and ethnic groups.

The politics of production

That being said, throughout this book I have stressed, like cultural industries scholars, that commodification is a fundamentally ambivalent process. Commodification is not inherently negative; it has enabling/constraining elements – it is ambivalent, contested and contradictory. In the context of the cultural industries, cultural production is always a process of commodification – whether it is a major television network adopting narrowcasting strategies in order to create an audience to sell to an advertiser, or an underground grime label, selling white-label 12-inch vinyl out of the back of a van. The point is that some paths of commodification offer more counter-hegemonic scope than others – though this is always contingent. A cultural politics of race in the context of the cultural industries depends on what route commodification takes. At times, a particular path of commodification allows a minority producer to challenge and defy racialized/gendered/sexualized formats or genre codes. As commodification has both constraining and enabling properties, then a successful politics of production depends not on resisting commodification, but on harnessing its enabling qualities.

The politics of production is an important companion to (rather than a substitute for) a politics of representation. If the latter entails the design and conception of representational strategies that disrupt and subvert the racial discourses that reinforce a Manichean colonial vision of difference and absolute racial types (which can involve different types of methods depending on context), the former is tasked with the opening up of representational practices; that is, removing the constraints placed on minority cultural production. What then might the politics of production in the cultural industries look like? This could be the subject on an entire book in itself, but to conclude I am going to sketch out a few ideas regarding what a politics of production could entail.

The first thing to stress it is that there is not one production space that is wholly enabling for minority cultural producers and their white collaborators. The politics of production that I conceptualise is based on Stuart Hall's Gramscian take on the politics of position within a struggle for hegemony; as capitalism attempts to totalize culture through the process of commodification, it leaves tears or stretches where its integrity is weakened, and this is where minority symbol creators need to stage their interventions. The rationalizing/racializing logic is not absolute, but variable, in intensity and reach and weight, according to different production circumstances. As such, at certain moments – depending on the interplay at specific moments between different political-economic and sociocultural forces – social actors can steer the commodification process in such a way that leads to the production of disruption and destabilization of racial discourses through cultural production. While it is not always predictable where a space is going to open up, a politics of production nonetheless should strive to find opportunities to prise open spaces. Despite its contingent nature, this should not prevent us from taking a normative position on what form an effective politics of production should take.

To begin, I argue that the opening up of representation practices depends on suspending economic rationales at key moments in production – enabling risk-taking. This would suggest that the corporate sphere with its profit-orientation is not conducive to minority cultural producers, but, as I showed in chapter 6, this is not always the case. On the reverse side of the coin, the subsidized sector does not always produce the widest representations of racial and ethnic minorities; the increasing liberalization of the cultural industries has made it more difficult to totally insulate cultural production from market forces, and in chapters 4 and 5 I referred to cases of minorities who have experienced the negative effects of arts funding governmentalities. In those instances where an aesthetic or political vision has been compromised, it is usually when commercial forces begin to dominate. There are many complex issues that arise from this, but if minority race-making practices are to be judged (at the very least) by their ability to resist being subsumed into a racialist nationalist narrative that marks non-whites as absolutely different to a national Self, then an awareness of how this ideology manifests through normative, commercial rationale, as I have shown in this book, is paramount to formulating effective cultural politics strategies. There are two ways that this needs to be tackled.

The first strategy entails a structural focus on policy and regulation. As I explored in chapter 3, minority cultural production is impeded by the dominance of a handful of media conglomerates, more interested in profit and expanding their share of the market – where minority productions/ audiences are considered a risky investment, and not attractive enough to advertisers. Political economists engaged with issues of race argue that such media are naturally conservative and use their outlets to espouse explicitly anti-immigrant rhetoric (Gandy, 1998; Blevins and Martinez, 2010: 232). Minority cultural production is undeniably affected by media concentration, and, as a result, regulation that breaks up oligopolies and facilitates independent production should be part of a politics of production. However, I want to stress that this is not enough by itself to really tackle the entrenched nature of racist ideologies within the cultural industries. For instance, as Ross (1995) suggests in her study of the UK independent television scene, while policymakers who determined that a set portion of a national broadcaster's programming had to be produced by independents (see Hesmondhalgh, 2013: 201) for a moment at least enabled the growth of the black independent sector, this was quickly replaced by a hierarchical system where (white) 'Super-Indies' became the preferred suppliers for broadcasters. To this day, such companies dominate the independent market. As such, regulation designed to break up monopolies, contrary to what Blevins and Martinez (2010) argue, needs to also entail a civil rights or (for want of a better term) 'diversity' agenda that at least engages with the specific challenges that minority independent media companies face.

Another area of policy that should constitute a politics of production concerns protecting public service media and ideals. While I have critiqued the development of public service diversity policies across different contexts, PSM still represents an absolutely crucial space for minorities, not least since it is one of the few sites in the cultural industries that proactively encourages participation from minority cultural producers. Again, there is not the space to go into detail here, but at the very least PSM needs to fully commit to a remit that is focused on covering different aspects of minority experience alongside a commitment to presenting them to the mainstream, that is, at prime time, on the main channels. This necessitates forms of regulation, management and the promotion of public service values that protect producers/commissioners from market pressures, allowing them to take risks. Moreover, I argue that a politics of production for PSM should entail a multifaceted approach that includes a multicultural policy, which recognizes race and racism as structural forces that characterize national life, but which is combined with the mainstreaming strategies of cultural diversity policies so that minorities do not feel ghettoized. I concur strongly with Georgina Born's (2013: 137–139) model for PSM and cultural diversity based on different layers of inclusion and facilitation, including (1) a space where the majority is committed to hosting divergent and contesting minority perspectives, (2) a space where the minority speaks both to the majority and to other minorities where PBS acts as a theatre/forum where cultural diversity is worked out, displayed and represented and intercultural exchange is mounted, and (3) a space where minority speaks to minority (intracultural communication), which, far from parochial, has the potential to contribute to the 'mainstream' public sphere (this includes the public support of minority ethnic media). A set of overlapping spheres such as this – based on a strong infrastructure and adequate funding – is the best way to ensure that the full range of minority experience – its pains, its beauty, its traditions, its innovations, its pasts, its futures – is captured.

The second strategy that should comprise a politics of production is focused on the agency of the creative worker and the experience of industrial cultural production itself. It states that, since cultural production is a contested process, minority cultural producers need to focus on their industry practice as much as they do on their craft. In other words, a politics of production necessitates minority symbol creators and collaborating cultural intermediaries continually reflecting upon their choices, decisions and strategies throughout the production process. Ideally, it means that, as much as possible, symbol creators are present (or have trustworthy representation!) at each key stage of production in order to guide the text appropriately through the commodity phase. Such steps are crucial to ensuring that a minority production does not succumb (fully at least) to the rationalizing/racializing logic of capital, particularly during the packaging and marketing stages of production. Deciding which organization to work with or target is an important component of this strategy. As stated, successful interventions can be held in different kinds of production settings, dependent on the autonomy experienced by the symbol creator and their access to appropriate networks of distribution and marketing. For instance, working with an established independent organization that prioritizes artistic or political endeavour over profit is a particularly productive space in which to produce challenging work, though this would probably mean a compromise in terms of the scale of the audience reached. While it may prove more difficult, interventions can additionally be staged in a corporate context, though preferably within an environment where individuals experience a degree of autonomy, and have more freedom to act on their ethics/instincts. Broadly speaking, working with corporations or bigger companies where commercial pressures are most felt will provide the minority symbol creator with larger distribution channels, bigger marketing budgets and greater rewards for their labour – certainly more so than working independently. In which case, the question becomes the degree to which cultural producers are willing to compromise their aesthetic and political vision in order to receive the benefits of working within a more profit-oriented organization, whether corporate or independent (though this raises many ethically complex questions that I do not have the space to address here). Effective cultural work can additionally occur through alternative modes of production and DIY strategies that reject the established forms of media, whereby the symbol creator retains full control over the entire production and distribution process. While we should resist utopian pronouncements on the liberating potential of the new digital forms of production, they have undoubtedly lowered barriers to entry for minority cultural producers, in particular, which effectively puts the means of production (of representation) entirely in their hands. Making and distributing work independently using the Internet gives minorities the full freedom to self-represent and self-define without any outside influence. There are instances when a filmmaker, author or musician has managed to reach huge online audiences totally independently, though the challenge remains in monetizing digital streams in order to further develop and sustain this sphere of minority cultural production.

What the examples I have provided here reiterate is that there is not one ideal production setting for minority cultural producers. Moreover, each scenario poses different sets of problems and cost/benefits. Nonetheless, each also represents a particular way in which the enabling properties of commodification can be exploited. A successful politics of production is essentially premised upon the extent to which the rationalizing/racializing logic of capital can be resisted, challenged or subverted. As I have demonstrated, it is precisely through such rationalizing techniques, that the counter narratives of difference are governed. In essence, it is rationalization through standardized procedure that restricts the autonomy of the minority cultural producer, compounded by increasingly commercially pressured and risk-averse cultural industries. Such is the imposition of neoliberal economic models upon the cultural industries, whether in the form of corporate management or media/cultural policy, that the reality of being able to totally evade rationalized, standardized production is impossible. Regardless, the potential for producing challenging forms of cultural production depends on the ability of symbol creators to negotiate these processes in a way that does not compromise their ethical, political or aesthetic vision. By deepening our understanding of how cultural industries make race, we can gain the insights, knowledge and tools that can intervene in and disrupt the persistent repetition of racialized images of the Other that saturate Western media.

References

Acosta-Alzuru, C. 2003. Tackling the issues: Meaning making in a telenovela. *Popular Communication*. 1(4), pp. 193–215.

Adams, T. and Cleary, J. 2006. The parity paradox: Reader response to minority newsroom staffing. *Mass Communication & Society*. 9(1), pp. 45–61.

Adorno, T.W. 1991. *The culture industry: Selected essays on mass culture* (ed. J. M. Bernstein). London: Routledge.

Ahmed, S. 2012. *On being included: Racism and diversity in institutional life*. Durham, NC: Duke University Press.

Alexander, C. 2009. Stuart Hall and 'race'. *Cultural Studies*. 23(4), pp. 457–482.

Alexander, C. 2008. The problem of South Asian popular culture: A view from the UK. *South Asian Popular Culture*. 6(1), pp. 1–12.

Alexander, C. 2006. Introduction: Mapping the issues. *Ethnic and Racial Studies*. 29(3), pp. 397–410.

Alexander, C. 2000. *The Asian gang: Ethnicity, identity, masculinity*. Oxford: Berg.

Alsultany, E. 2012. *Arabs and Muslims in the media: Race and representation after 9/11*. New York: New York University Press.

Amin, A. 2010. The remainders of race. *Theory, Culture & Society*. 27(1), pp. 1–23.

Ang, I., Brand, J.E., Noble, G. and Wilding, D. 2002. *Living diversity: Australia's multicultural future*. Special Broadcasting Services. Available at: http://epublications.bond.edu.au/cgi/viewcontent.cgi?article=1019&context=hss_pubs.

Back, L. 1996. *New ethnicities and urban cultures: Racisms and multiculture in young lives*. London: Routledge.

Back, L. 1995. Considering X amount of Sat Siri Akal! Apache Indian, reggae music and intermezzo culture. In A. Alund and R. Granqvist, eds, *Negotiating Identities: Essays on immigration and culture in present-day Europe*. Amsterdam: Rodopi, pp. 139–166.

Back, L. and Solomos, J. 2000. Introduction: Theories of race and racism. In J. Solomos and L. Back, eds, *Theories of race and racism: A reader*. New York: Routledge, pp. 1–32.

Back, L. and Tate, M. 2015. For a sociological reconstruction: W.E.B. Du Bois,

Stuart Hall and segregated sociology. *Sociology Research Online*. 20(3). Available at: http://www.socresonline.org.uk/20/3/15.html.

Balaji, M. 2009. Why do good girls have to be bad? The cultural industry's production of the other and the complexities of agency. *Popular Communication*. 7(4), pp. 225–236.

Banet-Weiser, S. 2007. *Kids rule! Nickelodeon and consumer citizenship*. Durham, NC: Duke University Press.

Banks, M. 2007. *The politics of cultural work*. Basingstoke: Palgrave Macmillan.

Banks, M., Ebrey, J., and Toynbee, J. 2014. *Working lives in Black British jazz*. Manchester: Centre for Research on Socio-Cultural Change. Available at: http://www.cresc.ac.uk/sites/default/files/WLIBBJ%20NEW%20 FINAL.pdf.

Banton, M. 2005. Historical and contemporary modes of representation. In K. Murji and J. Solomos, eds, *Racialization: Studies in theory and practice*. Oxford: Oxford University Press, pp. 51–68.

Basu, D. 2006. Hip-hop: Cultural clout, corporate control and the 'carceral cast'. In D. Basu and S. Lemelle, eds, *The vinyl ain't final: Hip-hop and the globalization of black culture*. London: Pluto, pp. 27–55.

Becker, H.S. 1984. *Art Worlds*. Berkley: University of California Press.

Bergner, G. 1999. On the subject of race in psychoanalysis. In A.C. Alessandrini, ed., *Frantz Fanon: Critical perspectives*. New York: Routledge, pp. 219–234.

Bhabha, H.K. 1997. Minority culture and creative anxiety. Presented at British Council 'Reinventing Britain' conference, 21 March.

Bhabha, H.K. 1994. *The location of culture*. New York: Routledge.

Bhambra, G.K. 2014. A sociological dilemma: Race, segregation and US sociology. *Current Sociology*. 62(4), pp. 472–492.

Blevins, J.L. and Martinez, K. 2010. A political-economic history of FCC policy on minority broadcast ownership. *The Communication Review*. 13(3), pp. 216–238.

Born, G. 2013. Mediating the public sphere. Digitization, pluralism and communicative democracy. In C. Emden and D. Midgley, eds, *Beyond Habermas: Democracy, knowledge, and the public sphere*. New York: Berghahn Books, pp. 119–146.

Born, G. 2010. The social and the aesthetic: For a post-Bourdieuian theory of cultural production. *Cultural Sociology*. 4(2), pp. 171 –208.

Born, G. 2004. *Uncertain vision: Birt, Dyke and the reinvention of the BBC*. London; New South Wales; Auckland: Random House.

Born, G. and Prosser, T. 2001. Culture and consumerism: Citizenship, public service broadcasting and the BBC's fair trading obligations. *Modern Law Review*. 64(5), pp. 657–687.

Brah, A. 1996. *Cartographies of diaspora: Contesting identities*. London: Routledge.

Braxton, G. and James, M. 2012. Laker legend to launch a TV network. *Los*

Angeles Times. Available at: http://articles.latimes.com/2012/feb/21/business/la-fi-ct-magic-johnson-20120221.

Busse, K. 2013. The return of the author: Ethos and identity politics. In J. Gray and D. Johnson, eds, *A companion to media authorship*. Oxford: Wiley.

Byerly, C.M. and Wilson II, C.C. 2009. Journalism as Kerner turns 40: Its multicultural problems and possibilities. *The Howard Journal of Communications*. 20(3), pp. 209–221.

Caldwell, J. 2008. *Production culture: Industrial reflexivity and critical practice in film and television*. Durham, NC: Duke University Press Books.

Callon, M., Méadel, C. and Rabeharisoa, V. 2002. The economy of qualities. *Economy and Society*. 31(2), pp. 194–217.

Camfield, D. 2016. Elements of a historical-materialist theory of racism. *Historical Materialism*. 24(1), pp. 31–70.

Campbell, C.P., LeDuff, K.M., Jenkins, C.D. and Brown, R.A. (eds) 2012. *Race and news: Critical perspectives*. London: Routledge.

Campion, M.J. 2005. *Look who's talking: Cultural diversity, public service broadcasting and the national conversation*. Oxford: Nuffield College.

Chakravartty, P. and Silva, D.F. da. 2012. Accumulation, dispossession, and debt: The racial logic of global capitalism. An introduction. *American Quarterly*. 64(3), pp. 361–385.

Chávez, C.A. and Stroo, S. 2015. ASPiRational: Black cable television and the ideology of uplift. *Critical Studies in Media Communication*. 32(2), pp. 65–80.

Chen, K.-H. 1998. Introduction: The decolonization question. In K.-H. Chen, ed., *Trajectories: Inter-Asia cultural studies*. New York: Routledge, pp. 1–53.

Chow-White, P.A., Deveau, D. and Adams, P. 2015. Media encoding in science fiction television: Battlestar Galactica as a site of critical cultural production. *Media, Culture & Society*. 37(8), pp. 1210–1225.

Christian, A.J. 2012. Beyond big video: The instability of independent networks in a new media market. *Continuum*. 26(1), pp. 73–87.

Christian, A.J. 2011. Race and ethnicity in fandom: Praxis. *Transformative Works and Cultures*. 8. Available at: http://journal.transformativeworks.org/index.php/twc/article/view/250/237.

Clarke, K.M. and Thomas, D.A. 2006. *Globalization and race: Transformations in the cultural production of blackness*. Durham, NC: Duke University Press.

Coffey, A.J. 2013. Representing ourselves: Ethnic representation in America's television newsrooms. *Howard Journal of Communications*. 24(2), pp. 154–177.

Conway, K. 2014. Little mosque, small screen: Multicultural broadcasting policy and Muslims on television. *Television & New Media*. 15(7), pp. 648–663.

Cornwall, A., Gideon, J. and Wilson, K. 2008. Introduction: Reclaiming feminism: Gender and neoliberalism. *IDS Bulletin*. 39(6), pp. 1–9.

Cottle, S. 2000. Introduction. Media research and ethnic minorities: Mapping the field. In S. Cottle, ed., *Ethnic minorities and the media: Changing cultural boundaries*. Buckingham: Open University Press, pp. 1–30.

Cottle, S. 1997. *Television and ethnic minorities: Producers' perspectives. A study of BBC, independent and cable TV producers*. Aldershot: Avebury.

Coulthard, G.S. 2007. Subjects of empire: Indigenous peoples and the 'politics of recognition' in Canada. *Contemporary Political Theory*. 6(4), pp. 437–460.

Crang, P., Dwyer, C. and Jackson, P. 2003. Transnationalism and the spaces of commodity culture. *Progress in Human Geography*. 27(4), pp. 438–456.

Curran, J., Fenton, N. and Freedman, D. (eds) 2016. *Misunderstanding the internet*, 2nd edn. New York: Routledge.

Daniels, J. 2013. Race and racism in Internet studies: A review and critique. *New Media & Society*. 15(5), pp. 695–719.

Dávila, A.M. 2012. *Latinos, Inc: The marketing and making of a people*, 2nd edn. Berkeley: University of California Press.

Davis, A. 2013. *Promotional cultures: The rise and spread of advertising, public relations, marketing and branding*. Cambridge: Polity.

Deane, P.S. 2009. *James Edwards: African American Hollywood icon*. Jefferson, NC: McFarland & Company.

Deuze, M. 2006. Ethnic media, community media and participatory culture. *Journalism*. 7(3), pp. 262–280.

Deuze, M. 2005. What is journalism? Professional identity and ideology of journalists reconsidered. *Journalism*. 6(4), pp. 442–464.

Downing, J.D.H. and Husband, C. 2005. *Representing race: Racisms, ethnicity and the media*. London: Sage.

Drew, E.M. 2011. 'Coming to terms with our own racism': Journalists grapple with the racialization of their news. *Critical Studies in Media Communication*. 28(4), pp. 353–373.

Du Bois, W.E.B. 1994. *The souls of black folk*. New York: Dover.

du Gay, P., Hall, S., Janes, L., Madsen, A.K., Mackay, H. and Negus, K. 1997. *Doing cultural studies: The story of the Sony Walkman*. London: Sage.

du Gay, P. and Pryke, M. 2002. Introduction. In P. Du Gay and M. Pryke, eds, *Cultural economy: Cultural analysis and commercial life*. London: Sage, pp. 1–20.

Duggan, L. 2003. *The twilight of equality? Neoliberalism, cultural politics, and the attack on democracy*. Boston, MA: Beacon Press.

Dwyer, C. and Crang, P. 2002. Fashioning ethnicities. The commercial spaces of multiculture. *Ethnicities*. 2(3), pp. 410–430.

Dyer, R. 1997. *White*. New York: Routledge.

Eide, E. 2010. Strategic essentialism and ethnification: Hand in glove? *Nordicom Review*. 31(2), pp. 63–78.

Ellis, J. 2000. Scheduling: The last creative act in television? *Media, Culture & Society*. 22(1), pp. 25–38.

Fanon, F. 1986. *Black skin, white masks*. London: Pluto Press.

Field, A.N., Horak, J.-C. and Stewart, J.N. 2015. Introduction: Emancipating the image – the L.A. rebellion of black filmmakers. In A.N. Field, J.-C. Horak and J.N. Stewart, eds, *L.A. Rebellion: Creating a new black cinema*. Oakland: University of California Press, pp. 1–54.

Fish, S. 1997. Boutique multiculturalism, or why liberals are incapable of thinking about hate speech. *Critical Inquiry*. 23(2), pp. 378–395.

Fitts, M. 2008. 'Drop it like it's hot': Culture industry laborers and their perspectives on rap music video production. *Meridians: Feminism, race, transnationalism*. 8(1), pp. 211–235.

Fitzgerald, S.W. 2012. *Corporations and cultural industries: Time Warner, Bertelsmann, and News Corporation*. Lanham, MD: Lexington Books.

Fleras, A. 2016. Theorizing minority misrepresentation. Reframing mainstream newsmedia as white ethnic media. In G. Ruhrmann, Y. Shooman and P. Widmann, eds, *Media and minorities: Questions on representation from an international perspective*. Bristol, CT: V&R Academic.

Florini, S. 2016. This Week in Blackness and the construction of blackness in independent digital media. In R.A. Lind, ed., *Race and gender in electronic media*. New York: Routledge, pp. 209–219.

Florini, S. 2015a. The podcast 'Chitlin' Circuit': Black podcasters, alternative media, and audio enclaves. *Journal of Radio & Audio Media*. 22(2), pp. 209–219.

Florini, S. 2015b. This Week in Blackness, the George Zimmerman acquittal, and the production of a networked collective identity. *New Media & Society*. Available at: http://dx.doi.org/10.1177/1461444815606779.

Fraser, I. 2004. The marketing of theatre. In F. Kerrigan, P. Fraser and M. Özbiligin, eds, *Arts marketing*. Burlington, MA: Elsevier Butterworth Heinemann, pp. 42–67.

Fraser, N. 1989. *Unruly practices: Power, discourse and gender in contemporary social theory*. Cambridge: Polity.

Freedman, D. 2014. *The contradictions of media power*. London: Bloomsbury.

Freedman, D. 2008. *The politics of media policy*. Cambridge: Polity.

Fuller, J. 2010. Branding blackness on US cable television. *Media, Culture & Society*. 32(2), pp. 285–305.

Fürsich, E. 2002. How can global journalists represent the 'Other'? A critical assessment of the cultural studies concept for media practice. *Journalism*. 3(1), pp. 57–84.

Galperin, H. 1999. Cultural industries in the age of free-trade agreements. *Canadian Journal of Communication*. 24(1), pp. 49–77.

Gandy, O.H. 1998. *Communication and race: A structural perspective*. Oxford: Oxford University Press.

Garnham, N. 2011. The political economy of communication revisited. In J. Wasko, G. Murdock and H. Sousa, eds, *The handbook of political economy of communications*. Oxford: Wiley-Blackwell, pp. 41–61.

Garnham, N. 2005. From cultural to creative industries: An analysis of the implications of the 'creative industries' approach to arts and media policy making in the United Kingdom. *International Journal of Cultural Policy.* 11(1), pp. 15–29.

Garnham, N. 2000. *Emancipation, the media, and modernity: Arguments about the media and social theory.* Oxford: Oxford University Press.

Garnham, N. 1990. *Capitalism and communication: Global culture and the economics of information.* London: Sage.

Garnham, N. 1987. Concepts of culture: Public policy and the cultural industries. *Cultural Studies.* 1(1), pp. 23–37.

Georgiou, M. 2005. Diasporic media across Europe: Multicultural societies and the universalism–particularism continuum. *Journal of Ethnic and Migration Studies.* 31(3), pp. 481–498.

Gillespie, M. 1995. *Television, ethnicity and cultural change.* New York: Routledge.

Gillett, C. 1996. *The sound of the city: The rise of rock and roll,* rev. edn. London: Souvenir.

Gilroy, P. 2013. 'We got to get over before we go under. . .'. Fragments for a history of black vernacular neoliberalism. *New Formations.* 80(1), pp. 23–38.

Gilroy, P. 2012. 'My Britain is fuck all' zombie multiculturalism and the race politics of citizenship. *Identities.* 19(4), pp. 380–397.

Gilroy, P. 2010. *Darker than blue: On the moral economies of black Atlantic culture.* Cambridge, MA: Harvard University Press.

Gilroy, P. 2004. *After empire: Melancholia or convivial culture?* New York: Routledge.

Gilroy, P. 2000. *Between camps: Race, identity and nationalism at the end of the colour line.* London: Allen Lane.

Gilroy, P. 1993a. *The Black Atlantic: Modernity and double consciousness.* New York: Verso.

Gilroy, P. 1993b. *Small acts: Thoughts on the politics of black cultures.* London: Serpent's Tail.

Gilroy, P. 1987. *There ain't no black in the Union Jack.* London: Hutchinson.

Goldberg, D.T. n.d. Obama's election was supposed to usher in a new post-racial era. Why has racist expression grown more vicious than any time since the 1960s? Available at: http://www.salon.com/2015/08/03/obamas_election_was_supposed_to_usher_in_a_new_post_racial_era_why_has_racist_expression_grown_more_vicious_than_any_time_since_the_1960s/.

Goldberg, D.T. 2012. When race disappears. *Comparative American Studies.* 10(2–3), pp. 116–127.

Goldberg, D.T. 2009. *The threat of race: Reflections on racial neoliberalism.* Oxford: Wiley-Blackwell.

Goldberg, D.T. 2005. Racial Americanization. In K. Murji and J. Solomos, eds, *Racialization: Studies in theory and practice*. Oxford: Oxford University Press, pp. 87–102.

Golding, P. 1978. The international media and the political economy of publishing. *Library Trends*. 26(4). Available at: https://www.ideals.illinois.edu/bitstream/handle/2142/6980/librarytrendsv26i4c_opt.pdf?sequence=1&isAllowed=y.

Golding, P. and Murdock, G. 2000. Culture, communications and political economy. In J. Curran and M. Gurevitch, eds, *Mass media and society*. London: Hodder Arnold, pp. 70–92.

Grabe, M.E., Zhou, S. and Barnett, B. 1999. Sourcing and reporting in news magazine programs: 60 Minutes versus Hard Copy. *Journalism & Mass Communication Quarterly*. 76(2), pp. 293–311.

Gray, H. 2016. Precarious diversity: Representation and demography. In M. Curtin and K. Sanson, eds, *Precarious creativity*. Oakland: University of California Press, pp. 241–253.

Gray, H. 2013. Subject(ed) to recognition. *American Quarterly*. 65(4), pp. 771–798.

Gray, H. 2005. *Cultural moves: African Americans and the politics of representation*. Berkeley: University of California Press.

Gray, H. 2000. Black representation in the post network, post civil rights world of global media. In S. Cottle, ed. *Ethnic minorities and the media: Changing cultural boundaries*. Buckingham: Open University Press, pp. 118–130.

Gray, H. 1995. *Watching race: Television and the struggle for blackness*. Minneapolis: University of Minnesota Press.

Gray, H. 1993. Black and white and in color. *American Quarterly*. 45(3), pp. 467–472.

Gray, H. 1988. *Producing jazz: The experience of an independent record company*. Philadelphia, PA: Temple University Press.

Gray, J. 1993. Cultural diversity, national identity and the case for public service broadcasting in Britain. In W. Stevenson, ed., *All our futures: Changing role and purpose of the BBC*. London: BFI Publishing.

Gray, J. and Johnson, D. eds. 2013. *A companion to media authorship*. Oxford: Wiley.

Greene, D. 1994. Tragically hip: Hollywood and African American cinema. *Cineaste*. 20(4), pp. 28–29.

Hage, G., 1998. *White nation: Fantasies of white supremacy in a multicultural society*. Annandale, VA: Pluto Press.

Hall, S. 2011. The neoliberal revolution. *Cultural studies*. 25(6), pp. 705–728.

Hall, S. 2000. Conclusion: The multicultural question. In B. Hesse, ed., *Un/settled multiculturalisms: Diasporas, entanglements, 'transruptions'*. London: Zed Books, pp. 209–241.

Hall, S. 1996a. New ethnicities. In K.-H. Chen and D. Morley, eds, *Stuart Hall: Critical dialogues in cultural studies*. London: Routledge, pp. 441–449.

Hall, S. 1996b. What is this 'black' in black popular culture? In K.-H. Chen and D. Morley, eds, *Stuart Hall: Critical dialogues in cultural studies*. London: Routledge, pp. 468–479.

Hall, S. 1995. Black and white television. In J. Givanni, ed., *Remote control: Dilemmas of black intervention in British film and TV; Report from the BFI African & Caribbean Unit Black & White in Colour Conference*. London: British Film Institute, pp. 13–28.

Hall, S. 1993. Which public, whose service? In W. Stevenson, ed., *All our futures: Changing role and purpose of the BBC*. London: British Film Institute, pp. 23–38.

Hall, S. 1985. Signification, representation, ideology: Althusser and the post-structuralist debates. *Critical Studies in Media Communication*. 2(2), pp. 91–114.

Hall, S. 1981. Notes on deconstructing 'the popular'. In R. Samuel, ed. *People's history and socialist theory* (History Workshop Series). London: Routledge & Kegan Paul, pp. 227–239.

Hall, S. 1980. Encoding/decoding. In Centre for Contemporary Cultural Studies, ed., *Culture, media, language: working papers in cultural studies, 1972–79*. London: Hutchinson, pp. 128–138.

Hall, S., Critcher, C., Jefferson, T., Clarke, J. and Roberts, B. 2013. *Policing the crisis: Mugging, the state and law and order*. Basingstoke: Palgrave Macmillan.

Hammou, K. 2016. Mainstreaming French rap music. Commodification and artistic legitimation of Othered cultural goods. *Poetics*. 59, pp. 67–81.

Hardy, J. 2014. *Critical political economy of the media: An introduction*. New York: Routledge.

Hartley, J. 2000. Radiocracy sound and citizenship. *International Journal of Cultural Studies*. 3(2), pp. 153–159.

Havens, T.J. 2014. Media industry sociology: Mainstream, critical, and cultural perspectives. In S. Waisbord, ed., *Media sociology: A reappraisal*. Cambridge: Polity.

Havens, T. 2013. *Black television travels: African American media around the globe*. New York: New York University Press.

Havens, T., Lotz, A.D. and Tinic, S. 2009. Critical media industry studies: A research approach. *Communication, Culture & Critique*. 2(2), pp. 234–253.

Heider, D. 2000. *White news: Why local news programs don't cover people of color*. Mahwah, NJ: Lawrence Erlbaum.

Henderson, L. 2013. *Love and money: Queers, class, and cultural production*. New York: New York University Press.

Hesmondhalgh, D. 2013. *The cultural industries*, 3rd edn. London: Sage.

Hesmondhalgh, D. 2010. Media industry studies, media production studies. In J. Curran, ed., *Media and society*. London: Bloomsbury, pp. 145–163.

Hesmondhalgh, D. 2009. Politics, theory and method in media industries research. In J. Holt and A. Perren, eds., *Media industries: History, theory, method*. Oxford: Blackwell Publishing, pp. 245–255.

Hesmondhalgh, D. 2008. Cultural and creative industries. In T. Bennett and J. Frow, eds., *The SAGE handbook of cultural analysis*. London: Sage, pp. 552–569.

Hesmondhalgh, D. 2002. *The cultural industries*. London: Sage.

Hesmondhalgh, D. 2000. International times: Fusions, exoticism, and antiracism in electronic dance music. In G. Born and D. Hesmondhalgh, eds., *Western music and its others: Difference, representation, and appropriation in music*. Berkeley: University of California Press, pp. 280–304.

Hesmondhalgh, D. 1996. Independent record companies and democratisation in the popular music industry. PhD thesis, University of London.

Hesmondhalgh, D. and Baker, S. 2011. *Creative labour: Media work in three cultural industries*. London: Routledge.

Hesmondhalgh, D. and Saha, A. 2013. Race, ethnicity, and cultural production. *Popular Communication*. 11(3), pp. 179–195.

Hesse, B. 2000. Introduction. In B. Hesse, ed. *Un/settled multiculturalisms: Diasporas, entanglements, 'transruptions'*. London: Zed Books, pp. 1–30.

Hill, A. 2001. Dyke: BBC is hideously white. *Guardian*. Available at: http://www.theguardian.com/media/2001/jan/07/uknews.theobserver1.

Holt, J. and Perren, A. 2009. Introduction: Does the world really need one more field of study? In J. Holt and A. Perren, eds, *Media industries: History, theory and method*. Oxford: Wiley-Blackwell, pp. 1–16.

hooks, b. 1992. *Black looks: Race and representation*. Boston, MA: South End Press.

Horsti, K. 2014. The cultural diversity turn: Policies, politics and influences at the European level. In G. Titley, K. Horsti and G. Hultén, eds, *National conversations: Public service media and cultural diversity in Europe*. Bristol: Intellect, pp. 43–60.

Hultén, G. 2014. A vulnerable diversity: Perspectives on cultural diversity policies in Swedish public service media. In G. Titley, K. Horsti and G. Hultén, eds, *National conversations: Public service media and cultural diversity in Europe*. Bristol: Intellect, pp. 147–166.

Hunt, D.M. 2005. *Channeling blackness: Studies on television and race in America*. New York: Oxford University Press.

Hunt, D.M. 1997. *Screening the Los Angeles 'riots': Race, seeing, and resistance*. Cambridge: Cambridge University Press.

Hunt, D.M. and Ramon, A.-C. 2015. *2015 Hollywood diversity report: Making sense of the disconnect*. Ralph J. Bunche Center for African American Studies at UCLA.

Huq, R. 1996. Asian Kool? Bhangra and beyond. In S. Sharma, J. Hutnyk and A. Sharma, eds, *Dis-orienting rhythms: The politics of the New Asian dance music*. London: Zed Books, pp. 61–80.

Huq, R. 2003a. From the margins to mainstream? Representations of British Asian youth musical cultural expression from bhangra to Asian underground music. *Young.* 11(1), pp. 29–48.

Huq, R. 2003b. Global youth cultures in localized spaces: The case of the UK New Asian dance music and French rap. In D. Muggleton and R. Weinzierl, eds, *The post-subcultures reader.* Oxford: Berg, pp. 195–208.

Husband, C. 2005. Minority ethnic media as communities of practice: Professionalism and identity politics in interaction. *Journal of Ethnic and Migration Studies.* 31(3), pp. 461–479.

Iosifidis, P. 2010. Introduction. In P. Iosifidis, ed., *Reinventing public service communication: European broadcasters and beyond.* Basingstoke: Palgrave Macmillan, pp. 1–6.

Jackson, P. 2002. Commercial cultures transcending the cultural and the economic. *Progress in Human Geography.* 26(1), pp. 3–18.

Jackson, P. 1999. Commodity cultures: The traffic in things. *Transactions of the Institute of British Geographers.* 24(1), pp. 95–108.

Jacobs, R.N. 2014. Media sociology and the study of race. In S. Waisbord, ed., *Media sociology: A reappraisal.* Cambridge: Polity.

Jacobs, R.N. 2009. Culture, the public sphere, and media sociology: A search for a classical founder in the work of Robert Park. *The American Sociologist.* 40(3), pp. 149–166.

Jakubowicz, A. 2014. 'And that's goodnight from us': Challenges to public service media in a culturally diverse Europe – an Antipodean perspective. In G. Titley, K. Horsti and G. Hultén, eds, *National conversations: Public service media and cultural diversity in Europe.* Bristol: Intellect, pp. 255–240.

Jenkins, C.D. 2013. Newsroom diversity and representations of race. In C.P. Campbell, K.M. LeDuff, C.D. Jenkins and R.A. Brown, eds, *Race and news: Critical perspectives.* London: Routledge, pp. 22–42.

Jerolmack, C. and Khan, S. 2014. Talk is cheap: Ethnography and the attitudinal fallacy. *Sociological Methods & Research.* 43(2), pp. 178–209.

Jhally, S. and Lewis, Justin 1992. *Enlightened racism: The Cosby Show, audiences, and the myth of the American dream.* Boulder, CO: Westview Press.

Johnston, A. and Flamiano, D. 2007. Diversity in mainstream newspapers from the standpoint of journalists of color. *The Howard Journal of Communications.* 18(2), pp. 111–131.

Jones, H. 2013. *Negotiating cohesion, inequality and change: Uncomfortable positions in local government.* Bristol: Policy Press.

Jones, H. and Jackson, E. (eds.). 2014. *Stories of cosmopolitan belonging: Emotion and location.* London: Routledge.

Jong, J. de 1998. Cultural diversity and cultural policy in The Netherlands. *International Journal of Cultural Policy.* 4(2), pp. 357–387.

Kaplan, E.A. 1999. Fanon, trauma, cinema. In A.C. Alessandrini, ed., *Frantz Fanon: Critical perspectives.* London: Routledge, pp. 147–158.

Kapoor, N. 2013. The advancement of racial neoliberalism in Britain. *Ethnic and Racial Studies*. 36(6), pp. 1028–1046.

Keith, M. 2005. *After the cosmopolitan? Multicultural cities and the future of racism*. New York: Routledge.

Kennedy, R. 2009. *Sellout: The politics of racial betrayal*. London: Vintage.

Khan, R. 2010. Going 'mainstream': Evaluating the instrumentalisation of multicultural arts. *International Journal of Cultural Policy*. 16(2), pp. 184–199.

Kohnen, M. 2015. Cultural diversity as brand management in cable television. *Media Industries*. 2(2).

Lee, S. 1995. Re-examining the concept of the 'independent' record company: The case of Wax Trax! Records. *Popular music*. 14(01), pp. 13–31.

Lentin, A. and Titley, G. 2011. *The crises of multiculturalism: Racism in a neoliberal age*. London: Zed Books.

Leong, N. 2012. Racial capitalism. *Harvard Law Review*. 126(8), pp. 2153–2225.

Leurdijk, A. 2006. In search of common ground: Strategies of multicultural television producers in Europe. *European Journal of Cultural Studies*. 9(1), pp. 25–46.

Lewis, P.M. 2008. *Promoting social cohesion: The role of community media*. Council of Europe's Group of Specialists on Media Diversity.

Lewis, P.M. and Booth, J. 1989. *The invisible medium: Public, commercial and community radio*. Basingstoke: Palgrave Macmillan.

Lipsitz, G. 1994. *Dangerous crossroads: Popular music, postmodernism and the poetics of place*. London: Verso.

Littler, J. 2017. *Against meritocracy: Culture, power and myths of mobility*. London: Routledge.

Malik, S. 2014. Diversity, broadcasting and the politics of representation. In G. Titley, K. Horsti and G. Hultén, eds, *National conversations: Public service media and cultural diversity in Europe*. Bristol: Intellect, pp. 21–42.

Malik, S. 2013a. 'Creative diversity': UK public service broadcasting after multiculturalism. *Popular Communication*. 11(3), pp. 227–241.

Malik, S. 2013b. The Indian family on UK reality television: Convivial culture in salient contexts. *Television & New Media*. 14(6), pp. 510–528.

Malik, S. 2008. 'Keeping it real': The politics of Channel 4's multiculturalism, mainstreaming and mandates. *Screen*. 49(3), pp. 343–353.

Malik, S. 2002. *Representing Black Britain: A history of Black and Asian images on British television*. London: Sage Publications Ltd.

Marcus, G. 1991. *Mystery train: Images of America in rock 'n' roll music*. London: Penguin Books.

Martin Jr, A.L. 2015. Scripting black gayness: Television authorship in black-cast sitcoms. *Television & New Media*. 16(7), pp. 648–663.

Mayer, V., Banks, M.J. and Caldwell, J.T. 2009. Production studies: Roots and routes. In V. Mayer, M.J. Banks and J.T. Caldwell, eds, *Production studies: Cultural studies of media industries*. New York: Routledge, pp. 1–12.

McChesney, R.W. 2013. *Digital disconnect: How capitalism is turning the Internet against democracy*. London: New Press.

McClintock, A. 1995. *Imperial leather: Race, gender, and sexuality in the colonial contest*. New York: Routledge.

McGill, L. 2000. *Newsroom diversity*. Arlington, VA: Freedom Forum.

McRobbie, A. 2016. *Be creative: Making a living in the new culture industries*. Cambridge: Polity.

McRobbie, A. 2004. A mixed economy of fashion design. In A. Amin and N. Thrift, eds, *The Blackwell cultural economy reader*. Oxford: Blackwell Publishing, pp. 3–15.

Medovoi, L. 2012. Dogma-line racism: Islamophobia and the second axis of race. *Social Text*. 30(2 111), pp. 43–74.

Meer, N. 2013. Racialization and religion: Race, culture and difference in the study of antisemitism and Islamophobia. *Ethnic and Racial Studies*. 36(3), pp. 385–398.

Meer, N., Dwyer, C. and Modood, T. 2010. Beyond 'angry Muslims'? Reporting Muslim voices in the British press. *Journal of Media and Religion*. 9(4), pp. 216–231.

Meer, N. and Modood, T. 2009. The multicultural state we're in: Muslims, 'multiculture' and the 'civic re-balancing' of British multiculturalism. *Political Studies*. 57(3), pp. 473–497.

Mellinger, G. 2003. Counting color: Ambivalence and contradiction in the American Society of Newspaper Editors' discourse of diversity. *Journal of Communication Inquiry*. 27(2), pp. 129–151.

Mercer, K. 1994. *Welcome to the jungle: New positions in black cultural studies*. New York: Routledge.

Miles, R. 1989. *Racism*. New York: Routledge.

Molina-Guzmán, I. 2016. #OscarsSoWhite: How Stuart Hall explains why nothing changes in Hollywood and everything is changing. *Critical Studies in Media Communication*. 33(5), pp. 438–454.

Molina-Guzmán, I. 2013. Commodifying black Latinidad in US film and television. *Popular Communication*. 11(3), pp. 211–226.

Molina-Guzmán, I. 2006. Mediating Frida: Negotiating discourses of Latina/o authenticity in global media representations of ethnic identity. *Critical Studies in Media Communication*. 23(3), pp. 232–251.

Mosco, V. 1996. *The political economy of communication: Rethinking and renewal*. London: Sage.

Moss, L. 2005. Biculturalism and cultural diversity. *International Journal of Cultural Policy*. 11(2), pp. 187–197.

Murdock, G. 1982. Large corporations and the control of the communications industries. In M. Gurevitch, T. Bennett, J. Curran and J. Woollacott, eds, *Culture, society and the media*. London: Methuen, pp. 114–147.

Murji, K. and Solomos, J. 2005. Racialization in theory and practice. In

K. Murji and J. Solomos, eds, *Racialization: Studies in theory and practice.* Oxford: Oxford University Press, pp. 1–28.

Murphy, M. 2012. *Multiculturalism: A critical introduction.* New York: Routledge.

Murthy, D. 2010. Muslim punks online: A diasporic Pakistani music subculture on the Internet. *South Asian Popular Culture.* 8(2), pp. 181–194.

Nakamura, L. 2013. *Cybertypes: Race, ethnicity, and identity on the Internet.* London: Routledge.

Nakamura, L. and Chow-White, P. (eds) 2012. *Race after the Internet.* New York: Routledge.

Napoli, P.M. 2008. Bridging cultural policy and media policy. *Journal of Arts Management, Law, and Society.* 37(4), pp. 311–332.

Negus, K. 1999. *Music genres and corporate cultures.* London: Routledge.

Negus, K. 1997. The production of culture. In P. Du Gay, ed., *Production of culture/cultures of production.* London: Sage, pp. 67–118.

Negus, K. 1996. *Popular music in theory: An introduction.* Middletown, CT: Wesleyan University Press.

Negus, K. 1992. *Producing pop: Culture and conflict in the popular music industry.* London: Edward Arnold.

Nelson, C., Treichler, P.A. and Grossberg, L. 1992. Cultural studies: An introduction. In L. Grossberg, C. Nelson and P.A. Treichler, eds, *Cultural studies.* London: Routledge, pp. 1–7.

Nickel, J. 2004. Disabling African American men: Liberalism and race message films. *Cinema Journal.* 44(1), pp. 25–48.

Nishikawa, K.A., Towner, T.L., Clawson, R.A. and Waltenburg, E.N. 2009. Interviewing the interviewers: Journalistic norms and racial diversity in the newsroom. *Howard Journal of Communications.* 20(3), pp. 242–259.

Nwonka, C.J. 2015. Diversity pie: Rethinking social exclusion and diversity policy in the British film industry. *Journal of Media Practice.* 16(1), pp. 73–90.

Oakley, K. 2014. Good work? Rethinking cultural entrepreneurship. In C. Bilton and S. Cummings, eds, *Handbook of management and creativity.* Cheltenham: Edward Elgar, pp. 145–159.

O'Brien, D., Laurison, D., Miles, A. and Friedman, S. 2016. Are the creative industries meritocratic? An analysis of the 2014 British Labour Force Survey. *Cultural Trends.* 25(2), pp. 116–131.

O'Loughlin, B. 2006. The operationalization of the concept 'cultural diversity' in British television policy and governance. *CRESC Working Paper Series.* Working Paper No. 27.

Parisi, P. 1998. The *New York Times* looks at one block in Harlem: Narratives of race in journalism. *Critical Studies in Media Communication.* 15(3), pp. 236–254.

Paterson, C., Lee, D., Saha, A. and Zoellner, A. 2015. Production research: Continuity and transformation. In C. Paterson, D. Lee, A. Saha and

A. Zoellner, eds, *Advancing media production research: Shifting*. Basingstoke: Palgrave Macmillan, pp. 3–19.

Pease, E.C., Smith, E. and Subervi, F. 2001. *The news and race models of excellence project: Overview connecting newsroom attitudes toward ethnicity and news content*. Oakland, CA: Maynard Institute for Journalism Education.

Peterson, R.A. and Anand, N. 2004. The production of culture perspective. *Annual Review of Sociology*. 30, pp. 311–334.

Pitcher, B. 2014. *Consuming race*. London: Routledge

Poindexter, P.M., Smith, L. and Heider, D. 2003. Race and ethnicity in local television news: Framing, story assignments, and source selections. *Journal of Broadcasting & Electronic Media*. 47(4), pp. 524–536.

Poole, E. 2002. *Reporting Islam: Media representations and British Muslims*. London; New York: I.B. Tauris.

Poole, E. and Richardson, J.E. 2006. *Muslims and the news media*. London: IB Tauris.

Pritchard, D. and Stonbely, S. 2007. Racial profiling in the newsroom. *Journalism & Mass Communication Quarterly*. 84(2), pp. 231–248.

Puwar, N. 2004. *Space invaders: Race, gender and bodies out of place*. Oxford: Berg.

Quinn, E. 2013a. Black talent and conglomerate Hollywood: Will Smith, Tyler Perry, and the continuing significance of race. *Popular Communication*. 11(3), pp. 196–210.

Quinn, E. 2013b. *Nuthin' but a 'G' thang: The culture and commerce of gangsta rap*. New York: Columbia University Press.

Rattansi, A. 2005. The uses of racialization: The time-spaces and subject-objects of the raced body. In K. Murji and J. Solomos, eds, *Racialization: Studies in theory and practice*. Oxford: Oxford University Press.

Rex, J. 1970. *Race relations in sociological theory*. London: Weidenfeld & Nicolson.

Rhys-Taylor, A. 2017. *Food and multiculture: A sensory ethnography of East London*. London: Bloomsbury Academic.

Riggins, S.H. (ed.). 1992. *Ethnic minority media: An international perspective*. London: Sage Publications.

Rivas-Rodriguez, M., Subervi-Velez, F.A., Bramlett-Solomon, S. and Heider, D. 2004. Minority journalists' perceptions of the impact of minority executives. *Howard Journal of Communications*. 15(1), pp. 39–55.

Robinson, C.J. 2000. *Black Marxism: The making of the Black radical tradition*. Chapel Hill , NC; University of North Carolina Press.

Robson, M. 1949. *Home of the Brave* (film). United Artists.

Rose, N. 1999. *Powers of freedom: Reframing political thought*. Cambridge: Cambridge University Press.

Rose, T. 1994. *Black noise: Rap music and black culture in contemporary America*. Middletown, CT: Wesleyan University Press.

Ross, K. 1995. *Black and white media: Black images in popular film and television.* Cambridge: Polity.

Ryan, B. 1992. *Making capital from culture: The corporate form of capitalist production.* Berlin: Walter de Gruyter.

Saeed, A. 2007. Media, racism and Islamophobia: The representation of Islam and Muslims in the media. *Sociology Compass.* 1(2), pp. 443–462.

Saha, A. 2016. The rationalizing/racializing logic of capital in cultural production. *Media Industries.* 3(1). Available at: http://quod.lib.umich.edu/m/mij/15031809.0003.101?view=text;rgn=main.

Saha, A. 2015. The marketing of race in cultural production. In K. Oakley and J. O'Conner, eds, *The Routledge companion to the cultural industries,* Abingdon: Routledge, pp. 512–521.

Saha, A. 2013a. 'Curry tales': The production of 'race' and ethnicity in the cultural industries. *Ethnicities.* 13(6), pp. 818–837.

Saha, A. 2013b. Citizen Smith more than Citizen Kane? Genres-in-progress and the cultural politics of difference. *South Asian Popular Culture.* 11(1), pp. 97–102.

Saha, A. 2013c. The cultural industries in a critical multicultural pedagogy. In D. Ashton and C. Noonan, eds, *Cultural work and higher education.* Basingstoke: Palgrave Macmillan, pp. 214–31.

Saha, A. 2012. 'Beards, scarves, halal meat, terrorists, forced marriage': Television industries and the production of 'race'. *Media, Culture & Society.* 34(4), pp. 424–438.

Saha, A. 2011. Negotiating the third space: British Asian independent record labels and the cultural politics of difference. *Popular Music and Society.* 34(4), pp. 437–454.

Said, E. 2004. *Power, politics, and culture: Interviews with Edward W. Said.* London: Bloomsbury.

Said, E. 1994. *Culture and imperialism.* New York: Vintage.

Said, E. 1991. *Orientalism.* London: Penguin Books.

Said, E. 1981. *Covering Islam: How the media and the experts determine how we see the rest of the world.* New York: Pantheon Books.

Semati, M. 2010. Islamophobia, culture and race in the age of empire. *Cultural Studies.* 24(2), pp. 256–275.

Sharma, S. 2013. Black twitter? Racial hashtags, networks and contagion. *New formations: A journal of culture/theory/politics.* 78(1), pp. 46–64.

Sharma, A. 1996. Sounds oriental: The (im)possibility of theorizing Asian musical cultures. In S. Sharma, J. Hutnyk and A. Sharma, eds, *Dis-orienting rhythms: The politics of the New Asian dance music.* London: Zed Books, pp. 15–31.

Sharma, S., Hutnyk, J. and Sharma, A. (eds) 1996. *Dis-orienting rhythms: The politics of the New Asian dance music.* London: Zed Books.

Sheng, A. 2009. Minoritization as a global measure in the age of global postcoloniality: An interview with Homi K. Bhabha. *ARIEL: A Review of International English Literature.* 40(1): 161–180.

Siapera, E. 2010. *Cultural diversity and global media: The mediation of difference.* Oxford: Wiley.

Singh, N.P. 2005. *Black is a country: Race and the unfinished struggle for democracy.* Cambridge, MA: Harvard University Press.

Sivanandan, A. 1990. *Communities of resistance: Writings on black struggles for socialism.* New York: Verso.

Skot-Hansen, D. 2002. Danish cultural policy: From monoculture towards cultural diversity. *International Journal of Cultural Policy.* 8(2), pp. 197–210.

Smith, S.L., Choueiti, M. and Pieper, K. 2016. *Inclusion or invisibility? Comprehensive Annenberg report on diversity in entertainment.* USC Annenberg: School for Communication and Journalism: Institute for Diversity and Empowerment at Annenberg (IDEA).

Spivak, G. 1993. Foundations and cultural studies. In S. Bordo, M. Moussa and H.J. Silverman, eds. *Questioning foundations: Truth/subjectivity/culture.* New York: Routledge, pp. 153–277.

Spivak, G.C. and Harasym, S. 1990. *The post-colonial critic: Interviews, strategies, dialogues.* Abingdon: Psychology Press.

Stevenson, N. 2002. *Understanding media cultures: Social theory and mass communication,* 2nd edn. London: Sage.

Thomas, D.A. and Ely, R.J. 1996. Making differences matter: A new paradigm for managing diversity. *Harvard Business Review.* 74(5), pp. 79–90.

Titley, G. 2014a. After the end of multiculturalism: Public service media and integrationist imaginaries for the governance of difference. *Global Media and Communication.* 10(3), pp. 247–260.

Titley, G. 2014b. Ireland, the 'migration nation': Public service media responses between discourse and desire. In G. Titley, K. Horsti and G. Hultén, eds, *National conversations: Public service media and cultural diversity in Europe.* Bristol: Intellect, pp. 125–146.

Toynbee, J. 2000. *Making popular music: Musicians, creativity and institutions.* London: Arnold.

Toynbee, J. 2013. Race, history, and black British jazz. *Black Music Research Journal.* 33(1), pp. 1–25.

Troyna, B. and Carrington, B. 2011. *Education, racism and reform.* London: Routledge.

Tsing, A.L. 2011. *Friction: An ethnography of global connection.* Princeton, NJ: Princeton University Press.

Valluvan, S. 2016. Conviviality and multiculture: A post-integration sociology of multi-ethnic interaction. *Young.* 24(3), pp. 204–221.

Wasko, J. and Meehan, E.R. 2013. Critical crossroads or parallel routes? Political economy and new approaches to studying media industries and cultural products. *Cinema Journal.* 52(3), pp. 150–157.

Watson, S. and Saha, A. 2013. Suburban drifts: Mundane multiculturalism in outer London. *Ethnic and Racial Studies*. 36(12), pp. 1–19.

West, C. 1990. The new cultural politics of difference. In R. Ferguson, M. Gever, T.T. Minh-ha and C. West, eds, *Out there: Marginalization and contemporary cultures*. New York: The New Museum of Contemporary Art / MIT Press, pp. 19–38.

Williams, R. 1981. *Culture*. London: Fontana.

Williams, R. 1973. Base and superstructure in Marxist cultural theory. *New Left Review*. (82), pp. 3–16.

Wilson, C.C. 2000. The paradox of African American journalists. In S. Cottle, ed., *Ethnic minorities and the media: Changing cultural boundaries*. Philadelphia: Open University Press, pp. 85–99.

Wilson, C.C. and Gutierrez, F. 1995. *Race, multiculturalism, and the media: From mass to class communication*, 2nd edn. London: Sage Publications, Inc.

Winant, H. 1994. *Racial conditions: Politics, theory, comparisons*. Minneapolis: University of Minnesota Press.

Winseck, D.R. 2011. *The political economies of media: The transformation of the global media industries*. Upper Saddle River, NJ: FT Press.

Wise, A. and Velayutham, S. 2009. *Everyday multiculturalism*. Basingstoke: Springer.

Wolock, L. and Punathambekar, A. 2014. Race and ethnicity in post-network American television: From MTV-Desi to outsourced. *Television & New Media*. 16(7), pp. 664–679.

Zhao, Y. and Chakravartty, P. 2007. Introduction. In Y. Zhao and P. Chakravartty, eds, *Global communications: Toward a transcultural political economy*. Lanham, MD: Rowman & Littlefield, pp. 1–19.

Zook, K.B. 1999. *Color by Fox: The Fox network and the revolution in Black television*. New York: Oxford University Press.

Index